6.95
D0597015

# PERSPECTIVES ON PERSUASION

# PERSPECTIVES ON PERSUASION

WALLACE C. FOTHERINGHAM
The Ohio State University

*ALLYN AND BACON, INC.* *BOSTON, 1966*

Library of Congress Catalog Card Number: 66–14155

Printed in the United States of America

# Table of Contents

## part one the concept of persuasion

## part two the potential and limitations of persuasion

## part three functional analysis in persuasion

# Preface

*All I say is by way of disclosure, and nothing by way of advice. I should not speak so boldly if it were my due to be believed.*

MONTAIGNE

Professors are notorious for believing that the fields they study and teach are far more important than the world has realized. Too few people are interested, they say; the significance of the subject has not been adequately appreciated. If the study of persuasion has a central problem, it is exactly the opposite. Everyone is interested—and rightly so. For whether there is an audience in the millions or an audience of one, persuasion is often a necessity. It can become the only available and effective means of influencing others. In a sense persuasion is not a field a person might go into, or a "subject" he may decide "to take up" or not. Rather, it is a part of living, the most sanctioned means by which one tries to influence others. It is a major means of satisfying a need to deal with one's environment. Furthermore, one might "take up" persuasion as a *study* of interpersonal influence or pursue it as a *career,* a professional competence. It is in support of these latter goals that this book is written.

One result of man's necessary interest in persuasion has been the generation of a medley of groups, courses, articles, and books largely concerned with this form of influence. There seems to be something for everyone. Toastmaster and toastmistress clubs flourish, as do adult courses such as those offered by the Dale Carnegie Corporation. Industrial corporations, large and small, provide training programs in communication and persuasion. Similarly, courses are common for students in junior high school, high school, and college. There are textbooks and courses for engineers, clergymen, businessmen, and Indian chiefs. There are texts in special forms of communication, many of which have substantial concern with persuasion—texts in public speaking, radio and television announcing, interviewing, counseling, discussion, and debate;

texts in writing advertising copy, sales letters, and editorials. Articles abound in popular magazines on how to influence others, and how to sell yourself and your ideas.

Concurrent with this flood of how-to-do-it material, a lively and growing theoretical literature continues to develop. Phenomena such as symbolism, language, meaning, cognition, learning, motivation, cultural patterning, personality, conflict, group influences, and homeostasis are being examined as explanations of persuasive effects. Other contributions to the "literature" are found in the numerous reportorial and critical accounts of contemporary persuasive events. The tactics of rightist groups, of the Soviet agency for agitation and propaganda, the civil rights campaign, the persuasive role of the President, managed news, and the progress in selling America abroad have become popular reading.

This proliferation of courses and writings about persuasion is particularly vigorous in modern, urban societies. It is here that the great occupational shift from producing things to handling people and symbols has taken place. Many more people are becoming vocationally involved with problems of persuasion. In this country, for example, the number of white collar workers began to exceed the number of blue collar workers in 1957. The trend is likely to continue, and with it a greater proportion of people engaged in persuasion. Contributing factors have been the mushrooming of the mass media industries, the automation of production, the rise in literacy throughout the world, the greater interdependence of individuals, groups, and nations, and the development of special interest groups and organizations with consequent competition between them to exert influence. It should be kept in mind, of course, that this gush of persuasive messages is received by someone. As receivers, most of us have felt a need to be more knowledgeable.

In approaching a subject, especially one of concern to so many people with diverse interests, we tend to make a choice of strategies. Among the possibilities, there are strategies for perspective as well as strategies of proof and evaluation. The objective of this book is not to prove beyond reasonable doubt particular theories or methods in persuasion, but rather to develop a coherent framework in sufficient detail to encourage further investigation of the knowledge gaps it exposes, and by means of this perspective to provide a basis for more workable decisions in the practice of persuasion.

Then, too, a strategy of evaluation is not an organizing principle for this book; it does not concern itself with questions of the moral value or the fate of various persuasive methods in different societies.

Such inquiries seek to arrive at moral judgments; they are more normative in spirit than empirical. Important as moral judgments are, they need not be the chief emphasis. Increased understanding of the relationship between means and effects, and between persuasion and other forms of influence can be sought before value judgments are made. Evaluation may in fact be better for having been preceded by a more dispassionate approach. For example, one may conclude from a more empirical approach, as the author has, that persuasion fares very well when evaluated against other means of influence.

The choice to seek perspective rather than proof or evaluation leads to another decision. From what perspective shall persuasive events be viewed, that of the source, the receiver, or the monitor? Careers in persuasion can be categorized into these three basic functions; some persons are primarily sources of persuasive efforts while others function chiefly as receivers or monitors. These categories, of course, are not mutually exclusive; a career may involve functions in more than one category. Usually, however, one is emphasized over the others.

Most of us find it easier to identify professionals who function primarily as sources—the propagandist, salesman, press agent, ghostwriter, advertiser, and editorial writer. Yet, upon reflection, vocations primarily concerned with receiving or monitoring persuasive efforts can be identified and generally agreed upon. Among professional receivers of persuasion are judges, interviewers, purchasing agents, administrators, and members of investigating committees or commissions. A judge, for example, trying a case without a jury, listens to testimony to be persuaded. His responsibility is to make up his mind, to be persuaded that one verdict has more merit than another. When he announces his verdict, his bases of influence are primarily power and authority, not persuasion; his position does not require that he function as a source of persuasion. Similarly a purchasing agent seeks to be persuaded of the merit of products he may secure for his organization. He is a professional receiver or listener to the persuasive efforts of salesmen.

Among professional monitors of persuasion are judges in jury trials, investigators of various regulatory agencies of persuasion such as the Pure Food and Drug Administration and the Federal Communications Commission, and in a free society various institutions such as the press, the broadcasting industry, the church, and the university. The jury trial judge, for example, stands between the attorneys (persuasion sources) and the jurors (persuasion receivers). He is presumed to be familiar with the Laws of Evidence and to use this body of rules governing courtroom persuasion to monitor the kind of messages to be presented to jurors (Wigmore 1942, and McKelvey 1944). When the judge fails in this monitoring function and the verdict is appealed, the persuasive practices of the trial are reviewed by an appellate court. Their responsibility is to determine if a proper trial was conducted, if the jurors (receivers) were subjected to improper persuasion. Similarly, the issue of managed news which arose in connection with the Cuban crisis of 1962 raised the question of the role of the press in regard to governmental persuasive efforts. Baldwin (1963) noted that "The fundamental obligation of a free press is to serve as a monitor of government." Schramn (1957), discussing responsibilities of the mass media, points to our constitutional guarantee of free speech and the consequent obligation of the mass media to exercise a monitoring function for receivers (citizens). The Television Code (1965) is additional evidence of recognition by that industry of a monitoring obligation and function. It is filled with rules and criteria to serve the industry in the control of the persuader's efforts to influence viewers (receivers).

Each of these functions—source, receiver, and monitor—involves a number of tasks. The amount of material relevant to all of these tasks is more than the covers of one book can contain, and more than can be adequately discussed in a typical college or university course. The choice made has been to emphasize the functions associated with sources of persuasion. Receiver and monitor functions will be discussed insofar as they interact with and contribute to an understanding of source efforts. Persuasion sources, of course, do carry on receiver and monitor functions. Sources, for example, must acquire content for persuasive messages and thus become receivers; and sources do have consciences and frequently stand between their own self-interests and the receivers of their messages. The point is that this emphasis on source functions should not imply a strict trichotomy of functions between sources, receivers, and monitors.

The chapters in this book will contain an examination of the findings of those who have studied the process of persuasion. Among the contributors are communication specialists, rhetoricians, semanticists, psychologists, sociologists, educators, industrial economists, business organization experts, political scientists and others. From the fields of applied persuasion—journalism, public relations, politics, television, social work, and business—many have written their experiences and observations. To bring this varied literature into a coherent whole posed two problems. The diversity of the writings and the vocabularies employed suggest a Tower of Babel. Consequently, an effort is made to use a consistent vocabulary throughout. Inasmuch as the content, in the author's view, is germane to persuasion conceived as a behavioral science, the vocabulary of those sciences is used.

The second problem is that there are in the literature great differences in the degree to which hypotheses are supported by carefully obtained evidence. Much of what is believed about persuasion has been a conglomeration of empiricism and ideology, of facts and prescriptions, of principles and proverbs. Theoretical explanations of persuasive effects do not classify easily as scientific. Typically, scientific theory is offered as valid for a specified situation. Persuasion theories are often proposed as general truth. We have been prone to over-generalize. The surrounding circumstances, however, play so large a part in determining relationships between independent and dependent variables that we can expect no element of a persuasion theory to be generally or categorically valid.

Consider some of the prescriptive notions and stock formulae in wide currency among those who seek to persuade. One of these is the notion that the persuader does well to speak and dress in accordance with the norms approved by his audience. This common sense view has a good deal of observation to support it. Yet, common sense has a way of filtering out exceptions, sometimes those that reveal important limitations of the rule. Rovere, in his biography, *Senator Joe McCarthy,* notes his effectiveness yet points out that "He was a master of the scabrous and the scatological; his talk was laced with obscenity . . . He belched and burped in public . . . He seemed to understand, as no other politician of his stature ever has, the perverse appeal of the bum, the mucker, the Dead End kid." Rovere concludes that the McCarthy exception was possible in a nation uneasy about a vast leveling process in which conformity and mediocrity seemed a threat. Research, morever, has specified several situations in which a negative communicator has significant effect, and reveals the shortcomings of this stock formula in persuasion.

Another notion holds that there is a substantial positive relationship between effect and amount of message presentation. Effect is thought to be significantly determined by the amount of message exposure; effect can be increased either by more messages or more audiences, or both. When audiences are not informed or not responsive, insufficient message presentation is viewed as the major explanation. Numerous persuasive campaigns are built on this formula. Election campaigns typically seek to saturate the voting public. Programs for advertising products, for getting messages behind the iron and bamboo curtains, and public information programs for safety, health, and forest conservation often adopt this prescription for effectiveness. Again, many instances support this common sense view, but there are too many significant exceptions to make such a stock formula categorically valid.

Similarly, the tendency to overgeneralize common sense and to erect stock formulae is found in such notions as: the greater the reward or punishment implied by a message, the greater the effect; in arranging messages, place your most effective one last; self-preservation is the strongest of human motives; the pen is mightier than the sword; a picture is worth a thousand words; a man convinced against his will is of the same opinion still; and the bigger the lie, if presented often enough, the more likely it will be believed. In contrast to the stock formula approach to persuasion, it is hoped that the perspective provided will underscore the situational determinants of effect. The originality and irregularity of people dictate caution in our observations and conclusions. Among the most widely accepted findings from the study of human behavior that bear on this problem of overgeneralization are: (1) people are different, highly variable one from another; and (2) people are on-going systems, highly variable from one time or situation to another.

One further orientation to persuasion provided in this book is that the persuasive effort can be viewed usefully as a system of interrelated and interdependent functions. This grouping of functions must also have direction—a specific objective. Generally, the concept of system implies more than one person or machine, more than one component. This is not essential; one individual in a particular circumstance could carry on all the functions of a persuasive system. In the careers of professional persuaders, however, functions tend to be acquired by or assigned to different individuals. This is the case whether the engaged individuals constitute a formal organization or a collectivity. Furthermore, persuasion by a group, differentiated in function, is more significant to the individuals engaged and to society. Thus, it holds more interest to those planning careers and to students of the persuasive process.

Consistent with a system or organizational view is the perspective that persuasion is more typically a campaign through time rather than a one-shot effort. Exceptions can be found, as in mail-order or door-to-door persuasion, but generally an effort is seldom limited to a single message. A structured series of messages is more often developed, using varied media, message forms, and codes. For this reason, this book is not limited to the study of a single code such as speech, writing, or graphics, nor to the production of a single message. Problems in composing the single message can be studied in existing texts, many of which are well done. For this book, a choice has been made to underscore the campaign character of persuasion and to expose the problems it creates.

Finally, the content of this book is selected to provide those who study or engage professionally in influencing others with information on the options available among the forms of influence. Persuasion is viewed as one particular form, either in competition with or used in conjunction with others. Among these other kinds of influence are those involving force, authority, habit stimulation, signal response stimulation, suggestion, and special interpersonal relationships. It is a thesis of this book that persuasion has more limitations as a form of influence than is generally maintained, even though it does have considerable potential. It is a further thesis that the decision to persuade is not necessarily the best. It is hoped that the discussion will provide a basis for comparing the assets and liabilities of various means of influence in making decisions to use persuasion.

# PART ONE

## THE CONCEPT OF PERSUASION

# Chapter I

## Concepts of Persuasion

Consider the following: a thief pointed a gun at you, asked for your money, and got it. Do you consider that the use of persuasion? A powerful nation offered a starving nation food in exchange for political affiliation; it was accepted. You observed a man lighting a cigarette in a TV commercial; almost immediately you lit one. Persuasion? A salesman wined and dined a customer; no sales talk was presented yet the salesman obtained an order. While riding on a bus you overheard a damning comment, not directed to you, about a political candidate. At election time, you voted against this candidate because you believed that comment. Has persuasion occurred? A dog snarled at you and you moved to the other side of the street. You talked yourself into buying a new car. You stopped a noisy apartment party by threatening to call the police. A psychiatrist influenced his patient to change his self-evaluation. A juror in the jury room changed his vote from not guilty to guilty when the first ballot revealed the majority of jurors favored a verdict of guilty. The press reported that the Soviet leader Khrushchev said, "We will bury you!" and you believed this. Are these examples of persuasion?

Perhaps you consider none of these as persuasive events. Whether you do or not, you have company. Students, reacting to these events and others, disagreed very much as to whether the events were instances of persuasion or not. Similarly, inconsistency seems to prevail among writers. Among them, the term "persuasion" is varyingly associated with such phenomena as brainwashing, subliminal stimulation, mass hypnosis, prestige suggestion, propaganda, euphoric and tranquillizing drugs, implanted electrodes, psychological conditioning, persuasion during sleep, and even miniature radios embedded in the brain. And one writer coined the term "coercive persuasion"—probably to the consternation of those who would view force and persuasion as antithetical.

The many concepts of persuasion in use have not seemed to diminish the amount of research on the subject. Abundance, however, is less important a characteristic of research than is direction. A plethora of explanations is more apt to indicate attention to different phenomena than a richness of theoretical thought, and can easily lead to confusion when there is extensive disagreement over what is an instance or not of any phenomenon. Thus, if there is no agreement on the nature of persuasive events, it becomes impossible to communicate hypotheses, conclusions, and implications about persuasion. Discussion degenerates into dogmatism, with many speakers but no listeners. The cafeteria of definitions available attests to the variety of views of persuasion.

## cafeteria of meanings: the dictionary

One reason for the disagreement about persuasion is the lack of a common and precise definition. Even a dictionary is not too helpful. "The dictionary nowadays is more a *Social Register* of words (and meanings) than a Supreme Court of Language" (*Time*, Oct. 6, 1961). In this case, one dictionary defines persuasion as (1) "the act of influencing" (e.g. He tried to persuade his friends to join him); (2) "that which serves to persuade" (e.g. Appeals to vital interests persuade more effectively than those to non-vital interests); (3) "power to persuade" (e.g. His ability to persuade developed with experience); and (4) "state of being persuaded" (e.g. The others were persuaded, but he remained unaffected). Obviously, this dictionary presents a variety of meanings in common use, none of which is developed precisely and in detail.

Note that the first meaning seems to emphasize the *act, attempt,* or *effort* involved in persuasion; the second meaning directs attention to the *stimuli* which induce persuasion. Perhaps it also includes the condition of the receiver which makes him more receptive. The third meaning suggests that persuasion is an *ability* or *power,* and the fourth presents persuasion as an *effect* or *response.* The use of such scattered meanings could account for some of the disagreement over which events involve persuasion. Rather than a cafeteria of vague meanings to choose from, detailed and limited meanings are needed.

## *cafeteria of meanings: expert definitions*

The numerous choices of the dictionary are not reduced by the definitions of writers on persuasion. Brembeck and Howell (1952) prefer to consider persuasion an *attempt.* For them, persuasion is "the conscious attempt to modify thought and action by manipulating the motives of men toward predetermined ends." With a similar emphasis on the attempt, Thayer (1961) sees persuasion as "a conscious effort made by people to affect other people's behavior in a specific circumstance or at a specific time." Similarly, Wright and Warner (1962) consider persuasion as "an active attempt to influence people to action or belief by an overt appeal to reason or emotion."

Other authors stress the *stimuli involved,* the *means* used to influence. Minick (1957) prefers "persuasion is discourse, written or oral, that is designed to win belief or stimulate action by employing all of the factors that determine human behavior." And Blau and Scott (1962) note that "in persuasion, one person lets the arguments of another person influence his decisions or actions." Wilson and Arnold (1964) similarly emphasize the stimuli involved as a basis for defining persuasion. Eisenson, Auer, and Irwin (1963) emphasize the means used. Thus, for them, "persuasion in public address is defined as the process of securing acceptance of an idea, or an action, by connecting it favorably with the listener's attitudes, beliefs, and desires." This last definition is part of a discussion of public address and probably is not meant to imply that persuasion should be defined differently in other communicative settings. In a still different vein, Johnson (1956) sees persuasion as primarily an *ability*: "there is a particular art, the art of persuasion, that has as its major purpose the control of the effects that words shall have."

On the whole, these definitions reveal differences in emphasis rather that contradictions. In common, they imply that persuasion is a particular means of influence. Some stress the attempt to employ persuasive means, others the stimuli involved, others the ability to use those means, and some the effects of those means. Each definition from this cafeteria has an advantage over the dictionary. Each provides a somewhat clearer basis for categorizing events, with more agreement on which are persuasive or non-persuasive. Yet, taken together these definitions specify no common basis for indentifying persuasive events;

types of attempts, stimuli, abilities, and effects, mixed together, would confound the effort. A choice is needed.

## definition or concept

Before making a choice, it is well to note that the above "definitions" are better thought of as concepts. This is so because persuasion is not a precise, simple term. It cannot be defined in the same fashion as voltage, mass, or specific gravity. In preciseness, definitions of persuasion are not comparable, for example, to the formula definition of an "average" in statistics ($\overline{X} = \Sigma X/N$), or to that for the area of a triangle ($A = \frac{1}{2}bh$). Rather, we have a generalized idea about a class of events when we use the term. We have concepts rather than definitions of persuasion.

A concept has several functions. It serves to suggest the boundaries of investigation, aids in deciding whether an event is to be included or excluded from the set of events to be studied, assists in the organization of knowledge, and facilitates communication about the subject. It makes a difference what concept is adopted, since it determines how things are perceived—sometimes with startling effect. Among the Trobriand Islanders, for instance, pregnancy is regarded as an act of spirits; as a result they find themselves unable to see resemblances between fathers and sons. The power of our concepts is no less in affecting what we observe. A concept focuses observation; it tends to establish priorities in investigation. If persuasion were viewed as an effect produced by words alone, for example, we would tend to focus only on events involving words, spoken or written. Similar effects, generated by non-verbal events, would be ignored and an important aspect of persuasion would be overlooked.

Reflection on the various dictionary and expert concepts will suggest how a class of events is likely to become the object of study. If, for example, persuasion is conceived as an *attempt*, we will be inclined to observe attempts, classify them, determine their frequency and origin, assess their predictability from other coexisting conditions. The study of the abilities involved in persuasion, the stimuli used, and the effects obtained would be ancillary to the central interest; they would be studied as aids in understanding attempts to persuade. The result would be quite a different body of knowledge about persuasion than that derived from the use of some other concept.

## *persuasion as effect*

Of the four concepts presented, the one emphasizing effect is the author's preference. It focuses on those phenomena typically measured in persuasion research. This fosters the development of better operational definitions of persuasion and thus promotes more exact scientific investigations. Katz and Lazarsfeld (1955) note that "all communication research aims at the study of effects." A review of the varied research in persuasion yields evidence that chiefly *effects* are studied and measured. It follows from this that without an effect there is no persuasion. A letter unopened or not delivered may represent an attempt, use verbal stimuli, and be ably written, but would not constitute a persuasive event.

The emphasis on effect underscores the dynamic, interpersonal nature of persuasion. Effect reminds us that persuasion is a process energized to produce desired behavior among intended receivers. Effect reminds us that persuasion is something that happens. Effect reminds us that a manuscript is not persuasion, that the ability to affect people is only a static potential until used, that an attempt is not evidence that effect has occurred. Emphasis on the outcome of the persuasive process, moreover, points to the realities by which our predictions and explanations are confirmed, rejected, or refined.

Additionally, a concept of persuasion should focus attention on the kinds of effects of widest interest to those in either research or applied fields. Thus it would attempt to stimulate study of interest to communication scientists, public relations practitioners, advertising men, preachers, politicians, and others vocationally or professionally involved.

With these considerations in mind, *persuasion is conceived as that body of effects in receivers, relevant and instrumental to source-desired goals, brought about by a process in which messages have been a major determinant of those effects.*

If a concept is to fulfill its functions, more than a skeleton statement of it is required. Its implications may not require an entire book, but they are not self-evident. It is the plan of Part One to explore this concept in some detail with the reader. This approach, involving several interrelated chapters, is designed to enable greater differentiation of persuasion from other means of influence, to suggest some of the significant foci of investigation and study, to aid in appraising the potentialities and limitations of persuasion as a form of influence, to expose the unsought effects of persuasive efforts and the problems these raise for the practitioner, and to reveal what and how one learns to be a more effective persuader. In short, some flesh is to be added to a skeletal perspective. To do this, several criteria of a persuasive event are proposed. These are: the effect must be (1) relevant, (2) instrumental, (3) largely generated by message impact, (4) involve the perception of choice for the receiver, and (5) be interpersonal.

# Chapter 2

# The Relevancy of Effects

Not all effects are of interest to those most concerned with persuasion. Consider, for example, a gubernatorial campaign in New York. Messages supporting each candidate are broadcast over New York City radio and television stations. Citizens of New Jersey, Pennsylvania, and Connecticut may receive these messages and be influenced. They do not, however, vote in New York. Or, if a persuasive speech energizes people to do what the speaker wants, it may be of no consequence that some listeners acquired a new and useful word for their own subsequent use. Or, if the goal of commercial television is to get and hold audiences for advertisers, other effects of programming may be viewed as irrelevant to that goal. One of these other effects, in the judgment of Vonier (1964), is that TV programming is homogenizing the values of Americans. Now, to view this effect as irrelevant is not to gainsay its possible social significance. Perhaps program producers should seek heterogeneity of values. The point is that, given a goal of securing audiences through programming, this side effect probably is irrelevant. The effect is not indicative of goal achievement.

## *the relevancy criterion*

When a persuasive effect in a receiver is said to be relevant, the term implies that the effect bears some close relationship and importance to the person involved. But at least two persons are closely related to any persuasive effect, the receiver and the source. To whom must the effect be relevant? To both. Obviously, any response in a receiver is relevant to that person. Thus, satisfying the requirement of receiver relevancy is no problem. Yet many receiver responses, as already indicated, may not be relevant to source goals. It is the intent, then, of the relevancy criterion to give emphasis to the study of receiver responses related to the goals sought by a source.

### RELEVANT EFFECTS

Some effects of persuasion may be relevant without being helpful to the persuader. Sometimes a listener is less favorable to a proposal, after hearing a message favoring it, than before. On other occasions, receivers may distort the message, discredit the source, or even over-respond with behavior in excess of that sought by the source and harmful to his goals. The civil rights crisis constitutes an example of such over-adoption by the receivers of persuasive stimulation.

If the effects sought by Negro leadership were support for and participation in orderly, non-violent, passive efforts to produce integration, the followers seemed initially to respond as desired, then over-respond. The violence in Los Angeles, St. Petersburg, Birmingham, Cleveland, Rochester, Philadelphia, New York City and elsewhere testify to this effect. At the national convention of the N.A.A.C.P. James Meredith, picked by that organization to be the first Negro enrolled at the University of Mississippi, was denounced for questioning the pressure tactic of a national civil rights march on Washington. The Rev. Dr. J. H. Jackson similarly opposed a mass Negro march on Washington. Dr. Jackson was a recognized leader, president of the National Baptist Convention, U.S.A., Inc., the largest Negro denomination in the U.S., with 5,000,000 members. Among Negroes, he was an influential man, but for his opposition to the proposed new tactic, he was booed into silence when he began to speak and attacked when he attempted to leave the speaker's platform at a large rally.

The relevancy view holds that persuasive effects should not be limited to "good" or "effective" persuasion. When study is based on the assumption that only those effects from "good" or ethical persuaders and only those effects which promote approved social goals or other ethical ends are worth attention, unfortunate restrictions are imposed on understanding. Bryant (1953) states the point well. "It doesn't matter whether the individual is a preacher or an agitator, a messiah or a mountebank, advocate or advertiser, they are all users of rhetoric and must be studied. The fact is that in their characteristic preoccupation with manipulating the public mind, they are one." In terms of effect relevancy, no distinction need be drawn, as is sometimes done, between persuasion and propaganda, the one attracting "good" men and the other "bad." The more useful distinction, as will be developed later, is that these two forms of influence differ in the means employed, not necessarily in the ethical character of the people or ideas involved.

Similarly, those effects which interfere with a persuader's goal warrant the same attention as those which promote it. The refusal to buy is as important to the advertiser as the explanation of buying behavior. Yet, desired effects are more typically emphasized. This is particularly the case with general, popular discussions of persuasion—e.g. Dale Carnegie's *How to Win Friends and Influence People* and Vance Packard's *Hidden Persuaders.* In fact, the general tendency of the "How To Do It" treatment of persuasion is to exaggerate the desired effects of persuasion and the ease with which they are obtained. Research findings, in contrast, have been noting in recent years the occurrence of unintended effects of persuasive efforts. Considerable interest has developed along with efforts to explain such undesired effects as forgetting, rejection, avoidance, distortion, resistance, and over-adoption. These as well as desired effects are significant in the study of persuasion.

## RELEVANT AND IRRELEVANT RECEIVERS

*Who* receives a message is an important dimension of response relevancy. The persuader not only seeks relevant effects, but seeks them in particular individuals and groups. The political party wants to affect registered voters; the advertiser is concerned with effects among potential customers. Effects in some receivers are more pertinent than in others. Contemporary perspective provides a richer view of the "audience," and promotes awareness of the significance of different audience elements to the persuader's goals.

Among those who can receive messages, four classes of persons, differing in relevancy, can be distinguished: (1) intended receivers—those in whom the persuader seeks to develop effects instrumental to his goals; (2) unintended receivers—those for whom the message was not intended and in whom unfavorable effects may be created; (3) irrelevant receivers—those in whom effects are unimportnat to the persuader's goals; and (4) interested third parties—those who will produce messages of their own relevant to the persuader's message and goal.

Theoretical and experimental literature reflect an overemphasis on the first group—the intended receivers—and especially those who directly receive the persuader's message. In contrast, other receivers—those intended to be reached indirectly, the unintended, the irrelevant, and interested third parties—have been relatively ignored. Several conditions contribute to this neglect. Among these are two limited and questionable concepts of audience; though formerly held, these have been subjected in recent years to theoretical and empirical challenge.

One notion now being challenged is the so-called "hypodermic needle model" of the communication or persuasion process, and the consequent view of audience it assumes. Wright (1959) and Rogers (1962) provide illustrative evidence of the limitations of this model. Usually, this view holds that a message acts directly on audience members, influencing each one directly or not. Each audience member is individually and directly "injected" with the message. Once it has been "injected," the message may or may not affect him, depending on whether it is potent enough to "take." Whether the message "takes" or not, the process of influence ends. Though there are many objections to this model, of particular concern here is the fact that receivers frequently pass along a message, or their reaction to it, to others not directly exposed. Thus, by diffusion, the audience may be considerably enlarged.

Closely allied to the "hypodermic needle" notion of the persuasive process is what might be called the myth of the passive audience. This views the audience as passive, capable of responding to stimulation, but not expected to initiate persuasion or reenergize the process started by the source. Among the influences leading to this notion were some of the early theories in business organization and the ideas developed by the behaviorists in psychology. March and Simon (1958) note that such early organization theorists as Taylor (1911) and Gilbreth (1912) assumed that members, particularly employees who constituted the audiences for management, were primarily "passive instruments, capable of performing work and accepting directions, but not initiating action or exerting influence in any significant way." It was not difficult to view persuasive settings similarly structured. Roles were differentiated. The persuader's role was to energize the process and provide the stimulus; the role of the audience was a passive one, to receive and respond to stimulation. The rise of labor unions, of course, put a substantial dent in the notion of the passive, uninitiating employee-audience.

Similarly, the early behaviorists in psychology wrote largely in terms of S-R (stimulus-response) relationships with little attention to the organism between the stimulus and response. Again, the responding organism was viewed as a passive element in the response picture. Later, of course, this view was revised and an S-O-R (stimulus-organism-response) model substituted. The earlier model, however, encouraged a passive concept of the responder. It likely contributed to stimulus-response, or passive audience views in the field of persuasion.

Illustrative of the evidence that contradicts these audience concepts is the study of Larsen and Hill (1954). The authors studied the dissemination of the news of the late Senator Robert A. Taft's death. Their results showed that more than 80 percent of those who learned of Taft's death through regular news sources attempted to diffuse the news or discuss it with others. By this means the original message was diffused to others not directly reached by a regular news source. The recognition of audience activity in diffusing a message to others has enlarged our view of who are the relevant intended receivers of a persuasive message. This is evident, for example, in a television commercial presented during a children's program and directed to children. Active diffusion of the message to parents is anticipated. A by-product, worth noting, of research on diffusion is the fact that both diffusion and non-diffusion become effects to be sought by the persuader.

Another condition that promotes an overemphasis on receivers who are directly exposed to a message is controlled experimentation. Experimental groups tend to be only those who are the immediate recipients of a persuader's message. They are the audience in which the measurement of effects is chiefly studied. Such a practice limits our view of an audience. Other persons to whom the message may be diffused tend to be ignored, since such potential audience members are not part of the experimental design. Even control groups not exposed to the message are used principally to demonstrate significant effects in the directly exposed audiences, so that the directly exposed audience is the experimenter's overriding interest. Our present knowledge of persuasive effects in other types of audiences comes largely, not from experiments, but from field studies and reports of observers not engaged in experimentation.

UNINTENDED RECEIVERS. Though intended receivers, reached directly or indirectly, are of primary concern in persuasion, it is easy to recognize the importance of the unintended receivers. You may recall the experience of Margery Michelmore, a Peace Corps worker stationed in Nigeria. She dropped a home-addressed postcard that commented on uncivilized conditions in Nigeria and seemed critical of life there. It was picked up, put in anti-American hands, and screechingly "ballyhooed." The persuader recognizes the relevancy of unintended receivers by trying to prevent diffusion of a message among them. Intended receivers are told to keep information "under their hats." When the boss speaks to an employee about a salary increase "in confidence," he seeks to prevent diffusion. His message, though designed to bring about an effect in one worker's behavior, may be disturbing to others. The administrator who speaks "off the record" to his staff makes it clear he wants to prevent diffusion. The labeling of letters and reports as "confidential," similarly, represents an effort to limit message distribution. The prevention of message diffusion can be a significant goal in persuasion.

Another type of unintended receiver is the "company man" in a labor union. Such a person pretends to be what he is not. He serves management but pretends loyalty to the union. It is in his pretense that he differs from typical undesired receivers. His role is that of pseudo-receiver; his real function is in being an informer. It is in highly competitive groups like unions and management, political parties, and nations that the informer is most likely to appear. A somewhat similar type of pseudo-receiver is the professional shopper—the Macy's man in Gimbel's or the Republican at a Democratic rally. Still another type is the professional heckler. He appears in the modest role of receiver, but with the intention of hindering the persuasion of legitimate receivers. In the winter of 1964, Governor Wallace of Alabama spoke on a number of university campuses. One student chapter of the N.A.A.C.P. circulated an announcement of a "welcome" to the Governor. Members and other interested persons were urged to meet at the auditorium entrance in order "to be seated in a solid block, front and center, to give the Governor our *Support*." While it might be argued that these types of unintended receivers are more often a problem of security than of persuasion, the persuader's goals unquestionably are threatened by their presence in the audience.

The likelihood of unintended elements in an audience varies with the message media used. The mass media, least of all, enable a persuader to exclude unwanted receivers. Radio, television, newspapers, or mass magazines provide little control over who receives a message. For this reason, the mass media best serve the persuader when he is not concerned with audience selectivity. Thus, messages for adults only, for Americans only, for Protestants or Catholics only are difficult to transmit via mass media without exposing them to unintended receivers.

Interest in the unintended receiver has increased substantially in contemporary life. This century is characterized by greater literacy, the vastly extended use of mass media, increased interaction among competitive groups, and growing interdependence of groups and nations. Each of these factors promotes interest in the unintended receiver. He has easier access to messages the persuader may not wish him to receive. Recently, Governors Ross Barnett of Mississippi and George Wallace of Alabama faced this problem because of nationwide television coverage. The messages they might use effectively with their own constituencies might generate effects, harmful to their goals, in other groups. Similarly, the televised political convention provides a more heterogeneous audience than one not televised. Messages that might arouse enthusiasm in the convention auditorium might lose votes with other groups. The increased prominence of the unintended receiver is not a security problem, but a persuasion problem.

IRRELEVANT RECEIVERS. The third group of persons in a position to receive messages are irrelevant to the persuader in respect to seeking message effects in them, but are of significance in aiding the persuader in affecting other receivers. Two distinct types can be noted. Goffman (1959) labels the first group "non-persons." Children, he points out, are often treated as unimportant listeners; adults often discuss children, in their presence, as if the children were non-persons. Servants, particularly in the nineteenth century, were similarly treated as non-persons. Of more interest today is the growing body of personnel involved in staging or servicing a persuasive event. These are recording stenographers, stagehands, janitors, broadcasting technicians, photographers, and secret police. From the standpoint of the persuader, they are perceived as non-persons.

The other type of receiver, in whom message effects are subordinate to services provided, could well be labeled the "shill." This label covers a variety of persons whose role is to furnish favorable but artificial responses to messages. These responses are artificial feedback designed to affect legitimate receivers. The shill is a pseudo-receiver, and one with a long history of usage. In ancient theatre, for example, it was the practice to hire a claque; this was a group of paid applauders who generally sat throughout an audience and provided a model of the desired response to others. They stimulated enthusiasm and acceptance of the performance and attempted to generate applause in others.

Today, in closely prepared persuasive events, the shill's performance may be included in the script. In television, the studio audience is partly used as a shill for the much larger viewing audience, prompted as it is to laugh and applaud on cue. People involved in "news events" are sometimes encouraged to act as shills for TV audiences. During the civil rights crisis a few years ago in New Orleans, Mayor Morrison declared he had observed a television cameraman set up a "scene" and then persuade a group of students to yell and demonstrate in response to his cues (Boorstin, 1962). Another example is the use of persons to begin the "discussion from the floor" following a speech. They, too, are involved in the pseudo-role of legitimate receivers. Still another example is the chairman's role at a public lecture following the introduction of the guest speaker. At this time he serves as a visible model of behavior for legitimate listeners. Regardless of personal feelings, his pseudo-role calls for him to listen with great attentiveness and to provide the audience with cues as to whether a particular remark ought to be reacted to with nods of approval, laughter, seriousness, or applause. One more example of the shill is found in the widely used testimonial in advertising. A celebrity or an ordinary person provide favorable but often artificial responses to a product. These are designed to affect legitimate buyers.

INTERESTED THIRD PARTIES. In every political campaign, in every charity drive, and in every promotion of a civic improvement there exists a group of receivers who are not receivers in the traditional sense. They are not the persons one seeks to persuade in the usual sense; the persuader more importantly seeks from them further diffusion of his message. They are third parties interested in using the persuader's messages to produce messages of their own. They are typically members of organizations able to secure audiences of their own and professionally engaged in communicating to those audiences. With the growth of organization life (Whyte, 1957), the number of such parties in the audience has increased greatly. Their presence warrants an enlargement of the traditional conception of audience.

One of the most likely interested third parties present at a persuasive event is the press. The relation of interested third parties to the persuader is exemplified in the experiences of the late Senator McCarthy in his hunt for Communist infiltration into government, churches, and educational institutions. Boorstin (1962) notes that "Senator McCarthy's political fortunes were promoted almost as much by newsmen who considered themselves his enemies as by those few who were his friends." This was because newsmen and Senator McCarthy were in the same business—communication and persuasion. Senator McCarthy aided the press in its role as the agent of the public to satisfy its expectation of news. Rovere (1959) reports

> He was capable of going into a tantrum before the television cameras and screaming "Mr. Chairman, Mr. Chairman, point of order, point of order"—and then making a beeline for the Gent's Room, the objective he had in mind when he began his diversion. Why not put nature into politics? He would tear passion to tatters—saying he could bear no more of the "farce," which made him "sick, sick way down inside"—and stage a walkout that would take him no farther than a corner of the room outside the sweep of the television cameras, there to observe calmly and be amused by the commotion he had caused. He often timed his walkouts for the newspaper deadlines.

The point here is not to indict McCarthy, but to note his recognition of the press as a special kind of audience, one which if its needs were considered was capable of helping him reach those larger audiences he sought to influence. Even though many newsmen disliked McCarthy, they had their own audiences to satisfy, to provide with news, and McCarthy and his charges were news to a hungry public. These audiences are characterized by excessive expectations and perhaps excessive need for news. Those who open the morning paper or turn on the radio newscast during breakfast expect them to report the momentous events that have happened since the eleven o'clock newscast the night before. Those on the way to work turn on the car radio for that news which developed since the morning paper went to press or was missed by the breakfast newscast. Similarly, persons returning home in the evening expect important events to have occurred during the day and the newscast to report them.

As Boorstin (1962) observes, "There was a time when the reader of an unexciting newspaper would remark 'How dull is the world today!' Nowadays he says, 'What a dull newspaper!' When the first American newspaper, Benjamin Harris' *Publick Occurrences Both Foreign and Domestick,* appeared in Boston on September 25, 1690, it promised to furnish news regularly once a month. But, the editor explained, it might appear oftener 'if any Glut of Occurrences happen.'" Mr. Harris today would find that, if there is no news that appears worthy of printing, the newspaper audience believes there is news and it can be found by the enterprising newsman. The successful reporter is one who can find the news that must be there, even if there is no invasion in progress, significant flood, major race riot, threatening strike, or important Supreme Court decision. In response to this demand for news, the press becomes an interested third party at a persuasive event.

Additionally, the press is involved as an interested third party because of a need to fill in the white spaces around the advertisements, or in broadcasting to fill up the dead space around the commercials. Newspapermen distinguish between what they call "hard" news and "soft" news. Though difficult to define, soft news is recognized in the reported interview, the comments or predictions of a "reliable" source, and the "news behind the news." To a considerable extent, the fill around the advertisements is soft news. By this means the press satisfies an audience need for "news" and at the same time encourages exposure to the advertisements which pay the bill.

A fuller recognition of the needs of the press and of their services to the persuader in diffusing a message apparently prevailed in the Kennedy political organization in 1960 than in the Nixon group. White (1961) observed that it was a practice of the Kennedy campaigners to provide the press immediately a stenotype transcript of what the candidate had said. This was done consistently whether Kennedy's remarks were made to a small village audience or in New York's Coliseum. "Chick" Reynolds, a stenotypist, was employed to do this. The Nixon campaigners, in contrast, did not provide such a service until late in the campaign.

One instance of the failure to appreciate the relevancy of this audience, the interested third parties, occurred with the Nixon farm speech. The candidate had worked on it intently for two days. When it was spoken, however, no one had explained it in advance to the press correspondents. As a result, the speech was often misinterpreted and apparently misunderstood by many of the reporters. Mr. Nixon did not seem to realize fully that these reporters had their own audiences, who would retransmit his message, diffusing it to a much larger audience than he would otherwise reach. The fidelity of these retransmissions depended, in part, on the accuracy of the reports. A copy of the speech would have insured such accuracy. Moreover, though Mr. Nixon had the editorial support of 78 percent of all newspapers whose publishers endorsed a candidate in 1960, it is a fact that newscasts and front page news items have substantially larger audiences than do editorial pages. The lesson was apparently learned. In the 1964 presidential campaign, the organizations working for both candidates made a determined effort to provide reporters with copies of speeches.

Other parties, through a need to satisfy their own audiences and their own goals, become interested in the persuader's effort. These parties include officers of service clubs, clergymen, university professors and administrators, and PTA program chairmen. Thus, it comes about that the persuader often finds these parties willing co-participants in the dissemination of his messages. To reach these other audiences, he finds it very important to use the press conference, the news release, and other techniques of providing interested third parties with messages for their audiences.

## summary

It is to be expected that receivers should find their own reactions to messages relevant. But more than this, reactions in receivers must have a bearing on the persuader's goals. This requirement of source relevancy applies in any effort to influence by whatever means. Moreover, effects in receivers may be morally bad or interfere with what the persuader wants, yet be relevant. Such effects should be studied as well as the good or desired results of persuasion. Another important aspect of relevancy is the receiver. Receivers can be grouped into four classes: intended, unintended, interested third parties, such as the press, who attend to a message to gather material for messages to their own audiences, and finally irrelevant receivers whose reactions are inconsequential to what the persuader seeks. Generally, intended receivers, particularly those who are directly exposed to a message, have been given the most attention in the literature and research on persuasion. This overemphasis, and the consequent limited view of the audience, has been fostered in the past by the notion that audiences are largely passive. A more contemporary view, supported by research and observation, holds that audiences commonly diffuse the persuader's message to others. It is this fact that increases the importance of interested third parties who diffuse messages and the many indirect receivers who are exposed to a message secondhand.

# Chapter 3

# The Instrumentality of Effects

The concept of instrumentality, and its contribution to a perspective on persuasion, is clarified in an illustration used by the author in an earlier publication (Fotheringham, 1963).

> "The biggest bargain in New York City is the nickel ride on the Staten Island Ferry." Thousands of tourists and New Yorkers agree. Should you take this leisurely ride from Manhattan past the Statue of Liberty to Staten Island, watch your fellow passengers. You will observe something relevant to . . . persuasion. . . .
>
> Even before the ferry has left the dock, some persons have climbed the stairs, crossed the decks to the rails and are looking about to see what is to be seen. Others are seated indoors, some of them examining papers from opened briefcases; these apparently are planning for or thinking about what they will do when they reach Staten Island. The first group is interested in the experience of crossing the harbor, the second merely concerned with getting across. Those in the first group become immersed in seeing, hearing, smelling, feeling, becoming acquainted with the moment; their purpose seems to be to *consume* the experience. For those in the second group, the ferry is a means, an *instrument* which enables them to pursue goals not yet attained.
>
> Fifty years ago, Max Eastman (1913) classified these groups as poetic and practical persons. He didn't imply that you and I were either-or, but rather that each person could be placed on a poetic-practical continuum (a continuous series of gradations from one extreme to the other). Each person possesses a particular mixture of the two traits.
>
> Since then, we have supplemented this trait theory of behavior. The behavior of people, we believe, is also affected by the situation they are in, their sets, attitudes, needs. For example, the tourist is more

likely than the office worker to be out on deck consuming the experience, partly because he is on vacation. Back home, his behavior becomes more instrumental (practical). Furthermore, the terms poetic and practical, in the hands of the behavioral scientist (Festinger, 1950), have been changed to *consummatory* and *instrumental*. The meanings are essentially similar.

The essential characteristic of instrumental behavior is that it is a *means* to some goal not yet achieved. In this respect, the ferryboat passengers differed. Some found their goals or needs satisfied in the excitement of the ride; for others, their goals were simply furthered by a transportation facility. Other illustrations of these differing emphases are not hard to find. Tourists and San Franciscans both ride that city's famed cable cars; for the tourist the experience may be a sufficient reward in itself, but for the daily user of the cable car the ride may be largely a means to some subsequent reward. Weekend joy-riding by car or airplane tends to be a consummatory kind of behavior. Many activities such as playing cards, fishing, reading, or walking can serve as rewards in themselves or be used as means to other goals.

Similarly, communicators differ. Some find their goals realized in the immediate responses of receivers; for others these responses are insufficient but do serve to further more remote goals. This basic difference among communicators arises from the different values placed on effects. Immediate effects, such as comprehension, recognition, approval or disapproval, and belief, may be valued as goals in themselves. For other communicators, they are valued for their instrumentality in generating some desired action. Thus responses are, from the source's view, consummatory when they reduce or eliminate his motivated state. The same responses are instrumental when they lead receivers to that further behavior, the source's goal, which satisfies his motivated condition. Communicators interested in effects primarily for their value in producing further behavior (action) are persuaders.

For those readers already familiar with the term "instrumental" in other contexts, the distinction between its use here and elsewhere should be noted. The term is commonly used in discussions of conditioning and learning. Those who discuss learning by conditioning speak of two types of behavior. One is activated by a specific external stimulus; this is referred to as respondent behavior, implying a response to an identifiable stimulus. An eye blink in response to sudden light is a typical example. The other is behavior which is difficult to account for on the basis of specific external stimulation; this behavior functions to bring an individual what he needs; it is behavior which is instrumental in achieving some goal. Because this type of behavior attempts to operate on or alter the surrounding environment, it is called operant or instrumental. From this view, all communicators, comedians, or advertisers engage in instrumental behavior; all attempt to change those around them to achieve a goal.

In this context, however, instrumental behavior refers to effects in others, not to the effort of a source to alter others. Discussions of conditioning generally are not concerned with the interaction and behavior of at least two people. Discussions of communication and persuasion, in contrast, typically consider behavior in both source and receiver. If the two meanings of "instrumental" are combined to reflect their differences, it could be said that communicators engage in instrumental behavior to achieve a goal; they look upon message effects in receivers, however, sometimes as the desired goal and sometimes as a means to further behavior in receivers. This further behavior is viewed as the goal. When communicators emphasize effects as instruments to further behavior, they are considered persuaders.

## persuasion: message effects valued for their instrumentality

When was the last time you heard a good joke, one that really "sent" you? Whenever it was, you probably told it to others. You may have told it to friends, acquaintances at a cocktail party, or a stranger beside you on a bus or train. If the listener was a stranger, you sized him up. Was he the sort who enjoys a good joke? Almost any listener, satisfying this criterion, would have been acceptable. You had no special audience in mind. If your listener laughed heartily, as you anticipated, you were satisfied. Your goal was achieved; the listener enjoyed the story. When the bus or train approached your destination, you may have glanced at your watch and noticed it was getting late. You mumbled an " . . . enjoyed-talking-with-you," and left. In telling the joke, the effect you sought was a consummatory one. You were interested primarily in the listener's immediate satistfaction as an end in itself and not as a means to further behavior. A consummatory response from a receiver, then, is behavior that satisfies a source's motive; the response is the source's goal, not a means to it.

In contrast, a salesman may have a good story to tell. In fact, he often has a large repertoire of stories. And he remembers them. He uses them in his business. For listeners, he prefers potential customers. A customer who enjoys his stories, he reasons, is apt to give him an order. The salesman doesn't dignify his thinking by calling it a theory of persuasion, yet he has one that runs something like this. When one sells, his goal is to get an order, but he doesn't ask for this immediately. Only a customer who is already sold will respond to this. With unsold customers, the first step is to give the customer something he wants—in this case, the pleasure of a good laugh. When the customer laughs, this effect produces another effect. He associates his pleasure with the salesman, and as a result likes the salesman. This in turn leads to the goal. Customers buy from people they like, other things being equal. The effect the salesman sought (laughter) was viewed instrumentally by him; it was a means to further desired behavior. Similarly, some television commercials generate amusement as an instrument or means to an end. Suppose the customer laughs but does not buy. The sponsor's goal has not been achieved although he may be pleased by the laughter. It is the instrumentality of the initial effect rather than the effect itself that is important to the persuader.

The two illustrations should not imply that a communicator seeks either consummatory or instrumental effects. An effect may have both consummatory and instrumental value; it may have value as an end in itself and as a means to a further end. A communicator may seek both. The professional comedian may find reward in the listener's enjoyment. Also, he hopes the word gets around and others come to enjoy his act. On the other hand, the advertiser may seek the remembrance of his product name as an initial effect; to him this effect has only instrumental value. It leads to the purchase of his product. Which is the persuader, the professional comedian or the advertiser? The answer is clearer when the question is restated; which one looked upon message effects more for their instrumentality in producing further behavior? Both men persuade, the advertiser more completely than the comedian.

Communicators may be positioned on a scale (see Figure 1) reflecting the kind of values they place on message effects. Persuaders are viewed as communicators who value effects largely for their instrumentality.

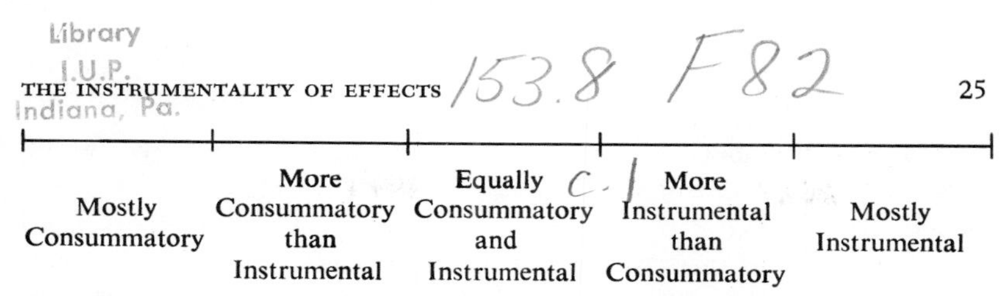


FIGURE 1. Ratio of consummatory to instrumental value placed on message effects by various communicators.

It follows from the fact that a communicator may value effects for their consummatory and instrumental qualities that no strict dichotomy exists between persuasive and non-persuasive messages. There is no clear-cut answer to the question, "Is the message persuasive or non-persuasive?" Rather, it is a matter of emphasis. Communicators attaching greater value to instrumental effects are primarily persuaders; those with little interest in such effects are primarily non-persuaders. The U.S. Weather Bureau, for example, prepares messages about tomorrow's weather. The principal effect sought is listener comprehension of the message. Other effects of the comprehension are of value to the listener, not to the Bureau. It generally seeks no specific further effects. The word "specific" is worth noting. It may be argued that the motives of Weather Bureau personnel may not be satisfied solely by message comprehension. Receiver use of the information may be a needed reward. Is comprehension, then, valued for its instrumentality? Are weather reporters persuaders? Simply to find satisfaction in the thought that others act *in some way* on one's information seems hardly to characterize the persuader. He seeks specific action—buy this product, vote for this candidate, join this group. In the case of an approaching hurricane, however, the Weather Bureau may shift emphasis and seek definite instrumental effects from its messages. The Bureau personnel want their messages to be the means of getting people to refrain from dangerous activities such as swimming, boating, fishing, and flying as well as flee from threatened areas in the hurricane's path.

Communicative efforts that dominantly seek effects as ends in themselves (consummatory effects) are exemplified in the referee's messages to the audience watching a televised football game. A whistle blows. A referee faces the television camera to communicate the infraction that has occurred. Viewers see him use a chopping motion of the hand against his leg and understand that a team is being penalized for clipping. Or the referee holds one arm above his head and grasps his wrist with the other hand: a holding penalty is being imposed. In such messages, comprehension is the communicator's goal; the effect is the goal, not an instrument to further behavior. The referee is not a persuader.

Some of the mass media organizations—radio and television networks and stations, newspapers, and mass magazines—are interesting in the values they attach to consummatory and instrumental effects. Are these organizations primarily persuaders? Indeed they are, but in quite a different way from political, social, or religious organizations and even other commercial groups. Mass media organizations are predominantly concerned with securing and holding an audience. Messages, in the form of variety, mystery, western, quiz, and news shows, are designed to achieve viewership or readership. The goal is to attract and have available an audience that can be sold to advertisers. That the audience enjoy a show is not an end in itself; it must lead to future watching of that show. The goal is continued viewing, or in the case of newspapers and magazines, continued purchase. These organizations value effects of their messages for their instrumentality in generating further behavior.

That mass media organizations view their presentations as instruments to retain audiences for sale to advertisers, moreover, seems to apply even to newscasts and documentaries.

Considerable criticism has been directed at the mass media organizations, particularly commercial television, for making the getting and holding of audiences their prime goal. Lindeman and Patureau (1964) remark that, "Like Roman emperors, the network executives wait for the boos and cheers of the crowd. If the TV ratings show that the crowd is unenthusiastic about a program, it is consigned to oblivion." The lack of enthusiasm, of course, means the goal of securing large audiences is not being achieved. Elsewhere in their article the authors quote Pat Weaver, a major TV executive.

> It is an economic fact that there is a limit to the amount of focus and interest that commercial TV can fulfill. They must aim at the mass taste at the broad lowest common denominator to get the most people to watch for the longest period of time. They want a viewer to sit for five hours in a sort of apathy, but they don't want to wear them out so they will turn the set off.

If the goal is to secure an audience, and receiver responses are dominantly valued for their service to this goal, then the shows provided by the mass media organizations eminently make good sense. Put simply, the type of message is provided which yields the desired goal. It also makes good sense, given this goal, that television networks and stations be primarily concerned with measuring audience size and composition rather than other effects less vital from their viewpoint.

Similarly, much of the news in daily papers and many articles in mass magazines reveal that a prime goal of these media is to secure an audience to be sold to the advertiser. The messages deal with popular interests, fads, curiosities, gossip, comic strips, sports, scandals, the sex lives of celebrities, the latest murder or exposure of corruption. The messages about a recent murder are not primarily intended to be instrumental in the reduction of this crime, but to foster continued readership.

It might well be argued that such a goal is socially unacceptable. It could be contended that the mass media should seek to produce effects which are instrumental in bringing about such socially approved goals as more informed voting, improved standards of taste, safer highway driving, and more tolerant behavior toward minority groups. If television is a "vast wasteland," along with much that appears in newspapers and mass magazines, it is not because these organizations do not seek to affect the behavior of their audiences. It is because the receiver behavior of most concern to them is to have them come back for more. Receivers tend to get what the largest number of them will continue to view or read.

It should not be concluded that mass media organizations cannot emphasize other persuasive goals. They could be and are used, on occasion, by society or groups within society to promote other goals. The prime example is the use made of the Soviet mass media system (Wright, 1959). It is used to sell a particular interpretation of events and to prescribe standards of conduct. It is less concerned with printing all the news that's fit to print or all the news that will promote continued readership. Nor, as a persuader, does it seek to provide orientation or comprehension as ends in themselves. As Brown (1963) reports "many important events, such as the crisis over Cuba or the Chinese aggression in India, are not made known to the Soviet citizen until days after they have occurred and government officials have decided how to present them." The Soviet mass media system, of course, is not concerned with selling audiences to advertisers. Government ownership permits an emphasis on other persuasive goals.

For one further observation in distinguishing between consummatory and instrumental effects, let us return to the example of the weather report. What the listener to a weather report does following comprehension suggests that the initial effects of a message, consummatory or instrumental or both, may have different values for the source and receiver. The receiver may not only comprehend the weather report, but find the information instrumental in planning a party or picnic. Receivers of telephone directories may find varied uses for the information; a researcher uses it to conduct a survey; a politician uses it to call potential voters; a salesman uses it to set up appointments. In persuasion, however, the instrumentality of effects is what is useful to the source's goal.

## instrumental effects and goals

The distinction and relationship between instrumental effect and goal are suggested by the following illustrations:

*Source:* Candidate for Governor.
*Receivers:* Eligible voters.
*Instrumental Effect:* To have receivers believe the state is falling behind economically.
*Goal:* To be elected Governor.

*Source:* Program sponsor—producer of consumer product.
*Receivers:* TV audience of adult consumers.
*Instrumental Effect:* To have listeners remember a product name.
*Goal:* To increase sales of company product.

*Source:* Adlai Stevenson, American U.N. Delegate.
*Receivers:* U.N. Security Council and other delegates.
*Instrumental Effects:* To have delegates believe Russia has built offensive missile bases in Cuba; to have delegates believe Russia has been deceitful in its declarations about Cuba.
*Goal:* To develop support for U.S. policy toward Cuba.

*Source:* Sales Manager.
*Receivers:* Salesmen for company.
*Instrumental Effect:* To create anxiety and fear for one's job.
*Goal:* To increase company sales.

Persuasive efforts in commercial advertising reveal something of the wide variety of instrumental effects that persuaders seek and at the same time clarify the distinction between them and goals. Among instrumental effects sought through advertising messages are: getting potential customers to visit stores and showrooms, encouraging customers to return coupons in order to secure leads for salesmen, impressing an industrial customer or distributor, creating awareness of the extent of a product line, increasing comprehension of the uses of new products, arousing awareness of new uses for old products, creating awareness of product warranties, developing recognition of a new brand name for a product, encouraging requests for samples, and creating an image of the company as a good employer, citizen, or neighbor. Wolfe, Brown, and Thompson (1962), in studying the advertising efforts of 300 companies, identified 91 different instrumental effects sought in conjunction with the pursuit of the company goals.

In the political field, the establishment of instrumental effects as a means to a goal is widely recognized. To become known, to be identifiable to voters is probably the most necessary product of political persuasion. A known name and an identifiable face can be counted on to produce votes. *Newsweek* (Oct. 1962) reported that Pat Brown, then candidate for Governor of California, distressed his supporters with his inability to be easily recognized. He had had eight years as attorney general and four as governor, yet still had failed to identify himself to many Californians. It was reported that "Early in the campaign, some Brown posters appeared showing the governor without his glasses. They were quickly taken down when it was seen that virtually no one recognized him." Of his opponent, Nixon, one Brown aide said almost jealously, "You could block Nixon's eyes out, and they'd still recognize him." In political as in commercial advertising, it would not be difficult to identify a wide variety of instrumental effects--name recogition, face recognition, wearing party symbols in the form of elephants or donkeys, wearing campaign buttons, and accepting a wide range of beliefs about the present and future. Similarly, persuasive efforts of clergymen, lawyers, physicians, lobbyists, government officials, and others reveal the variety and role of instrumental effects in generating goal behavior in receivers.

## limitations of the trichotomy of communication purposes: to inform, to persuade, to entertain

Readers may have noticed that the term "purpose" has not been used. There is partisan feeling in that omission; it has been deliberate. It is difficult to avoid using a term of such common currency, and which in many ways has genuine legitimacy. Yet its wide and varied uses reduce its value. It seems worth the effort to avoid some erroneous implications of the term. Its use is apt to confuse rather than clarify a concept of persuasion.

To begin with, the term "purpose" is avoided by those most concerned with the scientific study of the behavior of the human individual. Tables of Content and Indexes of contemporary texts in general psychology do not list "purpose" as such. The principal explanation of this avoidance is that other less ambiguous terms are available. Social and behavioral scientists employ such concepts as motivation, goal, need, and drive.

When the term "purpose" is used, as in persuasion texts, ambiguity is likely. Purpose is used to refer to instrumental effects sought, goals of the persuader, and his motives. For example, one can ask of a TV commercial, "What was the purpose?" The answers can be (1) to increase retention of the product name (instrumental effect), (2) to increase the purchases of the product (goal or final viewer effect), and (3) to make money (motive). It is desirable to distinguish between these phenomena; separate and distinct terms would help.

When we speak of communication purposes—to inform, to persuade, and to entertain—another difficulty develops. With particular relevance to persuasion, such language encourages thinking of final receiver effect and neglecting consideration of instrumental effects. The political candidate who says he seeks to persuade citizens to vote for him tends to view his messages as direct producers of final effects. The importance of intervening variables (preliminary effects) between message and final effect is underestimated. The result is less clarity about his persuasive task. In their study of the persuasive efforts of 300 companies, Wolfe, Brown, and Thompson (1962) concluded that the management of the advertising programs revealed a failure to develop clear-cut statements of specific objectives. They failed to specify receiver behavior in terms of instrumental effects. Ends (goal behaviors of customers) were thought about and were too often looked upon as the effects messages were to produce. Rather than one term—purpose—used interchangeably, two terms—instrumental effect and goal—would serve to reduce ambiguity and promote more effective consideration of both kinds of receiver behavior. It seems language interferes with our perceiving that persuasion has two kinds of objectives—instrumental behavior and goal behavior.

There is a natural tendency to view an effort to influence others in terms of its reward, the receiver behavior which is the persuader's goal.

It is the goal behavior that is rewarding, not the means of setting in motion a sequence of behavior leading to that goal. In fact, to think of receiver behavior in terms of its instrumentality involves recognizing that reward is not immediate, and is likely to be delayed and dependent on prior effects. In experimental studies of reward—psychologists use the term reinforcement—this much seems fairly certain: reward delay and uncertainty are difficult to accept. It is thus more pleasant to think of goals rather than means, which imply delay and uncertainty. For this reason, the persuader needs a tolerance for delayed reward and an increased awareness of the need to consider means more specifically. Distinct terms for means and ends encourage this.

Furthermore, the point has been made (Berlo, 1960; Thayer,1961) that it is a matter of habit for us to talk or write without a clear, specific objective. The habit-character of our persuasive efforts is confirmed in our own experience and that of others. Our messages, choice of audience, and message form and wording portray the characteristics of habit: failure to consider alternatives, lack of variability, and resistance to change even when unsuccessful. Our persuasive efforts have the "fixed" character of habit, rather than the "searching" behavior required in problem solving. We habitually fail to specify the precise effect to be achieved and the consequent behavior that this effect is to generate. This, in part at least, is due to vagueness and confusion about instrumental effects and goals.

One can speculate as to what effects this confusion has on a person motivated to persuade others. Stagner and Karwoski (1952) point out that we cannot identify motivation directly, but infer it by observing if behavior is that which motivated persons display. This behavior, the authors specify, has three primary characteristics: energy, persistence, and variability. The more highly motivated person expends more energy in a given situation; he doesn't give up easily; he varies his methods, if first efforts fail, as he continues to seek satisfaction. The habit-bound, confused persuader could be expected to display least of all this last characteristic of motivation, namely, variability, The much maligned back-seat driver, as a persuader, typically displays more energy and persistence than variability of messages in seeking goals. Failure to see the relations between messages, instrumental effects, and goals hampers variability in message production.

## *the goals of persuasion*

The ambiguity of the term "purpose" has fostered vagueness about the goals of persuasion. For some, the goal is to change the beliefs or actions of receivers, or both; for others, the goal is vaguely to affect other people's behavior, and for others to gain the acceptance of a belief or proposed action.

*The ultimate goal of all persuasive efforts is action.* The development of comprehension, feeling, belief, retention, confusion, uncertainty is instrumental to the goal of persuasion. These function to influence, direct, and control the actions of others. Those persons typically identified as professional persuaders—politicians, advertisers, propagandists, leaders of movements, evangelists, physicians, psychiatrists, lawyers, social workers—seek action from their audiences. Less than this is unsatisfying. In this sense, then, persuaders are not different from those who employ force or authority in influencing others. The goal of all such individuals is action on the part of those to be influenced.

The concept of action, in the study of persuasion, has been too restricted. Action has been conceived only as a change in behavior, the adoption of different behavior. Action has meant that the audience would do something, and something different from what they had been doing. Clearly, this restricted view does not square with the goals sought by persuaders. Among the millions of receivers of a cigarette, soap, or automobile advertisement, a great many already use the product. The advertiser wants them to continue purchasing his product. He seeks action in the form of continuance, not change. Service clubs are as concerned with persuading members to continue their membership as they are in securing new members. The American Medical Association's lobbyists have sought to deter legislative action on medical plans of which they disapproved. Parents commonly seek, often by persuasion, to deter the onset of undesired behavior in their children. Similarly, deterrence of behavior is a major objective of any society in its effort to exercise social control; the means of achieving it include persuasion. Finally, some persuaders seek the discontinuance of action. The persuasive efforts of Alcoholics Anonymous are directed largely to bringing about the discontinuance of action.

What is needed are categories of action that encompass the various forms of action persuaders seek, and provide distinctions between persistence and change, and between action and behavior that deters unwanted action. Four categories of action seem to fill this need. These four goals of persuaders are: (1) adoption, (2) continuance, (3) deterrence, and (4) discontinuance. In terms of action-goals, then, we can view persuasion as those instrumental effects to which messages have been a dominant contributor, and which are brought about to facilitate the adoption of, continuance of, deterrence of, or discontinuance of actions in others.

The utility of this set of action-goals is to be found in its value in understanding the behavior of different types of goals. We wonder, for example, about the popular politician whose messages avoid issues, are replete with platitudes, and are diversionary in intent. Grant that such a person stands to gain from continuant behavior among voters, then his messages and their effects become sensible. Of the four action-goals, for this case, continuance is the most sought from those who voluntarily expose themselves. These tend to be the people who have voted before for this politician. In such an audience, adoption, deterrence, or discontinuance are less desired goals.

Weaver and Strausbaugh (1964) describe the process of diversion by the persuader. Why would he seek to divert an audience? Consider their description from the viewpoint of deterrence or continuance as action-goals.

> A skillful persuader can sometimes send a questioner away perfectly satisfied, believing that he has received the answer he came for. . . . Sometimes the subject can be changed in the manner of free-association, wherein a word or concept in what started out to be the right answer is allowed to become the central subject of discussion and the original subject is forgotten.

As other action-goals of persuasion receive more extensive consideration, it is to be expected that theories and practices with respect to continuance, deterrence, and discontinuance will be refined, and tested through research efforts.

Among those who specifically theorize about persuasion, there is a consistent tendency to view adoption as the goal. This is revealed in the recommended structures of the persuasive effort, whether the effort be a one-shot appeal or an entire persuasive campaign. Monroe's motivated sequence (1939), for example, begins with getting attention and ends with adoption of action. Similarly, Minick (1957), Janis and Feshbach (1953), Brembeck and Howell (1952), Wolfe, Brown and Thompson (1962), Rogers (1962), Hoffer (1951), Schein, Schneier, and Barker (1961), Hovland, Janis, and Kelley (1953), Eisenson, Auer, and Irwin (1963), and Abernathy (1964) emphasize adoption or change of behavior as the goal of persuasion. To complement these discussions, what is needed are procedural steps (structures) for achieving other kinds of action-goals.

## instrumentality and the persuasive campaign

The concept of instrumentality encourages seeing persuasion as a campaign—a structured sequence of efforts to achieve adoption, continuance, deterrence, or discontinuance—rather than as a one-shot effort. Effects established in an earlier phase of a campaign are instrumental to the development of subsequent effects. The first effort to persuade others commonly accomplishes only part of the job; that part, however, is necessary for the success of the next phase and for the ultimate goal.

Scholars, concerned with the structural analysis of campaigns involving persuasion, typically observe the value of an earlier effect to a later effect. Schein, Schneier, and Barker (1961), for example, point out that the campaign by the Chinese Communists to influence American prisoners from 1950–1956 occurred "over time and consists of several successive stages or steps. These stages can be labeled unfreezing, changing, and refreezing." The initial phase of the campaign (unfreezing) is described as "an alteration by the agent of influence of the forces acting on the person such that the existing equilibrium is no longer stable." This effect was considered by the Chinese Communists to be necessary for and instrumental to the second phase (changing). This stage of the campaign involved "the provision by the agent of influence of information, arguments, models to be imitated or identified with, etc., which provide a direction of change toward a new equilibrium, usually by allowing the person to learn something new, redefine something old." The third stage, built upon the effects established in preceding stages, was that of refreezing. It provided "the facilitation by the agent of influence of the reintegration of the new equilibrium into the rest of the personality and into ongoing interpersonal relationships by the provision of reward and social support for any changes made by the person."

The point to be made is not that the "brainwashing" process, which used persuasion along with other means of influence, involved some new understanding or new theory of how to influence people. The underlying theory of behavior is old. Basically, "brainwashing" was based on a tension-reduction theory of behavior. The notion that our behavior will be directed toward tension-reduction is inherent in a whole family of theories or models of behavior. It underlies the homeostatic model of behavior discussed by Maccoby and Maccoby (1961), Heider's (1946) balance theory, Osgood and Tannenbaum's (1955) congruity theory, Asch's (1948) cognitive restructuring model, Festinger's (1957) theory of cognitive dissonance, and Newcomb's (1953) strain for symmetry theory. Tension reduction has been an important concept in motivation theory for a long time. It is implied in a variety of structures recommended for persuasive speeches. Monroe's (1939) motivated sequence was based on the presumed value of tension-reduction in changing behavior. The familiar problem-solution speech structure is consistent with this theory. The threat-reassuring recommendation structure discussed by Janis and Feshbach (1953), similarly, is based on this notion. In contrast to viewing "brainwashing" as the use of some new principle of influence, the point can be legitimately made that the process involved the recognition of the campaign nature of persuasion, and of the instrumental function of an early effect in arousing or facilitating a later effect.

Other campaign structures similarly reflect a recognition of the instrumentality of initial effects. It is found in Lifton's (1960) description of the program (persuasive campaign) used in the Chinese revolutional colleges. These were established to change Chinese peasants into dedicated Communists. The sequence of coordinated steps, as labeled by Lifton, were: group identification, emotional conflict, and finally, submission and rebirth. Hoffer (1951) and Berger (1963) both note the use of persuasion as one means of influence in revolutionary mass movements as well as the sequential character of their phases. For Hoffer, a mass movement passes through four phases; these are (1) the phase in which the status quo is discredited, (2) the provision of the new doctrine and slogans, (3) the activist phase, and finally (4) the consolidation or stabilizing of the changes made. Similarly, Berger comments on the sequential structure of revolutions.

> When we look at revolutions, we find that the outward acts against the old order are invariably preceded by disintegration of allegiance and loyalties. The images of kings topple before their thrones . . . this destruction of the peoples' conception of their rulers can be illustrated by the Affair of the Queen's Necklace before the French Revolution

> and the Rasputin case before the Russian. The ongoing insurrection of Southern Negroes [nationwide] against the segregation system in our own time was similarly preceded by a long process in which the old definitions of their role were discredited in the nation at large and destroyed in their own minds. The extraordinary passion of a charismatic movement only rarely survives for longer than one generation. Invariably charisma becomes what Weber called "routinized," that is, becomes reintegrated into the structures of society in much less radical forms. Prophets are followed by popes, revolutionaries by administrators.

The instrumental and sequential character of revolutionary stages explains why the "old guard" tends to be rejected. Those who cannot recognize that being "agin the government" is only a means to a later phase must be set aside. The intellectual and the fanatic who continue to discredit and disrupt, after the party they helped bring to power has become the orthodox authority, are now out of tune with the goals of the movement. In the American revolution, most of the early revolutionaries were not delegates to the Constitutional Convention held some years later. Leadership needs and goals had changed.

The revolutionary movement, clearly, changes its goals as it progresses from one phase to another. In the beginning, through persuasion and other means of influence, it seeks discontinuance as a goal. The *status quo* is discredited as a means of bringing about discontinuant behavior. The public is encouraged not to believe and ultimately not to behave as it formerly did. Following this, the goal of the movement becomes adoption. The objective is to influence people to adopt new behavior which supports the revolution. Once the movement has come into power, its goals become continuance and deterrence. It then seeks the continuation of the newly accepted behavior and the prevention of behavior which threatens the new order.

The instrumentality of one campaign effect on a subsequent effort can be seen in the *peredishka* or "breathing spell" technique used by the Communists (Meerloo, 1960). The campaign sequence employs waves of terror with in-between periods of relative calm and relaxed police activity. This on-and-off sequence is illustrated in the alternation of cold war propaganda with "dove of peace" messages and appeals for peaceful coexistence. In the thinking of totalitarian strategists, the intervals of calm and the absence of observable tension-producing incidents can be used to good advantage for political persuasion *pro-*

*vided some new wave of terror is anticipated.* The threat is instrumental in establishing persuasive effects during the "breathing spell."

The more familiar uses of persuasion (selling, preaching, courtroom advocacy, counseling, etc.) are better understood as campaigns, over time, in which initial effects are established for their instrumentality in bringing about or facilitating subsequent effects and ultimately the action-goal of the persuader. More often than not, the action-goal cannot be achieved by a one-shot effort. Thus, earlier persuasive efforts are more realistically viewed as efforts to establish initial effects and not to produce the action-goal *per se*. Wolfe and others (1962), for example, view the act of selling as a five stage campaign. In the first stage, the persuader seeks to create awareness of the product. Effort is directed specifically toward generating awareness; effort to produce purchase of the product, at this stage, is subdued. Following awareness, the second stage is to nurture acceptance of the product. In the third stage, preference for the product is sought. Then, effort is focussed on arousing intent to buy the product, and finally messages seek to develop action, or purchase of the product. This neat progression of stages, each instrumental to the final stage, is, of course, not followed in many sales campaigns. Some advertisements are conceived solely to create product awareness or solely to arouse intent to buy; others provide stimulation to produce one of several effects within the same advertisement. In the latter case it is assumed that individuals in the buying public are at different stages in the purchasing process.

The campaign structure of the persuasion involved in counseling and psychotherapy similarly reveals the instrumentality of earlier efforts. Rapoport (1960) outlines the basic steps involved. The first step involves "conveying to the other person that he has been heard and understood." At this point the person to be persuaded does most of the talking, responding to and guided by questions from the persuader (therapist). A subsequent inclination to listen to and understand the therapist is brought about by the experience of being heard and understood, rather than judged. As Rapoport notes, it is a novel and satisfying experience to be heard and understood. The second step involves "delineating the region of validity of the other person's stand." This means recognizing and appreciating the merit in the other person's view of reality. This procedure is in direct contrast with debate. The debater stresses the evidence, reasons, and conditions under which his opponent's position is not valid. Counseling and psychotherapy emphasize the conditions under which the other's position is valid. This second step is instrumental to the third, that of "inducing the assumption of similarity." The person to be persuaded is invited to listen to and seek to understand the persuader's view as was done for his viewpoint.

An analogous structure, applied mostly to public speaking and audiences of more than one, has been the object of several research studies. Authors have labeled it a "two-sided" or "both-sides" presentation. The initial experimental study of the effects of one-sided versus two-sided communications was done by the Information and Education Division, U.S. War Dept. (1947). Lawyers, debaters, and other public speakers, however, have for a long time been presenting "admitted matter" which essentially included those items of evidence and conclusions contrary to the speaker's position that he believed the audience would hold to be true regardless of subsequent argument.

The audience in the first experiment was composed of recruits being inducted into the Army in World War II. Early in 1945, the U.S. War Department was deeply concerned about the over-optimism regarding an early end of the war in the Pacific. The producers of the orientation program for recruits considered this issue: When most of the evidence supports a position while some evidence is contrary to it, is it more effective to present only those arguments supporting the position, or is it better to present both-sides—that is, to present arguments against as well as for the persuader's viewpoint?

The justification of such a communication structure is similar to Rapoport's structure for persuasion in counseling and psychotherapy. The "both-sides" presentation was based on such notions as (1) opposed audience members will listen and respond better when their view of reality is recognized, rather than threatened or ridiculed, (2) opposed audience members, when their side is not recognized, silently rehearse their counter-arguments and thus listen less well, (3) opposed audience members will be distracted, antagonized, and resistant when arguments on their side are omitted, and (4) this presentation will be perceived as more fair and ethical, thus enhancing the persuader's credibility.

The results of the experiment, in general, support the above hypotheses. The "both-sides" presentation was more effective with opposed audience members regardless of educational level. The method was also more effective with non-opposed audience members with high school educations or more. The "one-sided" presentation was more effective with non-opposed persons with less than a high school education. Subsequent studies of various aspects of this structure and the conditions under which it is effective are those of Lumsdaine and Janis (1953),

Thistlewaite and Kamenetsky (1955), Thistlewaite, Kamenetsky, and Schmidt (1956), Ludlum (1956), and Insko (1962).

At the beginning of this discussion of instrumentality and persuasive campaigns, it was stated that the concept of instrumentality encourages viewing persuasion more as a structured campaign than as a one-shot effort. Such a position implies that the latter view of persuasion has been overemphasized. This one-shot effort is exemplified in mail-order persuasion. No second effort is planned; no structure among efforts is formulated; the energy involved is minimal. Such persuasion is limited in usefulness. It achieves its greatest success when the producer and advertiser find out what people already want and then endeavor to supply it. The mail-order effort accommodates those who are already persuaded by clarifying and simplifying the purchasing action. That overemphasis of this view of persuasion is the case finds support in four conditions which operate as important contributors to the one-shot concept. These conditions are: (1) the high incidence of voluntary audiences, (2) typical procedures in the teaching of persuasion in Speech, English, Journalism, and other departments in colleges and universities, (3) the typical experimental designs to study persuasive effects, and (4) preference for immediate over delayed rewards from persuasive efforts.

The opposite of the "voluntary" audience is frequently called the "captive" audience. The terms are poor choices. They suggest an either-or dichotomy—an audience is either voluntary or captive. Secondly, the term "captive" implies that the audience has assembled involuntarily. Students in class, monks in a monastery, and soldiers in an enemy POW camp have all been labeled as "captive" audiences. Yet the first two groups would not feel forced to be an audience in the sense soldier-prisoners would. A more meaningful view of audiences would be to place them on a continuum from slightly motivated to highly motivated. The more highly motivated an audience, through reward or punishment, the more likely it will make itself available. The "captive" audience is essentially one that is characterized by consistent availability. An enthusiastic viewer of professional football on television is "captive," or more meaningfully, highly motivated to be in the audience. In contrast, voluntary audiences are weakly motivated, inconsistent in availability, and not to be counted on to be present throughout a structured series of messages.

So many audiences are weakly motivated (inconsistently available) that persuaders incline toward the one-shot effort to persuade. What might otherwise be a structured campaign is collapsed into a single effort. Over-emphasis results. In contrast, most of the theorizing about the structure of persuasive campaigns has come from those associated with consistently available or "captive" audiences.

The typical procedures in the teaching of persuasion have unduly stressed one-shot persuasion. Students are assigned a persuasive speech, theme, or editorial as an isolated effort in persuasion. Seldom are a structured series of messages assigned that could call the student's attention to the instrumental value of earlier efforts for subsequent ones. The student thus tends to leave such courses with a one-shot perspective on persuasion.

Despite the proven value of experimental research in persuasion, it has tended to over-emphasize the single effort. A hundred experiments, selected at random, would probably not turn up one specifically designed to study instrumentality and structure in persuasive campaigns. Subjects (audiences) are pre- and post-tested in connection with a single communication. Subjects are tested, retested, and retested over various periods of delay, but again with respect to a single message. Conditions are systematically varied under which a message is presented. Subjects with differing personality characteristics are studied with regard to message impact. Generally, the stimulus has been singular. It must be granted that the design problems generated by a campaign study are formidable, but the fact remains that experimentation has promoted a one-shot perspective on persuasion.

Other types of research, notably the field study and the repetitive survey, more frequently consider the impact of more than one message and sometimes attempt analysis of campaign structure. Such research, of course, lacks the rigor and control of the experiment. The establishment of the persuasive campaign as a more frequent object of research likely will require a variety of methods for its study. In any event, the products of research could do more to develop a campaign concept for students of persuasion.

Finally, in persuasion as in other activities, people prefer immediate over delayed reward for their efforts. A task that can be completed in one package and immediately rewarded is more likely to be attempted than a series of efforts sustained over time. The single, complete effort seems preferred even though the series of tasks over time may bring greater rewards. Such a preference favors a one-shot perspective on persuasion. Trying for the greater effectiveness can be increased if instrumental effects operate as sub-goals for the persuader. Awareness and observation of achieved sub-goals should provide sufficient reward to sustain the persuader through subsequent efforts to a final goal.

## summary

When one communicates, his interest can range from effects that are largely consummatory to those that are largely instrumental. A consummatory effect is one that is valued as an end in itself. This means that the communicator is essentially satisfied by the initial response in the receiver; obtaining this response is the communicator's goal. An instrumental effect, in contrast, is viewed by the communicator as a means to some end not yet achieved. This means that the communicator is not yet satisfied. The effect, however, is significant in that it is expected to generate further behavior in the receiver. This further behavior is the communicator's goal. In persuasion, message effects are dominantly valued, not as ends in themselves, but for their instrumentality. Moreover, a message effect should not be viewed as either persuasion or not persuasion. No such strict dichotomy exists; there are varying degrees of persuasive value attached to message effects. The more a message and its initial effects are valued as instruments to arouse further behavior, the more they are being used for persuasion.

Distinguishing among communication effects in terms of consummatory effects or instrumental effects has advantages over traditional classifications of purposes—for example, the three-fold classification, (1) to inform, (2) to persuade, and (3) to entertain. The emphasis on instrumental effects that characterizes persuasion reminds us more clearly of the distinction between effects and goals, and points up the fact that persuasion has two kinds of objectives—instrumental as well as final. Secondly, attention to the instrumentality of effects reminds persuaders that their satisfactions are apt to be delayed and dependent on careful development of prior effects. Finally, awareness of the instrumental relation of initial effects to goals refocuses attention on the campaign character of most persuasive enterprises.

# Chapter 4

# The Dominance of Message Effect in Persuasion

Consider the use of a popular concept of communication (Lasswell, 1948) rewritten and applied to persuasion. It would state that persuasion involves the study of *who* says *what* to *whom* with what relevant and instrumental *effects*. It is the response-producing value of *what* is said that differentiates persuasion from other means of influence. However, it makes a difference, in terms of effects produced, *who* says the *what;* it makes a difference to *whom* the *what* is said; it makes a difference in what *situation* the *what* is said. Messages occur inseparably in conjunction with other stimuli; for the receiver these arise externally and internally. Every persuasive event involves, in addition to a message, external components such as source, channel, occasion and other situational elements as well as personality factors in the form of needs, goals, prior experience, and abilities. Even in its simplest form, it is difficult to conceive of a persuasive event without them, and without their influence.

Though individuals often see things quite differently, people are somewhat consistent in their interpretations of the world about them, or in their interpretation of a message. Yet the same person may vary widely in his responses depending on the situation he is in. Both situational and personality factors must be considered in accounting for inter-individual and intra-individual differences in interpreting messages. Both sets of factors account for an individual's frame of reference. This refers to the perspective which the individual uses as a basis for interpreting incoming information, or in our case, messages. Here, however, our concern is with the situational contributors to frame of reference; it is among these external stimuli that a message is to have a dominant position.

## the message-stimulus and its context

Situational factors surrounding a message can be collectively thought of as context. These can serve to facilitate or inhibit a desired message effect, or be of sufficient significance to the receiver that they become the major determinants of response rather than the message. Among professional persuaders Burton (1959) illustrates the recognition of contextual factors in their influence on message effect. "Media research," he points out, "is learning more about the context in which the advertising message is placed, especially since so many highly-rated programs have had no, or little, influence in increasing sales." Among scholars, Dember (1961), in reviewing research and our existing knowledge of perception, concludes that "every bit of perceptual activity occurs in a context. . . . No perceptual event takes place independently of other events." The perception of a message and its meaning occurs in a context and is influenced by that context.

The so-called illusions provide numerous examples of the influence of context in perceptual events.

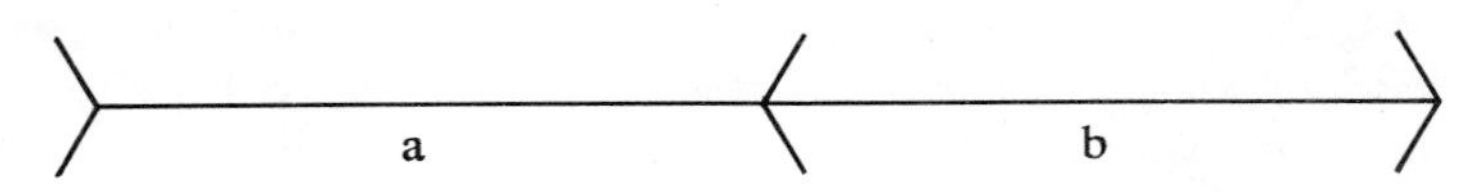


FIGURE 2. The Muller-Lyer illusion. The two arrowheads enclosing line (b) make it appear shorter than line (a) which terminates in two tails. The two lines are physically equal in length.

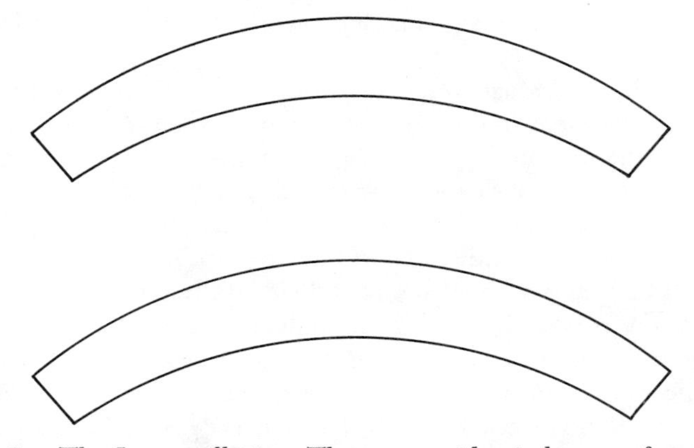

FIGURE 3. The Jastrow illusion. The two are identical except for position on the page. The upper, however, appears smaller than the lower.

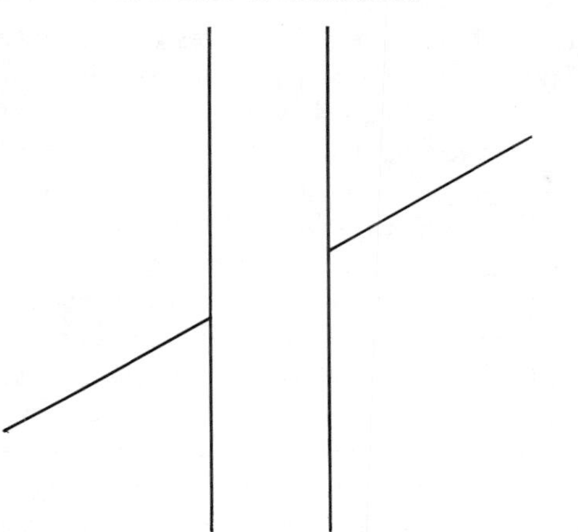

FIGURE 4. The upper and lower parts of the diagonal are continuous; the upper part, however, appears displaced upward.

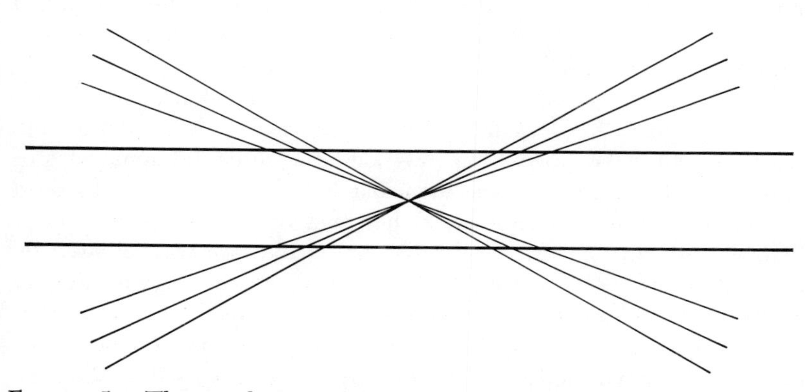

FIGURE 5. The two horizontal lines are straight and parallel, but appear bowed out.

Another example involves two series of symbols: 0, 1, 2, 3 and k, l, m, n. These are particularly interesting in that they are language symbols. Note again the influence of context, its tendency to affect our expectations and thus affect perception and meaning. The second symbol in each series is physically the same. In the first series, in a number context, it is perceived as a number, and in the second, in an alphabet context, as a letter of the alphabet. In this example, the context is the meaning of the surrounding elements. The implication for persuasion is that the context affects the meaning of a message.

The influence of contextual factors on message meaning as well as their role as major determinants of response is readily observed in more natural settings. When Khrushchev, former USSR premier, says, "We will bury you," the meaning aroused by that message is affected by that particular speaker and our view of U.S.–Russian relations. If we imagine the U.S. President saying these words to an audience of Russians, we are likely to attach a different meaning to them. The contextual element of time may affect the perceived importance of a message. If you receive a telephone call very early in the morning, before you usually get out of bed, the time of the call typically implies a message of importance and urgency. Similarly, a call after midnight, for most of us, is apt to be viewed as a matter of great seriousness. The medium used for a message, as a contextual element, affects meaning. Messages received by telegram, airmail, or long distance telephone are usually considered of some urgency or importance. The behavioral setting of a message affects meaning. A reprimand from the boss in the lunch room and in the presence of others, even though the same words are used, will have a different meaning than if given in the boss' office.

In his *Film Technique and Film Acting,* Pudovkin reported on a "little experiment in film editing." A simple, passive close-up of a well-liked Russian actor, Mosjukhin, was joined to three different strips of film. In one the actor's face was immediately followed by shots of a dead woman in a coffin. In another, a shot of a bowl of soup on a table followed the close-up. In the third instance, the face was followed by shots of a little girl playing with a funny, toy bear. According to Pudovkin, the effects on the audience were startling. They raved about the superb acting. They spoke of the heavy pensiveness of the actor's mood as he viewed the forgotten soup; they were impressed by the deep sorrow with which he looked at the dead woman; and they noted his light, happy smile as he watched the little girl at play. "But," says Pudovkin, "we knew that in all three cases the face was exactly the same."

Contextual factors, rather than the message, often become the major determinants of response. When an employee receives a memo from his boss suggesting he give priority to a certain task, he probably does as the message directs. He may respond, not because the message makes a major contribution to his response, but because he perceives the message-source as one having the legitimate right to direct his work behavior. The message, though necessary to his comprehension, may not be a major determinant of his response. The same message from someone else may not bring about the same effect. Communication has occurred but not persuasion.

Persuasion has not taken place when the message is not the major determinant of response. There are innumerable examples of such events. When the military officer orders one of his men to undertake an unpleasant task, it is the perceived right of the officer to direct the enlisted man's behavior and not the message that accounts for the response. Put the same message in the mouth of a civilian and the effect is very much altered. If, in the heavy traffic following a football game, a police officer directs you to turn right when you want to move straight ahead, it is not the message that largely determines your response but the perceived right of the officer to direct your behavior in that situation. In the 1964 political conventions, each presidential nominee "recommended" a vice-presidential nominee to his convention delegates. Opposition to William E. Miller existed among Republican delegates and to Hubert Humphrey among Democrats. Yet, in each instance, the delegates unanimously accepted the "suggestion," not because they were all persuaded but because of the perceived right of the presidential nominee to pick his running mate.

The compound of message with other influences makes the persuasive event a multiple-stimulus situation. The event does not exist without its associated components. Thus it is an over-simplification to say, "The speech convinced the audience," if we mean that it alone accounted for the effect produced. The message is only a partner in creating an effect, but in persuasion a major partner. Consistent with this, persuasion is conceived as those relevant and instrumental effects *of which messages have been a major determinant.*

## message impact vs. context as objects of study

Dember's line of thought about perception applies to persuasion specifically. It is context which imposes on the study of persuasion the complexity that makes it so bewildering and so fascinating. Contextual effects can be a source of contradictory results or limited conclusions for the person trying to investigate the isolated impact of message. For him, contextual determinants of the receiver's response must be controlled, rendered neutral, or manipulated in an experimental setting, and some measure of their contribution made. For others, context may be the very object of investigation.

A clear distinction should be made between studies of message effects and those of contextual variables which facilitate or inhibit persuasion. This distinction is exemplified in a study of Kelman and Hovland (1953). A tape recorded speech was used, preceded by an interview with the speaker, producing a "radio interview" form of communication. Three variations of the introduction were used; the speech itself was unchanged. The speech advocated more lenient treatment of juvenile delinquents. The introductions were altered to associate the message with speakers of differing credibility. The speakers were represented in the three variations as (1) a juvenile court judge, expert and fair, (2) a member of the studio audience, fair but non-expert, and (3) a member of the studio audience, a former delinquent with little respect for law and obviously biased and non-expert. The listeners were high school students. Measured immediately after the speech, opinion change was significantly greater when the speech was associated with the juvenile court judge or with the fair non-expert member of the studio audience than with the former delinquent. But after three weeks, when measured again, these differences were no longer found. The authors particularly point out that opinion change increased, after three weeks, for the speech associated with the unacceptable source. It was this increase, coupled with decreases for the other speakers, that made their effects quite similar at the later date.

This research was not a study of the effects of differing messages. Note that the *source* is the manipulated variable; the message is a controlled variable, the same speech for each audience. It is the relative effects of different *sources* that are revealed in the data. The study makes a contribution to our knowledge of the facilitating or inhibiting effects of sources, but little contribution to our knowledge of the message effects. The findings on opinion change after three weeks tend to confirm this. In explaining these results, the authors suggest that source and message may have become disassociated. Students no longer clearly associated the source and message. Such an explanation would explain the similarity of results after three weeks. This is as it should be; if source influence is sharply reduced, the same speech in all three variations should produce similar results. There is, however, a persuasive effect in the study apparently not of critical interest to the authors. Each "radio interview" was composed of two messages, an introduction and a speech. The introduction was designed to affect the listener's perception of the speaker. The results taken immediately after the speech provide evidence that different perceptions of the speaker were achieved. The three different introductions produced effects to which the introductory remarks were major contributors.

In contrast, research in which message effects were the central consideration is exemplified in the work of Janis and Feshbach (1953). The experimenters developed three illustrated speeches each 15 minutes in length on the topic of dental hygiene. The speeches differed in the amount of fear-arousing material. The message was the manipulated variable; the speaker and type of audience were controlled to produce similarity. The results contribute to our knowledge of the persuasive effects of different kinds of fear-arousing messages.

These two studies are not an argument for the rejection of the first type of study and acceptance of the second by the student of persuasion. The first is important in understanding the facilitating or inhibiting effects of non-message variables in the persuasive setting. The second, of course, is requisite to our knowledge of message impact. The point is that a distinction is required (1) to reduce vagueness in conceptualizing persuasion, and (2) to increase awareness as to whether contextual elements are facilitating message effect or have become the major determinants of response. Without this distinction, persuasion begins to mean the effects of any and all variables that exist in a communication setting whether or not the message is a principal factor in the receiver's response. To some extent compilations of persuasion research, such as Abelson's (1959), reflect this failure to distinguish between the study of message effects and context effects. This perhaps is the expected result of a vague concept of persuasion.

Discussion in the next chapter—Choice in Persuasion—hopefully will clarify further the meaning that the message be a major determinant of effect.

## significant contextual elements in persuasive events

Consider two well known historical events. The first was the Great Depression in the U.S., dramatically ushered in by the stock market crash of 1929. Three years later, in the Hoover-Roosevelt election, it was generally conceded that people voted more against the scapegoat Hoover than for Roosevelt. For the Democrats, the depression was a fortuitous event which greatly facilitated their persuasive efforts. The other event, in the 1930's, was the dramatic burning of the Reichstag. Marinus Van der Lubbe, the arsonist, was caught by the Nazis and tried in a German court. World observers were invited in order that he confess his crime in public. Psychiatrists who observed him on trial felt Van der Lubbe had been given special narcotics or sedatives. They observed that he behaved as if he were "punch-drunk." No opportunity, of course, was given to examine the man during his trial or after his conviction and hanging. It was not until the confessions of the Nuremburg trials, after World War II, that it became clear that the Nazis had used Van der Lubbe as a willing political tool. The government that punished and killed him had also been the one that had urged him to start the fire (Meerloo, 1960). The Reichstag burning was not a natural disaster or fortuitous accident capitalized on by the Nazis, but a planned event to facilitate their persuasion. Subsequent events showed that the Nazis were not interested in burning the Reichstag as a goal in itself, but in making the German people more receptive to Nazi claims that they should be given power to govern Germany. It is also probable that the Nazis felt the effects of their persuasion were too weak and too slow, and needed the spark that such an incident would provide.

One event was unintentional, the other planned. Both altered the context in which subsequent messages occurred, and facilitated their effects. The Reichstag burning, however, can be viewed both as a message and as an event which generated attention and receptivity to later messages. The incident doubtlessly was used by the German people as a sign; that is, it aroused its intended meaning. The event likely indicated political crisis to the Germans and the existence of weak leadership. As subsequent happenings demonstrated, the Nazis used the perceived crisis to gain better reception for their main message—that Hitler and the Nazi Party should be given the political power to lead Germany.

This illustrates that contextual elements may be events unplanned by the persuader or contrived events which may be used as messages to facilitate the main message which follows. It should be noted that a contrived context does not have to be intended as a message. The temperature of a meeting hall can be raised to the point of discomfort; uncomfortable seating can be provided. The meeting time can be scheduled late at night or before dinner to create a context favoring quick decision and insufficient discussion. The story is told that General MacArthur, when he did not wish thorough discussion of a policy, would not convene his staff meetings at typical times such as 9:00 A.M., 1:00 P.M., or 4:00 P.M. Instead he would call the meeting for 5:15 P.M., just a little before dinner. Presumably, he reasoned that hungry men, expected home for dinner, were more likely to agree without prolonged discussion (Ellis and Seidel, 1955). The physical setting in which a message occurs can serve as a facilitating contextual element. In his discussion of Presidential influence, Neustadt (1964) comments on the use of the White House to aid persuasion. He observes that it grows harder for Cabinet officers, Congressmen, and others to say "no" when they are seated in the President's oval office in the White House, or in his study on the second floor. The President and his message seem to acquire some of the aura of the surroundings.

One of the most common means of altering context, however, is found in the use of verbal messages. They are cheaper, more available, and more applicable. In a persuasive event, the messages presented commonly deal with a variety of subjects. For example, messages may refer to the speaker's credibility, his present or previous relationships with an audience, the occasion, the size and composition of the audience, as well as the speaker's topic. The use of such messages follows from the fact that these are contextual elements which serve to facilitate the main effect sought. If one of the main effects sought in a political campaign is to establish the belief that the incumbent administration is corrupt, it makes a difference not only *what* is said about that topic but *who* says it, *where* it is said, *when* it is said—in what context it is said.

Contextual effects, then, are instrumental to the main effects sought. As a reader, likely you have noted a similarity between the concept of contextual effect and an earlier discussion of instrumentality in persuasion. Of course, some contextual elements are not intended by the persuader, and often operate to inhibit rather than facilitate main effects. But they are instrumental in the sense that they are primarily of interest not in themselves, but rather for their bearing on those effects of more significant interest. They are a particular class of instrumental effects, occurring or made to occur in conjunction with the main message.

Research and the practices of professional persuaders suggest many of the facilitators of the main message effect. These often appear as part of the context surrounding the main message. Among these are the qualifications of the message-source, the message sponsor, the interpersonal relationship between source and receivers, the relevancy of the topic to the receivers, the reactions of relevant groups to the topic, the intent or goals of the source, the needs, desires, and goals of the receivers, the comparative merit of competitive or opposition sources, the media carrying the main message, the occasion that prompts the main message, and the similarity of difference between the position advocated and that of the receivers. These facilitators of main effects, of course, vary in importance and number from one persuasive event to another.

The influence of context on message effect warrants the attention of the professional persuader and the research-scholar. For the professional, contextual elements need to be appraised as a basis for altering them to facilitate the goal of his persuasion. Not only will people not beat their way to his door for his better mousetrap, they will not necessarily buy it when it is advertised by a clear message. That message needs the supporting effects of context. For the research-scholar, it follows from the fact of contextual effects that experiments should be designed to take account of more of the significant contextual variables and that field study should appraise context more completely. Sherif and Sherif (1956) are getting at this point in observing that

> Many writers who have surveyed studies on changing attitudes through communication have justly commented on the scarcity of well-planned experiments in the bulk of research reports. The research has other shortcomings. Lacking contemporary emphasis on the intimate relationship between attitudes and group processes, many early studies tried to measure the discreet effect of some form of communication on some people, without specifying their relationships to each other, to the communication, its source, the situation in which it was presented, or other prevailing influences. As a result, studies with similar problems and designs often yielded quite different results.

## stimuli—signs—messages

It is characteristic of living things that they are sensitive to stimuli impinging on them. We observe the laboratory rat withdraw from an electric shock, the worm withdraw from the prick of a fishhook, and the pet dog or cat rise to go outside when the door is opened. We observe people react to goldenrod in hayfever season, drive their cars into a service station when the gas gauge registers empty, and applaud or boo the words uttered by a speaker. It is commonplace to note that the world people experience is filled with such varied stimuli. Some are classified simply as stimuli; others are given more special classifications as signs or messages. What are the relationships between these three? What distinguishes a message from a sign or from other kinds of stimuli?

The term "stimuli," being the most inclusive, is useful to begin with. Two types of stimuli are capable of arousing response. The first involves "certain actual changes in physical energy which impinge upon the individual—changes in energy which lead to seeing, hearing, smelling, and tasting, to mention only a few of the kinds of experience which are associated with these changes" (Wickens and Meyer, 1955). The second type, though unavailable to the senses, is also capable of arousing response, as in thinking or in dreaming. A nightmare illustrates our capacity to respond to images and symbols generated by the activity of the mind. Such stimuli are absent to the senses. It is the first type of stimuli that concerns us in examining the nature of a message. Implicit in this view of stimuli is that changes in environment, external or internal, constitute an *input* into an organism's system. The system's *output* is varied, including phenomena such as sensation, perception, signification, symbolization, and behavior. The difference in these outputs provides a basis for distinguishing signs from other stimuli or inputs.

Gibson (1963) provides a useful distinction between sensation and perception as outputs. "Perception involves meaning; sensation does not. To see a patch of color is not to see an object. . . . To have a salty taste is not to taste salt, and to have a certain olfactory impression is not to smell, say, a mint julep. . . . To feel a local pain is not to feel the pricking of a needle. To feel warmth on one's skin is not to feel the sun on one's skin, and to feel cold is not to feel the coldness of the weather." More pertinent to persuasion, to hear sound is not the same as hearing your name, and to see black marks against a white background is not the same as seeing printed words. In persuasion, if a receiver is to function meaningfully, he must do more than see, hear, feel, taste, or smell stimuli. He must also interpret sensations in perception.

This interpretive output called perception needs to be further specified. It involves the arousal of various kinds of meaning—detection, identification, signification, and symbolization. Take, for example, a housewife opening the door and ringing a dinner bell. To hear a sound is not the same as hearing a bell. To identify this sound as a bell is not the same as interpreting it as an announcement that dinner is ready. It is in this latter response that the stimulus is used as a sign. It is used to indicate something beyond itself; it is used for more than detection or identification. In a household, the word "dinner" might be called out and used as a sign that dinner is ready. The French words "souper" or "dîner," however, might signify nothing and simply be identified as foreign words. Any stimulus may arouse meaning in the sense of being detected or identified. To be used as a sign, the object, event, signal, or symbol must function to indicate or stand for something beside itself. In reference to persuasion, the source employs stimuli with the intent that they be used by the receiver as signs.

## THE CONCEPT OF MESSAGE

A message is differentiated from other stimuli or other signs by its *function,* not its *properties. A message is viewed as a sign or group of signs—signals and/or symbols—intentionally used by a source to arouse signification or symbolization.* Sources use messages to affect receivers. Though a message is a stimulus, it differs in function from many other stimuli capable of producing response. Goldenrod stimulates an allergic person; a hot light bulb, when touched, burns; a flash of light affects the eyes. Such stimuli are not intentionally used to affect a receiver; neither are they typically used by receivers as signs. Also, a message is a sign or group of signs, yet it differs from gas gauges, speedometers and battery indicators. We use readings from these instruments as signs to indicate conditions that interest us, but the manufacturer (source) does not primarily provide them to affect our behavior in particular ways. They are there for us, to be used or not used as we see fit. Similarly, we may use a sonic boom as a sign of the presence of supersonic aircraft or observe wet streets as an indication of rain. Neither of these signs suggests an intentional effort by a source to arouse these meanings in receivers.

The part-whole relations between stimuli, signs, and messages can be illustrated (Fig. 6) by a set of circles, the smaller areas considered part of the larger.

Consider some examples. When a hunter and his dog discover signs of their quarry—paw prints, remains of the animal's feeding, excretions, and odors—these are used as signals to indicate the presence of the hunted game. Obviously, the hunted animal did not provide these to set the hunter on its trail. They are signs, but not messages. On the other hand, in the Boston great mail robbery in August, 1962, the thieves made efforts to affect the behavior of others. They set up a "detour" sign

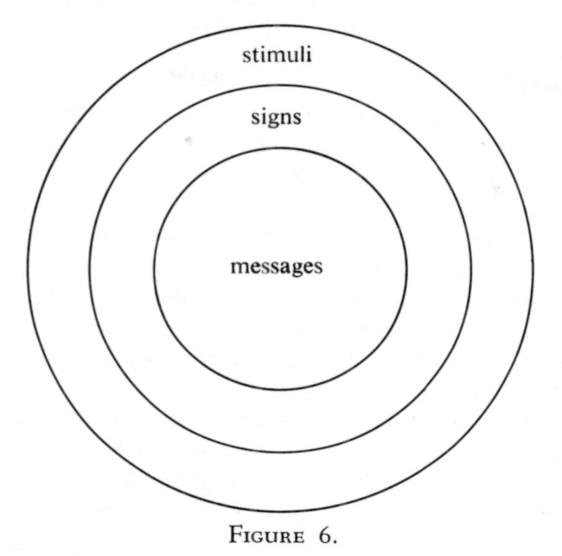


FIGURE 6.

to divert traffic off the highway while they committed the holdup. A "police car" and "police uniforms" were used to stop the mail truck, gain surprise, and avoid shooting. These were signs used to arouse meaning and affect others; they were messages.

A message requires *intent,* not only that the stimuli be used as signs by receivers, but also that they be used in such a way that the effects are relevant to source goals. What has been called unconscious propaganda by Doob, namely, stimuli that produce unintended effects on belief and action, does not satisfy this requirement. J. A. C. Brown (1963) reports an example:

> One social scientist went to the trouble of analysing a widely-used American text-book of arithmetic for schools and found that, in fewer than 200 pages, there were 643 problems which not only dealt with, but stressed the concepts peculiar to capitalism: rent, investments, interest, and so on. One might suppose it is no sin to take for granted existing economic practices; yet in a socialist country this would be regarded as propaganda and, quite recently, it was reported that Russian educationists were disturbed by the frequency with which the profit motive still reared its ugly head in their own text-books and were taking steps to change them in a more progressive direction. If arithmetic can be accused of bias [though unconscious], how much

more does this apply to the teaching of nationalist values through history, geography, and literature?

Were these 643 arithmetic problems messages? Not in their function of arousing meanings with regard to capitalism. The viewpoint taken here is that everybody, not only textbook writers, is continually though unconsciously propagating his own beliefs. The individual cannot help selecting examples, observations, illustrations, and language from a background that supports certain values and rejects others, and a background with which he typically agrees. The point, however, is that the stimuli he thus broadcasts, though used by others in the arousal of meanings, are no more messages than the paw-prints unconsciously left for the hunter. Without this restriction, all overt behavior used as signs by others becomes a message and the term is meaningless. Without this restriction, persuasion as a study becomes excessively broad and unrealistic in terms of the interests of professional persuaders.

In the area of sports, it is easy to observe the use of signs as messages. In baseball, part of the color of the game is the sign-making of the third base coach. In football, both the coach and quarterback use numerical signs as messages to their own team, but disguised from the unintended receivers on the opposing team. Similarly, it is easy to observe the use of signs as messages while driving a car. We are constantly being directed, as drivers, by signs indicating intersections, rest areas, towns or highways we are approaching, highway numbers, county lines, minimum and maximum speeds, and by signs directing us to stop, go ahead, slow down, and keep to the right except for passing. Some of these signs are composed of words and others not. All are signs. They function as messages; they are intentionally communicated to arouse meaning and affect behavior. It will be clarified in the next chapter—Choice in Persuasion—that such messages, however, are not persuasive. They do not satisfy the criterion that the receiver perceive himself to have choice.

Not only signs, but reports of signs, may be used as messages. Moreover, the report of signs is more typical in some forms of persuasion because it is more economical. It is cheaper for the public speaker or news writer to report signs than to produce them for others to observe. When the speaker presents "the facts" relevant to his thesis, his examples and statistics are not interesting in themselves, but in their capacity to arouse meanings. He intends that they be used by receivers as signs, and generate effects relevant and instrumental to his goals.

## SIGNS: SIGNALS AND SYMBOLS

In the preceding discussion, the term "sign" had considerable prominence. Two classes of signs are commonly differentiated: signals and symbols. These are the two basic types of stimuli that make up the persuader's message. Because people respond differently to signals and symbols, their differences are a matter of concern to the persuader. Relations and distinctions between these terms were stimulated by the thinking of Langer (1951) and Morris (1946).

SIGNALS AND SYMBOLS ARE DISTINGUISHED BY THEIR USE, NOT THEIR PROPERTIES. In distinguishing between signals and symbols, where one starts the search is important. One can begin by searching for a *property* possessed by signals and not by symbols, or a *quality* found in signals not found or found in less degree in symbols. This approach assumes that a signal is a signal is a signal, and does not become a symbol in some instances. The capacity of a stimulus to be used signally on one occasion and symbolically on another is, however, obvious. That which can act as a sign—a sound, word, gesture, condition, object, or event—may function as either a signal or symbol; the same word may at one time be a signal and at another a symbol. The distinction which seems valid upon examination is that signals and symbols differ in their function, not in properties or qualities possessed. Whether a sign is a signal or symbol seems to depend on the *use* made of it.

The shift of the same term from signal to symbol is exemplified in our uses of proper names. Suppose a John Doe is a mutual acquaintance, and I mention his name to you. You may turn and look toward the door. You use his name as a signal of his presence. On the other hand, you may respond by repeating some gossip about him "behind his back." This is just what you would not do in his presence. You use the term "John Doe" to *talk about* him, not as a signal of his presence. The signal and symbol for John Doe, his name, in this case initiates an act appropriate to his absence and inappropriate to his presence. It is used as a symbol and stimulates thinking about John Doe. If while you are reporting gossip, I should look toward the door, interrupt and change the subject, or raise my eyebrows, or shake my head, you would stop. This behavior would be interpreted as a signal that John Doe is entering the room. Your response to this signal, discontinuing your gossip, would be behavior appropriate to his presence. Not only does a sign used signally announce the presence of its object, it may also indicate the past existence or future presence of an object. A piece of pottery, for the archeologist, may be used to indicate the prior residence of an ancient tribe; a low thermometer reading may be used to predict the formation of ice on a pond. In all instances, signals point to that which was, is now, or will be, reality.

Signs used symbolically, on the other hand, are not indicators of an observable reality. To conceive of something is to think about it, to formulate one's view of it. When we form our notions of what characterizes a "left-winger" or "right-winger" we are using these terms symbolically. We are likely, of course, to believe these conceptions correspond to reality. The functional difference between signals and symbols is illustrated in Figure 7. The diagram depicts *three* elements necessary for the use of a sign as a signal: (1) a person or animal using the sign, (2) a signal or stimulus which, through association with an object, indicates its existence, and (3) the object, event, or condition indicated. The border enclosing signal and object is meant to suggest their association.

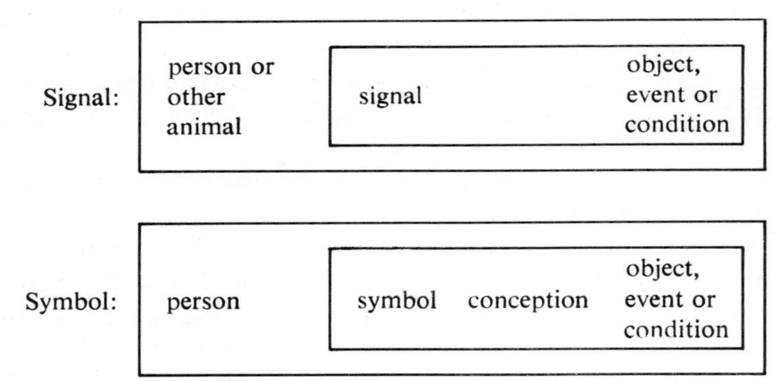


FIGURE 7. Essential elements in the use of signs as signals or as symbols.

*Four* elements are necessary for the use of a sign as a symbol. The symbol arouses a conception of an object, event, or condition. The conception, in turn, is presumed to reflect what characterizes the object. The symbol, conception, and object are bound together (associated) for the person. The symbol does not point to or indicate the object's presence; it is not an announcer of things; it is not an observable part of an object or an observable event associated with an object. In this sense, a symbol is not real—physically real. Rather, the symbol is the name of the conception held about an object. It is important to note that the conception of an object stands between the symbol and the object. When "John Doe" is used as a symbol for an acquaintance, it refers to your conception of the man, all those assets and liabilities you conceive him to have. You presume, in turn, that this conception fits John Doe.

In a similar vein, Sherif and Sherif (1956) take the position that

> It is useful to distinguish between symbolic [sign] reactions which are perceptually symbolic [used signally] and those which are conceptually symbolic [used symbolically]. The achievement of a conceptually symbolic level makes possible a standardized language system, an achievement which is unique to mankind among all animals. It makes possible the formation of concepts which encompass increasingly broader ranges of specific objects and situations.

It is the capacity to use signs symbolically or conceptually that makes it possible for man to categorize objects, conditions, or events and thus talk about them collectively.

Signals and symbols, then, arouse different kinds of meaning. The signal arouses meaning in the sense of signification; it develops a signal-object association. This is the meaning it generates, so that signal and object are associated in such a way that the signal indicates and announces the object. The symbol arouses meaning in the sense of conception, either denotation or connotation. It generates a meaning so that symbol, conception, and object are all associated in such a way that the conception aroused fits the reality it stands for. Thus, we use symbols to talk *about* the reality of an object, not to announce it.

When signs are used as signals, they tend to become time-bound and situation-bound. The term "Fire!" in an inappropriate situation would not act as a signal. To shout "Fire!" while bathing in the ocean would produce puzzlement or amusement. Someone might shout back, "What about fire?" Such a person would find himself unable to use the stimulus as a signal; to him, it can't announce a prevailing condition. His question implies it must have been used as a symbol. Unlike signals, symbols are not bound by time or situation. This permits us to talk, with symbols, about objects or events in their absence. The sign, when used as a symbol, refers to or is associated with the conception of an object, while the sign, used as a signal, indicates the object.

Care has been taken to avoid suggesting that signals or symbols mean anything *in themselves.* Note that the signal-function involves *three* elements, one of these being the person or animal using the signal.

Also, for the symbol-function, the person using the symbol is a necessary element. Meaning exists in the person, not the sign. The sign (signal or symbol) functions to arouse a meaning in the user. Meaning does not exist independently. In the diagram presented, the outer border enclosing the elements of the signal or symbol was drawn to suggest the necessity of the sign user as an indispensable element in these functions.

Implicit in this viewpoint is that signs or messages are stimuli, not containers of meaning. The fallacy of believing that words, pictures, artistic products, or other messages contain meaning is common. It is implied in such frequently heard remarks as: the facts speak for themselves; that statement means exactly what it says; I told him exactly what I wanted him to do. Facts, of course, do not transmit meaning; they arouse it, different meanings for different people. For those who would persuade, recognition of this common fallacy has advantages. It enables the persuader to realize his task is to do more than encode his message; he must encode it in such a way that it will arouse desired meanings in receivers. Awareness of this belief helps the persuader to appreciate the tenacity with which the receiver holds on to his meaning as the true one.

In short, the search for distinctions between signals and symbols should be carried out by viewing them as responses, not as stimuli. It is the way a stimulus is responded to that makes it a signal, symbol, or neither. These two uses are only two of several responses possible to incoming stimuli. A stimulus used signally arouses the kind of meaning which indicates or announces the existence of an object or condition. Used symbolically, a stimulus generates the kind of meaning which represents or stands for one's conception of an object or condition. In contrast, when signals or symbols are viewed as stimuli rather than as responses, no distinctions can be made that hold up. The same stimulus may be used as a signal, symbol, or neither.

ARBITRARINESS IS NOT A USEFUL DISTINCTION BETWEEN SIGNALS AND SYMBOLS. It is widely held that signals and symbols have different properties, for example, that symbols are arbitrary and signals not. Miller (1951), for instance, made such a distinction.

> Words cannot be distinguished from other stimuli on the basis of their representative role or their organization into patterns. What, then, is the distinguishing mark of a verbal stimulus? The principal distinction is that words have an arbitrary significance. Words signify only what we have learned that they signify. The fact that we say "chair" and

not "stuhl" is a matter of social coincidence. In contrast, the association between the light rays reflected from a chair and the chair itself is not arbitrary, but universal. Stimuli that are arbitrarily associated with objects are usually called *symbols*.

Arbitrariness as the distinctive property of symbols, or of words in particular, gets us into trouble in classifying signs. Many signs that are not words have an arbitrary character. All these are by no means used as symbols; many are used as signals. Among non-words used as arbitrary symbols are the cross, the hammer and sickle, the American eagle, and the flag. Arbitrary signs used as signals are classroom bells, railroad flashers, yellow caution lights, red stop lights, green go lights, and turn signals on automobiles. They signify only what we have learned they signify. The association between these signals and the objects or conditions they signify is not universal. The fact that a signal necessitates only correlation (association) with an object, and may not be involved in a cause-and-effect relation, permits no limit to what a signal may arbitrarily mean. Bells, for example, signify that a horse race is starting, a cake in the oven is done, a bus passenger wants to get off at the next stop, somebody is at the front door, someone wants us on the telephone, a typewriter line is ended, a class hour is ended, a transaction is recorded in a cash register, it is time for dinner, it is time to get up. Sirens, buzzers, clickers, lights, and flashers could have been arbitrarily selected to signalize these events.

### THE VALUELESSNESS QUALITY OF SIGNS

Signs—signals and symbols—lack, in themselves, intrinsic value. Though signals and symbols are not easily distinguished by different properties, they do have in common the tendency to be unimportant and uninteresting in their own right. Such is the characteristic of the sounds of speech and the letters of the alphabet. Sounds and letters, having little interest value as such, are excellent stimuli for the generation of meaning. Such stimuli make it possible for the listener or reader to use them in meaning arousal without being aware of or distracted by their presence. So typical is our disinterest in a speaker's speech sounds, for example, that when we do notice them the speaker is considered defective. For speech clinicians, one of the characteristics of defective speech is the use of sounds which call attention to themselves.

We respond to bells, chimes, buzzers, alarms, gongs, whistles, door knocks, red lights, stop signs, directional arrows, detour signs, the swastika, the cross, the hammer and sickle, the star and crescent, the flag, the CBS eye, the NBC peacock, the judge's robes, the policeman's badge, the military officer's bars or oak leaves, mink coats, Cadillacs, college degrees—and natural phenomena like rings around the moon, ground hogs on February 2, furry caterpillars in late summer, the first robin in the spring—and phenomena like words, gestures, shrugs, winks, frowns, the sign language of the deaf, the thumbed nose, the Churchillian "V" for victory, and the exclamation point. We call them signs: signals and symbols. Furthermore, we attach meanings to demonstrations, riots, picket lines and other events. We use them as signs. The best of these are those which arouse the least interest in themselves. Our most commonly used signs have this characteristic.

Hockett (1959, 1960) presents a similar view. A comparative linguist, his analysis of language yielded 13 components. His thesis is that no real dichotomy can be drawn between humans and other animals in the sense that humans alone have language. Rather, methods of communication, animal and human, can be placed on a continuum in terms of the number of language components used. It is one of these, the specialization feature of language, that emphasizes the valuelessness of signs.

The specialization feature of a language specifies that a communication stimulus is specialized if its direct energetic consequences are biologically or mechanically irrelevant. A mother may seat her infant for dinner in his high chair in much the same way that dishes and silverware are set at the table. Even though the mother has influenced the child's behavior, communication has not taken place because the energy used to influence had direct mechanical relevance in altering the child's position in space. In contrast, when the husband comes to the table in response to his wife's call that "Dinner is ready," communication has taken place. The energy involved in the speech has not mechanically altered the husband's position in space. The wife's use of sound energy has been *specialized* in that it has been irrelevant to the consequences. The energy employed in the epithet "Drop dead!" does not have the same consequences as a death ray. The words "Drop dead," spoken to someone unfamiliar with English would have little stimulus value; the energy of the death ray, and the consequences, are independent of language facility. Similarly, to "punch someone in the nose" is not to use a sign or message. The consequences are biologically relevant.

That a sign has little intrinsic value is not surprising when the relation between a sign and an object or event is examined. One can usefully begin by noting how a signal is artificially made in a laboratory. The widely known experiments of Pavlov with dogs on what is called conditioning will illustrate. The essential procedure involved, first, the ringing of a bell. In other experiments the clicking of a metronome was used. The results were similar. To the bell stimulus, the dog responded by turning its head toward the source of the sound and seemed to show little more than curiosity about this event; the dog, however, did not salivate. No association between the sound of the bell and food existed for the dog. Having demonstrated the lack of association, the dog then was subjected to a *pair* of stimuli; the bell was rung and then followed by the presentation of food. This presentation of a *pair* of stimuli was repeated until the sound became associated with the offered food. At that time, salivation occurred in response to the sound alone. It was not necessary to present the food. The bell had taken over the stimulus function. The bell became a signal of the object (food) for which the response (salivation) was really appropriate. The experiments demonstrated that the sound of the bell was, *in itself,* of little interest and importance to the dog. Only when it became associated (paired) with an object of importance (food) did it become important. Signs, then, are trivial events which have become associated with important events. It is, however, through this association that signs, and consequently messages, become important forms of influence.

Psychologists, as you know, speak of the bell in its artificial association with the food as a conditioned stimulus. It could be called, just as satisfactorily, a conditioned signal; it indicates, it *means* the *presence* of food. In contrast, stimulation of the animal's taste buds is called an unconditioned stimulus; it can evoke the salivation response without the aid of any training period to build up an association. Studies of conditioning have spawned a whole new vocabulary to denote various aspects of the findings. One more term is of interest in this discussion, the term "extinction." It was found that after a subject (dog) had been conditioned, the power of the conditioned stimulus (bell) to elicit the salivation response could be eliminated, at least temporarily. The bell was presented repeatedly without the food. The dog ceased to respond to it. This phenomenon was called "extinction." The bell seemed to be important only because of its association with the food. When the association was withheld, the interest value of the bell was sharply reduced. Similarly, when we have learned through association that a word indicates an object or condition, we respond to the word-signal.

When the word-signal ceases to be a good predictor of the object or condition, it suffers extinction as a stimulus. If, for example, words like "crisis," "breakthrough," and "emergency" too often fail to indicate their referents, our response to them declines. It is the old story of crying "wolf" too often when there is no wolf.

Similarly, symbols as well as signals lack intrinsic value. Symbols such as the cross, "V for Victory" and The Star of David are important only for the meanings they generate. To the person unfamiliar with the symbol and for whom it has no meaning, it has little interest in itself. Until the swastika was selected by the Nazis as a symbol, it was familiar to scholars of ancient cultures as a good luck symbol but to most people it meant little and was therefore uninteresting. In some future time, it is possible that the meaning this symbol arouses for most people will be insignificant; the symbol will then cease to have much interest value.

## ASSOCIATION: THE CRITICAL QUALITY OF SIGNS

For the persuader, the important feature of a signal or symbol is the strength of association it has with what it indicates or represents, the likelihood that the meaning it will arouse can be predicted.

Implicit in the remark, "Actions speak louder than words," is the notion that natural signs are more powerful than artificial ones (words), and perhaps that naturalness is a critical quality. A natural sign, with no association for the receiver with what it could signify, is useless. A city-reared youngster left in a forest abounding with natural signs would find them without meaning. Natural signs, including facts, inconsistent in what they mean to a receiver, are relatively useless in the formation of messages. It is only when they are highly associated, for the receiver, with a particular meaning that they are of maximal value in messages.

Many "artificial" signs with high association, of course, occur in our experience. A classroom bell consistently indicates for students and instructor the beginning or end of a time period. The bond or association of sign and referent has been built up through prior associations. For those in the classroom, the bell is an excellent predictor of the condition it signifies. Similarly, a red light in a theatre or auditorium is strongly associated for us with an exit; on a super-highway, the words, "Next Exit: 29 Miles," are accepted to indicate distance to the next outlet off the highway. For many of us, the meaning aroused by the Flag or Cross is fairly consistent. Other signs have lower correlation (association) for us with the conditions or conceptions they are presumed to represent. Red-headedness, we believe, does not consistently indicate a hot temper; turn signals from an approaching car do not always indicate correctly the intentions of the driver; a mink coat ceases to consistently arouse the idea of wealth.

Signs, natural and artificial, vary in the degree of association they have for receivers with the object, event, condition, or concept they stand for. The degree of association depends on who uses the sign; people vary in their beliefs of how consistently a signal predicts an object, event, or condition; they vary in their certainty that a concept, aroused by a symbol, fits the reality it represents. This fact, this variance in strength of belief, is the important aspect of signs in the study of persuasion, not whether they are natural or artificial.

Returning to conditioning experiments, the relative unimportance of naturalness to sign strength is worth noting. The sight and smell of the food are natural stimuli. A natural stimulus indicates that of which it is a part, while an artificial stimulus (bell) indicates something of which it is not an inherent part. These two types of stimuli are not as different as one would suppose. Both are conditioned; extinction can be achieved with both. If, for example, the smell of food is presented and the food withheld, the dog will become disturbed, reduce his salivation response, and gradually cease to approach the empty food pail. In another experiment, done with fish, extinction of a natural signal was vividly illustrated. As every fisherman knows, minnows are a preferred food for pike. For the experiment, a pike was placed in a tank of water (see Fig. 8). A glass partition was placed in the tank, confining the

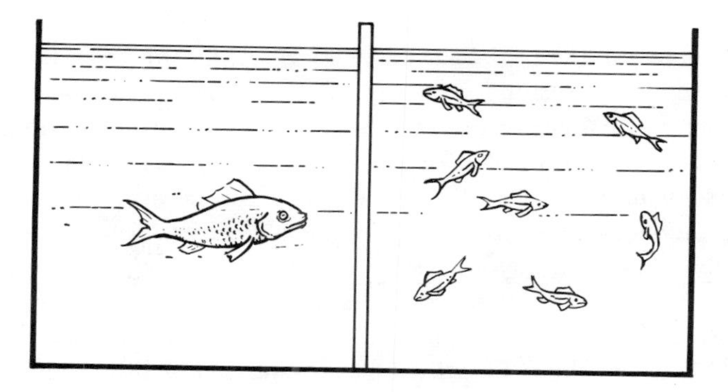

FIGURE 8.

pike to one end. In the other compartment, minnows were placed. The pike attempted to attack the minnows, and hit the glass partition. After repeated trials with no success, the pike ceased to attack. The natural stimulus was extinguished. The glass partition was removed and still the pike made no effort to attack the minnows.

Extinction, of course, can occur in human behavior. When a fist is thrown toward your face, the "natural" response is to flinch or blink. Yet, if the fist never hits the face, you can learn not to flinch or blink. Extinction occurs for the natural stimulus—the sight of the approaching fist. Like the bell, it lacks inherent value, *in itself,* as a stimulus, but has acquired it through association with the pain of being struck. Similarly, verbal threats that do not materialize cease to produce response.

The natural-artificial categories fail to emphasize the most important distinction, the differences or presumed differences in the degree of association between signal and object. What have been called "natural signs" are those which are considered to have a causal relation or correlate perfectly with their objects. Consider, for example, the spots and blurs on an X-ray plate. To the trained eye, these signals indicate the presence of tuberculosis. The disease, we say, causes the tell-tale spots and blurs; they are a part of the condition they signify. As a result, treatment is confidently recommended; the degree of association between cause and effect is presumed to be very high. Predictability from signal to condition is consistently successful. In this sense, the dog in Pavlov's experiment dealt with a signal of similar high association with the object. In its experience, the smell of food consistently indicated the presence of food. This signal was an excellent predictor. The bell, on the other hand, was in the dog's experience not a predictor of food until it was associated through conditioning.

Furthermore, the term "natural" has several meanings and leads to difficulty in distinguishing between signals. What, for instance, is a thermometer or barometer reading? Such readings and the instruments that produce them do not exist in nature. Yet they are perceived as natural signs to most of us; that is, heat is a natural aspect of weather and the thermometer instrument simply enables us to perceive it more accurately. Rain is a natural aspect of weather; a falling barometer indicates its approach. In the same fashion, weight is indicated by a needle on a dial, acidity by the redness of litmus paper, time by the hands of a watch, light by a light meter, and sound by a sound-level meter. These are natural properties (stimuli) of objects or events in a way that the sound of a bell is not a property of food, yet we perceive them by means of "unnatural" instruments.

Reference to thermometers, barometers and other instruments which "unnaturally" produce signals suggests another fact about signals of interest in the study of persuasion. *Technological advances along with an explosion in communication have increased the use of "artificial" signals.*

Increasingly, we learn to associate man-made signals of events with the events themselves. We answer the ring of the telephone, watch the needle on our speedometers, heed directional lights from approaching automobiles, respond to a classroom bell, and fill the gasoline tank when the gauge indicates "empty." At a more professional level, we learn in using the polygraph for lie detection to watch for the appearance of particularly high peaks among the oscillations being made by the stylus. These wiggles of the stylus are interesting chiefly because we associate them with the condition of the person being tested. Some wiggles are signs to the professional of a person's disturbance when he is lying. The event which holds interest is the lying; signs of it are interesting only because of association. An untrained observer would probably have, other than vague curiosity, little interest in the wiggles.

With the advance of scientific procedures, especially the development of new instruments to aid observation, scientists have extensively changed the signals they observe. Experiments such as those of Galileo with his weights and Franklin with his kite are more and more rare. These men were observing the actual objects of their curiosity—the falling weights and the key on the kite. Similarly, Pavlov observed the flow of saliva, not a sign of it. In contrast, today's scientists are watching index needles, the tracings on a revolving drum, the spots and blurs on sensitive plates, and the marks a subject makes on an answer sheet. Observation has increasingly become indirect; readings take the place of genuine witness of the event itself. The sense-data of modern science are apt to be spots, blurs, tracings, lights, marks, and dial readings. They are not, in themselves, the phenomena of interest to the scientist; the phenomena which do interest him are associated with these signals as their supposed causes (Langer, 1951). This is not an argument that scientists associate these signals with the events which caused them by a process of conditioning. We associate (learn) by other means than conditioning. The point is that the signals we use, and those that may be used in persuasive messages are more and more becoming "artificial" and indirect.

Similarly, the lives of all of us reflect a great shift in what we observe. Our observation of the environment about us has become more indirect. Increasingly, we take readings in place of observing "natural" signals—readings of thermometers, barometers, dial needles to indicate the speed of our automobiles, gas gauges, air pressure gauges for automobile tires, lights on stoves and toasters, and business indexes such as car loadings, unemployment figures, and the consumer's price index. Increasingly, we observe artificial signals. This shift has made us less dependent on and less able to profitably observe events. We no longer can step outside and read the weather directly with confidence; we do not need to. Our principal interest is still in the weather; the thermometer reading is interesting only because of its association with it. What this means is that people have become more dependent on signals and messages to indicate conditions about them. Moreover, this reflects the ease with which people accommodate themselves to signs as substitutes for direct observation, and accounts in part for the increasing role of communication and persuasion.

FURTHERMORE, IN ENCODING MESSAGES, ASSOCIATION, NOT FAMILIARITY, IS THE CRITICAL QUALITY OF SIGNS FOR THE PERSUADER. In recent years, a great deal of attention has been given to the "readability" and "listenability" of messages. Formulae, such as those of Flesch and Dale-Chall, have been devised to measure readability. Factors in these formulae stress word-familiarity as a desirable characteristic. For example, the number of syllables per word is counted; polysyllabic words are less familiar and thus reduce readability. Also, the proportion of words in a message included in the 3000 most frequently used words in English is determined. Again, familiarity is stressed.

Studies of readability have adequately established that word-familiarity is critical to knowing the denotative meaning of words and to message comprehension. From this orientation, writers and speakers engaged in persuasion—sales-letter writers, face-to-face salesmen, advertisers, preachers, speech writers, political speakers—are being advised to be more readable or listenable through the use of more familiar words. Familiarity is useful in persuasion because such words have more predictable association of sign and meaning in receivers. The meanings apt to be aroused by the word "fire" can be better estimated than those generated by the word "conflagration." The latter, being unfamiliar to some receivers, may arouse no useful meaning to the persuader in his audience.

The emphasis is misplaced. Familiarity, *per se,* is not critical in persuasion. The development of product-names illustrates this. In the marketing of soaps and detergents, we see such names as *Joy, Thrill, Cheer, All, Breeze, Zest,* and *Tide.* These are familiar words, but their critical quality is the connotative meanings they arouse. Similarly, when the 1964 Republican nominee for President, Barry Goldwater, said in his acceptance speech, "Extremism in the defense of liberty is not a vice. . . ," the stormy response aroused was not the result of using a three-syllable word. It was the meanings people *associated* with the word "extremism." As Goldwater stated later, his meaning might have been better conveyed by the word "dedication," a four-syllable word. Thus, the task of encoding a message in persuasion requires primary attention to the meanings receivers associate with the signs used.

## the variety of signs available for persuasion

The signs—signals and symbols—available as elements in persuasive messages include *any* stimuli capable of generating meanings sought by the persuader.

The number and variety of building blocks—signals and symbols—available for the development of persuasive messages are extensive. It is too restrictive a view to limit message elements to words. Included among the stimuli capable of arousing meanings in receivers are facts, reports of facts, statistics, examples, fortuitous or contrived events and reports of these events, labels, trademarks, slogans, product names, bells, sirens, alarms, shrugs, winks, smiles, frowns, gestures, badges, uniforms, membership buttons, mink coats, yachts, money, Ph.D. degrees, and titles of offices held. Hall (1959) in his book *The Silent Language* notes how even time and space can be used to arouse meaning. In an office situation, a person's appointment can be delayed or shortened to convey meaning. We make an effort to arrive for our appointments on time, but not too early, lest we convey a meaning we do not wish. Similarly, where we seat someone for an appointment is meaningful; to seat someone on the other side of the desk suggests a different meaning than seating him by one's side. Finally, even silence can be used to arouse meaning. The major limitation on the choice of stimuli is not the type of stimuli, but their capacity to generate desired meanings in selected receivers.

## THE EVENT AS A TACIT MESSAGE

A significant type of sign-message is the event-message. Such a message involves the intentional contrivance of an event to arouse a particular meaning beyond itself in observers or in those to whom it is reported. It is a tacit message, one that is unspoken, unexpressed in any conventional code. The Nazi burning of the Reichstag, mentioned earlier, is an example of the event-message. Demonstrations, picketing, and rallies often fall into this category. Such planned events have been extensively discussed by Boorstin (1962) and labeled by him as pseudo-events. The label could be improved upon. The kind of message of concern here is an intentionally created event, but one that is not perceived by observers as a pseudo-event or as one that is fictitious and unreal in the sense of an event on a theatrical stage. The event, on the contrary, is perceived as real; the participants in the event portray themselves; the situation in which they behave lacks the control and neat predictability of the pseudo- or theatrical event. This view rules out the completely planned and controlled event typically found in television commercials or on other theatrical stages. These are dramatizations, not real events, deliberately created to convey a message.

As part of the integration campaign, Negroes on Easter Sunday, 1963, sought entrance to all-white churches in Birmingham, Alabama. The participants were not acting the parts of others. Doubtlessly, the event was perceived by observers to involve real, not theatrical, behavior. To the extent to which this event was created to arouse a particular meaning and affect behavior, it was a message. If it was used to arouse the meaning that white people violate the Christian principles they profess even in their churches, then it was an event-message. Similarly, Dulles (1963) appraises Soviet arrests of American and other Western tourists as event-messages. He concludes, "It is unrealistic to think that U.S. and Western tourists in the Soviet Union can be of much use in intelligence collection. But for propaganda reasons, the Soviets continue to arrest tourists now and then in order to give the world the impression that U.S. espionage is a vast effort exploiting even the innocent traveler." Note that it is not requisite to an event-message that its "reality" be valid. What is required is that it be perceived as a real event, not a dramatization, and that the "selves" of the participants be judged, not their acting ability.

Events are used to create other effects than meaning arousal through their use as messages. The varied uses, moreover, are not mutually exclusive. The event maker often seeks several benefits from his effort. What is to be distinguished is the dominant use of an event in a particular case. Among uses other than as a message, an event may be designed chiefly to influence by force and not be conceived as a message in an effort to communicate or persuade. The event of an invading army may be carried on with little thought or concern about the meaning it may arouse. Also, an event may be contrived to provide a context in which a message is to be interpreted and not be enacted as a message in its own right. The care with which the Nazi rallies of the thirties were designed reflects concern with manipulating the context in which a message was to be heard. Then too, events are sometimes used dominantly to distract audiences from thinking about and reacting to a quite different matter. The circuses of Ancient Rome were events manufactured to distract the people from their economic hardships.

On other occasions, event makers seem dominantly engaged in counteracting competitive efforts to persuade. The event is designed to prevent or harass an opposition in its effort to present its message. An historic instance is described by Tannenbaum (1962); the event he describes as a competitive tactic has numerous contemporary parallels. In this particular instance, a rightist group, the Action Française, set about to prevent one of France's well known professors from speaking critically of Joan of Arc. Professor Thalamas had been scheduled to give a series of eight lectures at the Sorbonne in November, 1908.

> Thalamas had already become a controversial figure for his "debunking" of Joan and her exploits, and the Action Française was not going to allow him to defame France's most glorious heroine in the halls of her greatest university. A contingent of Camelots and students of the Action Française broke up Thalamas' first lecture with whistles and catcalls. Thereafter the police and the university authorities tried to control access to the auditorium in order to prevent further disturbances. But some of the students of the Action Française knew the secret byways of the Sorbonne and managed to get in from the roof. As a crowning act of defiance, they dashed up to the podium and gave the professor a sound thrashing.

The event-message is to be distinguished from agitation. The goals of the latter are to arouse feeling, to unstructure the environment of those for whom it is planned, and in general to heighten motivation. Persuasion, and with it the event-message, implies the establishment of a particular view or meaning or feelings toward a particular object as a means of bringing about a definite action-goal. Agitation generally precedes persuasion and is a preparation for it. Turner and Killian (1957) observe that

> For many issues serious efforts must be devoted not only to propagandizing persons to a particular point of view, but to preparing them—making them receptive—before the propaganda can be attempted. Efforts may also be necessary to stir people up about the positions which they accept so that they will contribute to an effective public. Frequently these efforts to ready people to listen to persuasive attempts and to stir them into becoming ardent advocates are referred to under the term agitation.

More extensive consideration of the uses of events than they have received, particularly as agitation to increase reception of subsequent messages and as messages in their own right, would contribute to a fuller understanding of the persuasive process. Little, if any, space in texts on persuasion is devoted to these two quite relevant uses of events. Professors and other authors, those who write texts on persuasion, tend to be men of words rather than action. As a result, they are likely to underestimate the role of event-messages and agitation in the process of persuasion.

The event-message does have advantages as a message type. It is dramatic. By providing emotional stimulation, it draws an audience. Because it draws an audience, it is newsworthy and is more likely to be rebroadcast and diffused by the news media. Its occurrence can be planned when needed, and it is easier to witness. It can be planned for the convenience of observers, made to happen during "prime evening television time" for the convenience of the public. The event-message seems well suited for mass audiences, especially those in which illiteracy is common. Neustadt (1964), in analyzing a President's task of persuading a citizenry, makes the points that (1) his persuasion is aimed at an audience habitually inattentive, and (2) he persuades less by telling than by doing or not doing. Because of its dramatic qualities, the event-message is probably remembered longer. Because of its "reality," it probably has greater persuasive power as a message.

At the same time, the event-message has disadvantages. It may involve a considerable amount of money, energy, and even danger. Though it is largely non-verbal, it is doubtful that its intended meaning is easier to grasp. The event does not specify the conclusion or specific meaning the persuader desires to convey. Research findings support the notion that audiences need the desired meaning explicitly stated. Otherwise, many receivers draw an unsought meaning from the message.

Moreover, Fine (1957) found in an experiment that a message explicitly stating a conclusion effects more opinion change than one not stating a conclusion. For this reason the event-message is typically followed up by more verbal messages to guide meaning. It does, however, enlarge the audience for the subsequent messages and probably improves receptivity to them. Finally, not all messages are acceptable in the form of events. For example, you may demonstrate against segregation, yet apparently not against the high cost of steaks. Those who demonstrate must be perceived to have no other choice, and to have exhausted conventional message forms and communication channels.

## summary

This discussion of the message criterion in identifying persuasive events supports several conclusions of value: (1) Message influence does not occur in isolation; various factors contribute to a message context. Contextual factors may be the major determinants of receiver response, or serve to facilitate or otherwise influence message effect. (2) In classifying an effect as persuasive, it is useful to require that the message has been a major contributor to the receiver's response. This helps limit persuasion within the much broader field of communication, and directs attention to those events of most interest to students of persuasion. (3) The concept of message is more restrictive than the concepts of stimulus and sign. This focuses study on those events in which a sign or group of signs have been used *intentionally* to arouse meaning in receivers. (4) Two types of signs—signals and symbols—are available as the building blocks of persuasive messages. They differ in the *response* made to them by receivers, not by possessing different *properties*. Both signals and symbols derive their value from the meanings they are able to arouse. (5) The important feature of a signal or symbol is its perceived degree of association with what it indicates or represents, and not whether it is artificial or natural. Sign-familiarity, not critical in itself, provides better prediction of what meanings the sign may arouse. For the persuader, this sign-meaning association in the receiver determines the credibility of the sign, the extent to which it is believed to indicate or stand for something other than itself. (6) Finally, the variety of stimuli available to the persuader, which may be used signally or symbolically by receivers, is extensive. Recognition of this variety helps in the identification of the multi-varied forms of persuasion, and provides a grasp of the many elements suitable for composition of persuasive messages.

# Chapter 5

# Choice in Persuasion

Concepts of persuasion typically consider choice a requisite of a persuasive event. The receiver must be free to accept or reject. He can refuse, without significant penalties, to respond as a source may desire. Burke (1955), for example, states that persuasion involves choice. It is directed to others insofar as they are free to choose. When people must do something, persuasion is unnecessary. In the case of the criminal condemned to death, his choice of action is restricted. There is no need to persuade him to enter the gas chamber. Thus, the persuasion of the priest is restricted to bringing about attitudes of repentance and resignation. Only in this area does the condemned criminal retain choice. Other writers commonly associate persuasion with choice and the democratic process (Miller, (1946); Brembeck and Howell, (1952); Minick, (1957)). They see persuasion as more compatible with free than authoritarian social organizations. Freedom to choose is conceived as the *sine qua non* of the persuasive process.

## choice versus the illusion of choice

Choice, like many other terms relevant to the study of persuasion, is borrowed from the vernacular of society. In everyday usage, the word conveys the idea that a person, confronted by various pressures and alternatives, is capable of selecting among the alternatives and thus of responding to a situation in more than one way. This capacity to exercise some control over response is explained in terms of man's "inner freedom," and assumes the existence of such a capacity for selection. Viewed this way, choice necessitates a belief in a person's capacity to interfere with and alter cause and effect (stimulus-response) relationships, and to operate as a force whose effect cannot be predicted.

Such a concept does not qualify as a scientific one. Empirical science operates from certain assumptions, one of which is that every effect is capable of being explained and predicted from prior causes. This is the assumption of universal causality. Any phenomenon, any response that is its own cause or by its nature unpredictable lies outside the domain of scientific investigation. Yet choice, in common usage, has these qualities. It arises apparently without being determined by forces outside itself; the response associated with the exercise of choice is "free," not predictable or determined by other causes. For these reasons, as Berger (1963) notes, "No amount of scientific search will ever uncover a phenomenon that can be designated as free. Whatever may appear as free within the subjective consciousness of an individual will find its place in the scientific scheme as a link in some chain of causation."

## DETERMINISM AND CHOICE

The scientist's working assumption of universal causality is called determinism. From this viewpoint, the scientific psychologist, for example, speaks of choice in a different sense than the vernacular. For him, the experimental rat faces choice points as he runs a maze. The term, in his usage, does not imply freedom to choose for the animal, but that a situation exists in which behavioral variability is possible, though still determined and predictable from causal factors. Choice, then, for the determinist means only that the response possibilities are greater than one. As we ascend the phylogenetic scale, animal behavior becomes more variable. In one-celled animals, response variability in different situations is highly limited. Though greater variability exists for the insect, the experimental rat, or guinea pig, the kinds of response are still limited. Behavioral variability, or "choice," is greatest in man. How he can react to words, a picture, or a flag is highly varied, though capable of prediction as the determinist sees it. In other words, though man's response possibilities are greater, he still is not presumed to have freedom in choosing among them.

The scientific model of man, based on a deterministic image, does not square at all with our subjective experience of "choice." Every individual seems to perceive himself to have choice. Even under excessive external constraints, we still perceive ourselves at least free to believe or not believe, free to like or dislike. The universality of the individual's perception of his personal freedom stands perhaps as the most potent argument against determinism. Immergluck (1964) poses the contradiction, the determinism-freedom issue in this way: "We are faced with a dilemma: Scientific observation leads to one conclusion, self-perception to another. How can we reconcile these contradictions?" His discussion and resolution of the issue are relevant to the understanding of choice in the persuasive process. The case for determinism is widely accepted for physical phenomena, but challenged as an explanation of psychological events. We find it easy to live with the notion that inanimate processes are lawful and predictable, that changes in weather, highway surfaces, and steaks broiled over a charcoal fire are effects of causes. We believe such changes are linked in causal chains to antecedent conditions and are totally explained by them. In our "Age of Science," we are convinced that knowledge of natural laws will result in control of natural events. For us, the proof is all around in the impressive advances in the physical sciences. The behavior of electricity, sound, light, and other inanimate phenomena, we agree, is measurable and predictable. Definite hesitancy and doubt, however, exist over accepting even the possibility that life processes and particularly "psychological" events are determined by similar strict cause-and-effect laws. We are not ready, or perhaps are unable to believe that the behavior of living things is capable of similar accurate prediction.

Some acceptance of a thorough-going determinism has taken place in these latter areas. At one time, we attributed choice and willfulness to animals; some animals were held to be responsible for their behavior and tried in court for their crimes. In the nineteenth century, however, the noted biologist Johannes Muller led a well-substantiated presentation of the mechanical nature of animal behavior. But he was unwilling to extend his conclusion of the deterministic character of behavior to man. In Immergluck's terms, Muller could be regarded as a "behaviorist" who exempted man.

At the human level, the determinism-freedom dilemma is confused by the common tendency to associate loss of freedom with *external* factors only. *Internal* constraints are likely to be ignored. Conditions within the individual, though otherwise recognized as causal factors in behavior, are somehow not brought into the picture in appraising freedom to choose. Our discussions of political, religious, and economic freedom, of course, are primarily concerned with external constraints on freedom. But this emphasis hampers consideration of internal determiners of behavior and the ultimate thesis that all human behavior may be lawful and therefore not free.

Opposed to the deterministic view is the argument that man's behavior is so patently unpredictable that the concept of choice is necessary to any reasonable explanation of it. When prediction goes much beyond reflexive behavior, it frequently breaks down. We can predict an eye-blink or a knee-jerk, but predictions of an individual's response, for example, to the experience of college are much less accurate. Some we predict will succeed end up failing; others considered "failures" succeed. Certainly, the record of the physical sciences in predicting effects is amazing, while that of the behavioral sciences is frankly disappointing.

To the charge of failure to predict, the determinist answers that, at present, measuring and accounting for all causative factors in human behavior cannot be done and are therefore not practical. When we do not know the experimental conditions in a study of animal behavior, we are tempted to label the animal's behavior as random, a synonym for choice. Yet, the impracticality of accounting for all causation is not proof that freedom to choose exists. In this connection, Immergluck observes

> It would be impossible, practically speaking, to calculate the precise course and time span involved in, say, the descent of an autumn leaf from the top of a particular tree to the ground. Obviously, the large number of unknown determining variables would make such calculation impossible, in any precise mathematical sense. At the same time, however, no one would doubt for a moment the intrinsic operation of strict lawfulness pertaining to this event, nor would anybody, because of the practical unpredictability and uncertainty, imbue the leaf with any kind of "free-will" attribute.

This amounts to saying that limited knowledge of the determiners of behavior leave the issue unresolved.

## CHOICE: A NECESSARY ILLUSION

A resolution of the freedom-determinism dilemma, suggested by Immergluck, states that the sense of choice we have about our actions is an illusion, but a necessary one for psychological health. We fool ourselves; we must. Our subjective experience of freedom to choose constitutes an "error," a perceptual distortion of reality we are unable to shake. Analogous to the visual illusions illustrated in the previous chapter, is the perceptual illusion in which we are trapped. Though we may "know" through measurement that the lines of the Muller-Lyer illusion are equal in length, our visual experience continues to deny this. Perhaps as the arrowheads and arrowtails in this illusion somehow are involved in bringing about error, so the demands of self-image are such that the erroneous notion of choice continues despite contradictory evidence.

It is doubtful that man can live with the idea that his thoughts, feelings, and actions are wholly determined. His image of self, as it seems to have evolved in all cultures, apparently requires a conviction of some degree of choice, a belief that he is not helplessly at the mercy of circumstances, external or internal. He may not be the "captain of his soul," completely the master of circumstances, but neither is he without some power to decide, some capacity to select his responses. Here, in this belief, may be one of the significant distinctions between humans and other animals.

## persuasion and the perception of choice

The implications of the possible illusionary character of choice are relevant to the study of persuasion. Assuming that man unavoidably makes the "error" of believing he has choice, it follows that persuasion involves not choice, but the perception of choice. The frequently used thief-gun-and-victim illustration clarifies the role of perceived choice. It is said that the victim has no choice, that he is forced to comply with the thief's demands. Alternatives, however, do exist. The victim is not forced in the sense that he has no alternative (no behavioral variability) except compliance. He can refuse to turn over his wallet, can run, or he can attack the thief rather than submit. And we occasionally read of an attempted robbery in which these atypical responses are made. These are alternatives, but the typical victim sees them as highly unequal. Submitting has significantly greater value to him than refusal, escape, or attack. Furthermore, the victim does not perceive himself as the principal agent in determining his response. He tends to say, "There wasn't anything I could do." But when perceived choice occurs, the individual sees his participation quite differently. He sees himself playing the *leading* role in determining his response. It is this characteristic which is essential to "choice." Ignoring internal determiners, the individual perceives self rather than some external agent or condition as the decisive factor in response. This seems to be the distinction between force and choice as stimulus situations, between compliance and acceptance as responses. Force involves a situation in which the individual perceives external, not internal factors, as the principal determiners of his response. The persuasive event is characterized by a "choice" situation and involves responses perceived to be self-determined.

Note that it is not the gun, *per se,* that rules out the thief-gun-victim situation as a persuasive event. The thief's gun is a message, but the effect is not persuasive. The gun is used by the victim as a sign. It indicates the thief's intent to use the gun to overcome resistance. The gun is a message, a sign used intentionally to affect the behavior of others. The effect, however, fails to meet the choice criterion. The victim does not perceive himself as the principal agent of response. For the thief, the gun is used as an instrument of force, not persuasion.

Sometimes it is claimed that the persuader seeks to make receivers feel they have no choice of action other than that which he desires. Indeed, efforts are aimed at having the desired action viewed as the most rewarding by receivers. Other actions are discredited and the desired action presented favorably in order to widen the desirability gap between possible courses of action. These efforts, however, are not designed to result in the perception of "no choice." The most persuaded voter may feel his candidate is the only reasonable choice; the car buyer may believe his purchase represents the best buy, the best choice by far. Yet, both still perceive themselves to have made the choice. Neither the voter nor the car buyer sees himself forced against his own preference to act as he did. The point is that the persuaded person not only approves of his action as the best in given circumstances, but perceives himself its chief selector.

If there is no choice, only an illusionary perception of it, of what value is persuasion? Are not receivers merely puppets whose responses are totally determined by external and internal conditions? Why seek to arouse in them the illusion that they have chosen their responses? The reason is that the perception of choice, illusionary or real, becomes an important internal determiner of behavior. It generates a harmony between one's feelings, beliefs, and actions. The receiver is more apt to approve of his "choice" of response, and to believe in the action that he takes. Such harmony has influence on his behavior. In this connection, it is interesting that the word persuasion is derived from *per suasio,* meaning influence "through sweetness." In the contemporary language of the behavioral sciences the notion of sweetness would be expressed as an harmonious relationship between the affective, cognitive, and overt components of behavior.

Those who use force or authority seek to produce actions in others with or without harmonious affective and cognitive components. If necessary, the action obtained need not be liked or believed in by the receiver. The resultant behavior may thus be highly disharmonious with the receiver's feelings and beliefs. In such circumstances, the user of force or authority uses messages to produce action as a direct effect of comprehending the message, and of recognizing the "no choice" character of the situation. Persuasion, on the other hand, brings about action as the result of harmony among the affective, cognitive, and overt dimensions of receiver behavior. The user of persuasion does not seek action directly or without a necessary consideration of affective and cognitive responses to his messages.

If choice is an illusion for the receiver, it is also for the persuader. Perhaps he does not really choose to persuade. Perhaps he too is a puppet in the hands of external and internal circumstances; even his words are not chosen, only perceived to be. In Chapter II, the "hypodermic needle" and similar models of the persuasive process were criticized for their inadequacy in understanding an audience. They also hinder our understanding of the source, the persuader. They are linear rather than circular concepts of persuasion. In essence, these views hold that the persuader supplies "freely" the initiative in the persuasive event. He directs a message at receivers; the "injected" message "takes" effect or does not and that ends the process of influence. Energy moves linearly from source to receiver.

Contemporary thought (Berlo, 1960; Eisenson, Irwin, and Auer, 1963; Bauer, 1964) supports a circular model. The major implication in this context is that the source is affected by the audience before, during, and after he presents a message, and indeed, like the receiver, is responsive to a variety of external and internal conditions. In his use of persuasion to influence others, he is responding to a situation he perceives is one of "choice" or "no choice" for him. As with the receiver, it is expected that his effort will be better if harmony exists in the affective, cognitive, and overt components of his behavior. Moreover, it seems particularly doubtful that an individual could regard his persuasive efforts and their effects as totally determined. He needs the perception of choice to make any sense of a persuasive endeavor.

## FORCE AND CHOICE

Our society tends to make the agent of effect the distinguishing feature between force and choice. Typically, the crime of rape rests on the belief that the female was forced. There may be alternatives but not choice. Self-selection of response is not the major factor; the superior strength of the male is assumed to account for the effect. Similarly, confessions under duress are considered the result of force, not choice. The power of those holding the prisoner, civilian or military, is considered overwhelming if employed to elicit a confession. The confession is not self-selected. The Korean conflict dramatized the application of force in obtaining confessions and declarations of conversion to Communism. Although the Chinese use of coercive interrogation has been widely publicized (Schein, 1956; Condon, 1962), intimidation and inquisition, subtle and crude, have existed as long as mankind itself. They are not Johnny-come-latelies as competitors of persuasion. Religious wars served the function of advancing conversion through force. Meerloo (1960) is of the opinion that we learned the more subtle techniques of coercive interrogation from the Inquisition of the Middle Ages. Galileo, for example, was intimidated into "repudiating" his belief in the solar system concept advanced by Copernicus. And at a later time, "witches" were made to "confess" their sexual union with the Devil.

Force, as a determiner of behavior, is society's definition of a situation, not the individual's perception of it. The martyr, "choosing" death rather than concede to the will of his captors, may perceive choice in a situation that society would define as force. To say a person was forced certainly does not literally mean "There was nothing else he could do." It is difficult to conceive of a situation in which the human individual does not have response alternatives. Thus, the notion that force limits response to one alternative, outside the area of reflexive behavior, may be as much an illusion as the idea of choice. In this context, force is most usefully viewed as a situation in which society considers conditions, not self-produced, the dominant determiners of only one reasonable and highly typical response among those available.

When, in the judgment of society, an individual "has no choice," this does not mean he is without other alternatives, only that the culture accepts his response as the only reasonable one. The assumption is that conditions, usually external and not-self-produced, are the determiners of a single response. No other is typical or normal. The individual is absolved of personal accountability. This group perception of a situation varies from one culture to another. Suicide in the Japanese culture may be approved as the only reasonable alternative in a given situation, but rejected by other cultures as a "choice".

Usually, the behavior of those who are forced is socially disapproved because it threatens in some way the stability of the social order. We commonly speak of force in connection with disloyal confessing under duress, revealing military information, opening a safe for thieves. If the social verdict declares force the dominant determiner, the individual is not held accountable for an otherwise punishable offense. However, one can be forced to engage in socially approved behavior. In our society, those who enact their roles in the execution of a criminal are excused of personal responsibility, and by their jobs "forced" to do cruel things. Judges are "required" to order this kind of killing by a law which is external to them. There are those who "must" witness the execution, and those who "must" physically perform it. These people are viewed as anonymous, mechanical beings representing the "law," the "state," or the "will of the people." To say that they have no other alternative is a fiction. They could quit their jobs. Yet so believed is this social fiction that many find themselves sympathizing with the poor judges, wardens, and executioners who "must" carry out the duties of their jobs (Berger, 1963). Similarly, the copy writer and TV announcer are often seen as mechanical beings not held accountable for misrepresenting a product or aiding in the distortion or suppression of facts. Yet they, too, have alternatives.

For the individual, the "existence" of force or choice depends primarily on his perceptions. He may not be aware of the available alternatives. What is a choice to one individual may represent force to another; one perceives himself the agent of response selection while another feels overwhelmed by external conditions. When American POW's "confessed" or "rejected democracy," there was a tendency to claim these men had choice. Some of these men may have violated norms in their responses, but this is not equivalent to saying they perceived themselves the selectors of response.

The tendency to accept and excuse oneself through the fiction of "no other alternative," even if socially approved, has been called by Sartre, the existentialist, "bad faith." The term refers to the practice of defining behavior as necessary, as forced, when in fact it is voluntary. Sartre, though he rejects the fiction of force in many situations, nevertheless accepts the illusion of choice. For him, "bad faith" is a flight from freedom, an evasion of the "agony of choice." The point maintained here is that though the reality of force and choice can be legitimately disputed, in the study of persuasion, it is the individual's *perception* of choice that is important.

## BASIC COMBINATIONS OF ALTERNATIVES

Often the perceived values of alternatives are highly unequal. As the victim says, "It's only money, not my life." Similarly, excessive reward can create the judgment that the alternatives are not at all equivalent. In the "long, hot summer" of 1964, it was reported that a $25,000 bribe was enough to tempt an informer to aid the FBI in locating the buried bodies of three civil rights workers murdered near Philadelphia, Mississippi. The reward may have been sufficient for the informer to say to himself, "For that kind of money, what choice do I have?" Similarly, the businessman, though desiring to be honest, may be tempted into a "deal" which will net him a handsome though unethical reward.

For the individual, the value of an alternative seems to have two dimensions—an affective and a cognitive. The affective dimension refers to the individual's feelings of like or dislike for the alternative; he dislikes being shot or killed more than being robbed. These feelings alone are insufficient to predict response. Does he believe he'll be shot if he refuses? The cognitive dimension deals with his belief in the probability of various consequences implied by the alternatives. In the armed robbery illustration, he may believe the stick-up man will not shoot. If this is his belief, he perceives the association of sign (gun) and consequence (being shot) not to be particularly high. Both dimensions, affective and cognitive, are involved in attaching value to a possible response. The persuader's task, through messages, is to alter these dimensions in a way that increases the value of his action-goal to the receiver.

Not only are the values of alternatives significant to a persuader's success, but the type or combination of alternatives is relevant. Dollard and Miller (1950) describe three basic combinations. For these authors, behavioral alternatives are valued in one of two ways: they are to be avoided or approached. Basic combinations, then, would bring together approach-approach alternatives, approach-avoidance, and avoidance-avoidance alternatives. Choosing between a new car and a luxury vacation would exemplify the approach-approach combination. Similarly, the businessman's choosing between his self-image of honesty and the rewards in a deal for a "fast buck" is involved in the same basic combination of alternatives. When his choice is between getting caught and making quick money, an avoidance-approach combination exists; he seeks to avoid detection and is attracted to the financial gain. The informer, bribed in Mississippi, was faced with the same combination. In an earlier illustration, however, the gunman's victim faces a combination of avoidance-avoidance alternatives. He wants to avoid being shot as well as giving up his money. Largely for simplicity in discussion, only two-alternative combinations are described. Clearly, we commonly face situations in which we are aware of more than two alternatives.

Viewing an audience in terms of the response alternatives it perceives could be a useful form of analysis and suggest the means to more effective persuasion. Gibson (1962), for example, provides evidence that, in the approach-avoidance issue of censorship, messages stressing the avoidance response to censorship were significantly better in changing attitude than messages emphasizing the approach or attractive alternative of non-censorship. Several hypotheses of interest to persuasion arise from a consideration of these combinations. (1) Persons for whom alternatives are perceived most equal in value are more responsive to persuasion. For such persons conflict and uncertainty exist; they are more ready to seek a basis for decision from someone else. In that conflict is itself an undesirable state, such persons are motivated to change. (2) An approach-approach combination of alternatives is the quickest and easiest to resolve. Persuasion is apt to have more success more quickly in generating action favoring one of these choices. (3) In that the tendency to approach a goal is stronger the nearer a person perceives it to be, it is important in persuasion that the nearness of the goal be indicated. This is another way of saying that the prospect of immediate reward encourages adoption. (4) Avoidance grows stronger the nearer the individual perceives the disliked alternative to be. The prospect of immediate punishment (negative reinforcement) acts as a deterrent. (5) When both approach and avoidance alternatives are weak, though perceived as equal, and conflict between them will be weak. The motive for change is weak and persuasion less likely to succeed. (6) When the persuader's goal is adoption, building reward strength is more useful than reducing avoidance strength. When the persuader's goal is continuance, change is avoided by maintaining the perception of unequal values and thus preventing the rise of conflict. When the persuader's goal is deterrence, building avoidance strength is preferred over reducing approach strength. When the persuader's goal is discontinuance, the creation of conflict followed by the strengthening of avoidance is preferred. (7) Persuasion as a means of influence is probably least successful when an avoidance-avoidance combination of alternatives exists. Other means of influence, not involving the perception of choice, are potentially more useful. In persuasive campaigns seeking the discontinuance of smoking, for example, their limited success may be associated with the alternatives perceived by the smoker. He neither wants to give up the pleasures of smoking nor does he want the health risks involved.

## *the perceived exercise of choice*

An individual may see himself as the principal agent of response yet feel that he has not exercised choice. The experience of making a choice, of using judgment, does not occur. Judgment, and consequently choice, are suspended. In such situations, the individual does not see his behavior as forced or external, but views himself as the primary source of his behavior. He often explains by saying, "That's the way I am," or "I don't know; it's a habit, I guess." Thus, the perception of choice does not insure the exercise of it; it only provides a setting in which it may occur. Persuasion, among the various means of influencing others, is conceived as that type characterized by the exercise of choice.

### HABITS AND PERSUASION

Habit is a much used word. And rightly so. It refers to a broad segment of human behavior. We speak of habits of speech, eating, driving, working, and of the habits of smoking, drinking, biting fingernails, and using narcotics. They are useful and harmful; they relieve us of the need to make decisions and they promote efficient behavior; they also interfere with learning, a change to more desired behavior. Habits are also useful or detrimental to those seeking to influence others. For the person who habitually votes for Republicans, all that is needed, when the candidate is a Republican, is so to identify him. When the candidate is a Democrat, this voter's habit is a roadblock to success. It is comforting to a cigarette company to have a large group of smokers who habitually smoke its brand. The faithful are complimented by being reminded "We Tareyton smokers would rather fight than switch," or

"I'd walk a mile for a Camel." Such habitual behavior, of course, is an obstacle in launching a new cigarette.

Does eliciting a habitual response from an individual constitute a persuasive effect? Certainly what the individual does is often in harmony with his feelings and beliefs. It is quite possible for one to enjoy a habit and even have a good opinion of it. One does not, moreover, perceive the cause of habit behavior to be external. For these reasons, it is concluded that habit behavior does not involve force. The tendency then is to reason that if it is not force, it must be persuasion. This either-or reasoning overlooks the possibility it may be neither type of influence. Consider a few examples of habit behavior. A "pusher" offers marijuana to a user. A sale is made. The user was not forced to buy, but was he persuaded? A cool bottle of beer is pictured on television and a habitual beer-drinker goes to his refrigerator. Has persuasion occurred? A habitual "yes-sayer" is asked to sign a petition or agree with a motion made in a committee. He agrees. Is the individual who habitually says "yes" persuaded?

It seems to me that influence through the stimulation of habit responses is best viewed as neither force nor persuasion. The nature of habit responses suggests why. They are characterized by (1) short latency periods, (2) high probability of occurring, and (3) high resistance to extinction. The short latency period refers to the brief time elapsing between the occurrence of a stimulus and the response to it. The high probability of occurring indicates the consistency of the response following stimulation. And resistance to extinction refers to the persistence of the response even though it is not reinforced (rewarded).

The short latency period makes of habit a type of behavior in which the experience of choice does not occur. Behavior occurs often without awareness. The fingernail biter is often made aware of his behavior after someone else calls it to his attention. The fast automobile driver is already speeding before some incident or near accident makes him aware of speed. In habit behavior, then, the experience of choice is infrequent or non-existent. Moreover, the stimulus for the habit response is frequently not consciously perceived and thus is not used as a sign by the individual to stand for something beside itself. It follows that habit producing stimuli are not messages and that habit behavior is not a persuasive effect. They can be used to influence others, but not persuasively.

Unlike persuasive effects, the habit response is typically consummatory; it is an end in itself and not a means to further behavior.

Meaning is not aroused through messages as a method of generating further behavior in the form of action. Like force, habit stimulation seeks action directly with little concern or necessity for harmony between that action and its affective and cognitive aspects. In that habit behavior need not be based on behavioral harmony it is possible to influence others, through their habits, to continue the use of drugs, cigarettes, or alcohol while they at the same time disapprove of their actions.

## SIGNAL RESPONSES AND PERSUASION

Similar in characteristics to the habit response is the signal response, a term used rather widely in recent years. Its consideration is particularly relevant to the study of influence and the distinctive features of persuasion. So often is the stimulus arousing a signal response a word or other sign used in persuasion that signal behavior is apt to be considered a persuasive effect. Essentially, the signal response is a particular kind of habit. Its chief distinction is in the stimulus which arouses the response. The stimulus is a perceived specific signal or one of a class of highly similar signals. In driving a car, for example, we apply the brake in response to perceiving a red light as a traffic light. Our response, however, like other habits, is characterized by immediacy, high likelihood of occurring, and high resistance to extinction. In fact, driving an automobile is an example of a series of signal responses. We react to such things as turn signals, signs indicating speed limits, detours, stop streets, construction areas, slippery highway conditions. Our behavior is not habitual in the usual sense. Driving by habit, such as habitually driving fast without attention to signs, leads to the obituary column. Driving is characterized by constant watching for signs and responding signally.

On the television show, "Candid Camera," a stunt was presented in which a traffic light was set up on the sidewalk and far from any street intersection. Apparently people were found and filmed who, *as pedestrians on a sidewalk,* would stop in front of the light when it flashed red. This is a signal response. Choice is not perceived or exercised; the behavior is automatic, not evaluated in the mind before it is carried out, and seemingly done without anticipation of the consequences. The individual is influenced as a result of conditioning, not persuaded. When the association of the traffic light (sign) and traffic intersection (condition) has sufficient strength, the sign seems no longer to be used to indicate an intersection but is reacted to in its own right. Though called a signal, it is no longer used by the individual to arouse meaning in the sense of standing for something beside itself. On the basis of its function, it should be classified broadly as a stimulus, not specifically as a signal.

Such stimuli occur in many communication events. Weaver and Strausbaugh (1964) observe that obscene words are frequently reacted to signally. Name-calling, the use of words like Communist, left-winger, pinko, wop, nigger, red neck, kike, and hillbilly are apt to be reacted to signally. The clergyman's "Let us pray," the neighbor's "Good morning" to which we respond automatically, and the National Anthem to which we rise are frequently responded to signally. The consequent behavior, however, is not the effect of having been persuaded.

In describing the testing and training program for the sit-in demonstrations used in the civil rights campaign, Lomax (1963) provides a dramatic example of signal response behavior.

> I watched Len Holt and his assistants from CORE as they schooled Negro students for nonviolent protest.
>
> The students were seated at a long table resembling a lunch counter. Holt, or one of his assistants, would play the part of the white man. The white man walked along the counter blowing smoke in the students' faces; he called them names: "nigger," "coon," "black bastard." When these failed to provoke any reaction, the white man would push and shove, and, finally in desperation, hit. The Negro student who fought back or got angry flunked the course. The only way to pass—and thus be allowed to participate in a real-life lunch counter sit-in—was to bear it all without a whimper, without anger.

In such a role-playing setting, one would suppose that trainees would not get angry in response to words and other artificial behavior. They knew the "white man's" behavior was not real and they knew as trainees they were not to get angry or fight back. Yet, so immediate, invariant, and resistant to extinction are signal responses that, though knowing they were not to respond to them, some trainees nevertheless did. Some of them must have found their reactions so quick and unthinking that they wondered afterward why they got angry and fought back. It is because of the power of such stimuli that they are frequently used by some seeking to influence others. The fact that they are potent, and often in the form of words, does nonetheless not qualify them as producers of persuasive effects.

## SUGGESTION, MOTIVATION RESEARCH, AND PERSUASION

If quotations linking suggestion with persuasion were all that were needed to establish it as a major producer of persuasive effect, an ample supply exists. Several texts on persuasion have devoted chapters or sections of chapters to its use. Such frequent reference to suggestion entitles it to consideration as a possible means of generating persuasive effects. As the term is used, however, two different notions of what is involved are used. The first conceives of suggestion as the process of arousing uncritical change of attitude toward an idea because of its association with another idea already in the mind. Prestige suggestion, for instance, implies that the receiver uncritically accepts an idea from a prestigeful speaker because of its association with him. Testimonials and commercials by television personalities are a practical application of this notion. The other use of the term views suggestion as the process by which an idea is aroused in the receiver without direct statement. The idea is only implied in the source's messages and inferred by the receiver. Terms such as innuendo and intimation refer to this process. In our folklore, and to some extent the practice of boy-girl relationships, the girl uses suggestion, not any direct statements, to generate the idea in the boy's mind that she is available to him for dating. Similarly, the politician does not directly declare his desire for a political nomination, but implies it through other statements. We hear him say, for instance, "No responsible man could carelessly turn down an honest draft."

The first concept of suggestion has had rough going among psychologists in recent years, largely beginning with Asch (1948). The doctrine of suggestion, Asch notes, was oriented originally to the *formation* of social misconceptions. The history of human thought abounds in examples of widely held beliefs that are inadequate, bizarre, or simply unsustained by any evidence. How these were formed and became widely believed was the question to which suggestion was offered as an answer. At that time the terms suggestion, prestige, and imitation were virtually interchangeable. Later, much broader application of the idea was made, and in the thinking of many scholars it became the theory of the formation and *change* of opinions and attitudes. The linkage of suggestion and imitation was weakened. It is this more general usage of the term that became associated with persuasion.

Asch's chief criticisms, however, of this general application of suggestion are that there are flaws in the research designs used to study suggestion and that a more valid explanation can be made of the effects obtained. Commonly, suggestion research used statements or quotations and assigned a source to them, a different source to different groups. Examples are:

> Those who hold and those who are without property have ever formed two distinct classes
>
> Karl Marx
> John Adams (correct)
>
> I hold it that a little rebellion, now and then, is a good thing, and as necessary in the political world as storms are in the physical.
>
> Jefferson (correct)
> Lenin

The typical results were that people approved the statements more when associated with an approved source. These findings were attributed to suggestion, an unthinking (non-cognitive) approval or disapproval of an idea because of the source with which it was linked. The theory rests on several tenuous assumptions. It assumes that emotional responses, divorced from cognitive processes, determine the changes in evaluating the idea. Liking or disliking the source of the idea alone does the job. Meaning, belief, opinion, or knowledge with respect to the idea have no bearing on response. As one experimenter put it, evaluation changes "regardless of the merit of the quotations." The second assumption made in this theory, one generally involved in studies of prestige effects, is that the object of judgment, usually a statement, has a fixed, unchanging meaning. It is assumed that the meaning of a statement does not change for the receiver, that only his evaluation of it is influenced by the source. The fallacy lies in the notion that messages have meaning in themselves, fixed and unchanging. The opposite position is a better fit with the facts of observation; that is, that meaning is in people and does change under the influence of contextual factors.

In line with this latter view, Asch rejected the doctrine of suggestion as an acceptable explanation of effects. In his words, "Authorship functioned not as a source of prestige but as a context for the determination of meaning." Thus, a change in the source changes the context; the result is a change in meaning *in the receiver*. Meaning is not an invariant property of messages. In this connection, Asch noted that "The specific content [meaning] of an event or utterance is a function of the perceived relation between it and its context." Rather than suggestion as an explanation of effects, Asch concluded that what occurs is "a change in the object of judgment rather than in the judgment of the object."

This view maintains that message meaning changes, that meaning is revised or restructured by the receiver. This process has been called cognitive restructuring. In one set of experiments (Lewis, 1947), it was concluded that suggestion phenomena are more satisfactorily explained by this concept. The receiver changes the meaning of the message. The effect produced is a response to a changed message meaning and not the occurrence of an uncritical, emotional response to suggestion.

Regarding this use of the term suggestion, two conclusions relevant to persuasion can be drawn. The first is that these supposedly uncritical responses are not persuasive effects. Such responses presuppose that the source, not the message, is the major determinant of effect. The second conclusion is that many of the effects attributed to suggestion are more satisfactorily explained as cognitive restructuring. In other words, these effects are instances of persuasion, not because of suggestion but because of the influence of context on message meaning. Message meaning retains its position as a major determinant of effect. One conclusion that should not be made is that suggestion effects do not exist, for they do, although their frequency in typical communicative events is sharply reduced. Certainly, clear examples of suggestion are to be found in studies of hypnosis. When the hypnotist suggests that a subject raise his hand, that his leg is numb, or that he is thirsty, the responses are characterized by uncritical acceptance of the source's suggestions. Moreover, the concept of suggestion has wider usage in the field of hypnosis than in those of social psychology, sociology, or persuasion. The important point, in this context, is that neither the effects of suggestion nor of hypnosis meet the criteria of persuasion. The perception or experience of choice is not involved; the message is not a major determinant of effect.

The occurrence of suggestion—that is, uncritical acceptance of an idea from others—can take place, however, without hypnosis, and without an appeal to cognitive restructuring as a more valid explanation of effects. Coffin (1947) demonstrated that persons uncertain of their abilities to handle a problem generally accept suggestions uncritically. Apparently, when people perceive themselves ignorant or uninformed about a problem, they are more prepared to accept suggestions; the perception of being wholly incapable of dealing with the problem makes appraisal of the suggestions seem futile—thus, uncritical acceptance. In contrast, persons who perceive themselves as trained to deal with a problem will be critical of a suggestion, and accept or reject it on the basis of their appraisal.

In Coffin's experiment, 16 mathematics problems were prepared and assembled into what was called the "Richardson Number Facility Test." The subjects were students in classes in elementary psychology and in mathematics classes in calculus. As a result, students varied in background from one-half year of mathematics to seven and one-half years. For each problem in the test, space was provided for working the problem. In these spaces, suggestion-messages were penciled in. These were "hints" about the answers or about a procedure for doing the problem. Most of the suggestions recommended incorrect procedures. The presence of these suggestions was justified in this way: it was explained that the test had been found to require more time than was available, so they were there to save time.

The tests of the 49 students involved as subjects were scored in terms of whether they accepted or rejected the suggestions offered. The tendency of the untrained person to accept and the trained person to reject the suggestions is revealed in the results (see Table 1).

TABLE 1

RELATION BETWEEN SUGGESTIBILITY AND TRAINING

| Years of mathematics training | Number of students | Average number of suggestions used | Per cent of total |
|---|---|---|---|
| 0.5–1.25 | 15 | 9.1 | 62.8 |
| 1.5–2.25 | 9 | 7.4 | 48.8 |
| 2.5–3.25 | 9 | 6.3 | 40.3 |
| 3.5–4.75 | 11 | 5.2 | 33.2 |
| 5.5–7.50 | 5 | 5.4 | 35.6 |

By way of additional clarification, the author divided the students into those with "elementary" mathematics training and those with "advanced." Elementary training was defined as less than three years of college mathematics, and advanced training equivalent to three or more years. For these two groups, 65.5 per cent of the 29 elementary students were suggestible while only 10 per cent of the 20 advanced students were similarly responsive. Such findings support the point that suggestion tends to occur among people perceiving themselves untrained to solve a problem independently.

The Coffin experiment left unresolved the question of whether suggestion can take place without the aid of prestige influence. Students surely perceived their professors as the source of the penciled-in "hints." As a result, the association of the suggestions with prestigeful professors could contribute to their ready acceptance by untrained students. To substantially reduce the prestige factor, I carried out a related study using marked examination booklets. The idea for the experiment grew out of the fact that students often mark up an examination booklet by putting check marks opposite answers they have chosen before they mark their answer sheets. Sometimes these booklets are used again among other students taking the test at a later time. Consequently, for the experiment, clean test booklets were deliberately marked up.

The test involved was part of the examining procedure for a course involving several hundred students. The type of test questions used were "best" answer rather than "right" answer questions. For the experiment, this was desirable in that "best" answer questions provide, in most students' experience, more uncertainty about which choice to make. Within the test, five consecutive questions were selected to be marked. Small check marks were placed opposite the least preferred choice in each question. These checks were partially erased to imply that a previous student had made an effort to clean up his test booklet.

These tampered booklets were given to a group of 103 students while 112 other students received clean booklets. In the former group, 34 students used one or more of the checked, but unsatisfactory, answers. These 34 students averaged 4.38 of a possible total of five checked choices. Apparently, when a student accepted this kind of nonprestigeful suggestion, he accepted it quite consistently. In the control group of 112 students, with unmarked booklets, only 10 students used one or more of these five answers; on the average they used only 1.11 of the answers in question. The two groups made very similar average scores on other questions in the test, showing there was no significant difference in their abilities to score well. It was concluded that uncritical acceptance of suggestions, for some people in situations involving uncertainty, occurs even though the suggestions were not aided by a prestigeful source. In summary, suggestion in the sense of uncritical acceptance does occur, but to a much more limited extent than formerly claimed. It further seems more associated with receiver uncertainty than with source prestige. This implies that its use is apt to be more effective following the establishment of uncertainty in receivers than if it is attempted solely by means of prestigeful sources. Such a technique is a competitor to persuasion as a means of influence, not an example of it. Choice is not exercised, except as dependence on another. Furthermore, receiver uncertainty, not the message, is the major determiner of effect.

A set of techniques and theory for influencing people, often described in terms similar to those used in explaining suggestion as an uncritical, emotional response, is covered by the label "motivation research." Louis Cheskin, one of its prominent advocates, defines it this way (Packard, 1957).

> Motivation research is the type of research which seeks to learn what motivates people in making choices. It employs techniques designed to reach the unconscious or subconscious mind because preferences generally are determined by factors of which the individual is not conscious. Actually in the buying situation the consumer generally acts emotionally and compulsively, unconsciously reacting to the images and designs which in the unconscious are associated with the product.

Packard, who described these procedures for the general reading public, points out that these motivation analysts team up with "symbol manipulators"—advertisers, public relations specialists, fund raisers, politicians, clergymen, and personnel experts—"to channel our unthinking habits, our purchasing decisions, and our thought processes by the use of insights gleaned from psychiatry and the social sciences. Typically these efforts take place beneath our level of awareness; so that the appeals which move us are often, in a sense, *hidden.*" The title of his book, *The Hidden Persuaders,* and its content consistently classify this form of influence as persuasion and those who use it as "professional persuaders." Yet it is implied that the receiver acts without choice. The theory explains response in terms of satisfying some human need of which the receiver is unaware. Nevertheless, it seems to me that motivational research and its use to influence others is properly viewed as persuasion. Consider some examples of its use.

The advertising message for Gleem toothpaste, on the basis of motivation research, was changed to make Gleem a toothpaste "for people who cannot brush their teeth after every meal." The motivation analysts explain that people, having been told since childhood to brush after every meal, feel guilty for not doing so. The sales message provided a means, through the use of Gleem, of reducing the sense of guilt. Various banking institutions have employed motivation analysts to explain their losing customers to loan companies despite the fact that most banks offer personal loans at lower interest rates and often are more lenient in accepting loan applicants. The analysts concluded that people see a bank as "a kind of parent, a parent capable of scolding or withholding approval," of making one feel like an "unreliable adolescent," while the loan company gives no impression of stern morality and parental judgment. Banks were told to soften their image. In the home freezer field, it is a fact that for many people a home freezer is an uneconomical purchase, yet sales boomed following World War II. The motivation analysts explained that wartime uncertainties created a need for security and safety. In childhood, these are associated with mother and she with assuring the availability of food. The freezer thus represents the assurance that food will always be available, and satisfies the need for security. Freezer merchandisers were advised to stress this "squirrel factor" in their sales messages (Packard, 1957).

Clearly, Mr. Average Man, even in the privacy of his own thought, is not going to explain his behavior in terms of guilt feelings, resentment of parental authority and judgment, and desire to return to the womb or to the security of childhood. Such factors as determiners of behavior are foreign to his way of explaining behavior. But to say he is unaware of such factors does not preclude the perception and experience of choice on his part. The individual who purchases a toothpaste to reduce guilt feelings is not likely to say, "I have no choice." He not only perceives choice, but is apt to give a "reason," or a rationalization, for his purchase. There is a cognitive dimension in his response to the advertiser's message; he has an opinion as well as a feeling about the message. Though his opinion may be incorrect, and his explanation of his behavior unsound, his response is not purely emotional.

Moreover, rather than call his behavior compulsive, it is useful to recall the earlier discussion of the determinism-freedom dilemma. There it was pointed out that the determinist sees all behavior as the result of knowable causes and sees choice as an illusion. A determinist might easily use the term "compulsive" to imply behavior without choice. It must be remembered the social scientists—psychologists, sociologists and psychiatrists—who provide these esoteric explanations of behavior following motivation research are very likely deterministic in their outlook. It seems to me that they are saying that responses to some messages are determined by internal causes and not by the exercise of free choice, but are not saying the individual does not perceive choice and have the experience or "illusion" of exercising it. Consequently, the effects developed by these teams of motivation analysts and symbol manipulators are best viewed as persuasion.

The reader will recall that two meanings of suggestion were described at the beginning of this discussion. The first was appraised, along with "motivation research," as a method of bringing about uncritical responses. The second notion of suggestion describes it as the use of innuendo or implication to lead to a conclusion not directly stated. The words of Iago in *Othello* and their effects exemplify this notion. They also exemplify influence by persuasion. As a concept in the study of persuasion, however, suggestion by words is too narrow because it restricts a message to a statement, and hence is misleading. In persuasion, events, pictures, objects and actions can be and are used to set in motion inferences by the receiver. He infers from these non-verbal stimuli an idea not directly observable. What a refusal to admit Negro demonstrators to a white church in Birmingham is apt to mean to observers of this event is not directly observable or stated. No one directly says, "The white man does not practice, even in his churches, the Christianity he preaches" or "This Negro church attendance is not sincere, only agitation." These are inferences or meanings aroused by the event.

Calling inferred meanings suggestion, and thus coupling these effects with the former use of the term, however, implies that the receiver's behavior is uncritical. The receiver's inference from the event is influenced by the event maker, and may be invalid in the judgment of others, but this is not to say it is unthinking and entirely emotional. To draw a conclusion from words or other stimuli is a cognitive act, involving the formation of belief and opinion. The response is not automatic; the perception and experience of choice exists. The effect is persuasive. Fortunately, the term suggestion is unnecessary for this kind of effect. Inference, as a term, adequately implies conclusion-drawing as a kind of effect prevalent in persuasive events.

## SUBLIMINAL STIMULATION, SLEEP TEACHING, AND PERSUASION

In the autumn of 1957, James Vicary, a marketing researcher and psychologist, conducted a demonstration of subliminal stimulation. During the presentation of the movie, *Picnic,* at a Fort Lee, New Jersey, movie house, Vicary flashed on the screen, at 1/3000 of a second every five seconds, the messages "Drink Coca-Cola" or "Hungry? Eat Popcorn." These messages were exposed so briefly that members of the audience were unaware of their presence. They were subliminal, below the level of perception. That is, they were not detected, identified, and certainly not consciously used as a group of signs for meaning arousal. After six weeks of this demonstration, Vicary reported that Coca-Cola sales in the lobby went up 57.7 per cent and popcorn sales rose 18.1 per cent (Brean, 1958).

This demonstration led some to conclude that large numbers of persons can be influenced by messages they do not see or hear. Congressmen advocated legislation against subliminal stimulation. The Women's Christian Temperance Union became concerned for our youth should brewers use this kind of advertising. Some advertisers felt it was an unethical means of influence. The National Association of Radio and Television Broadcasters, which includes all three major TV networks, banned the use of subliminal stimulation by its members. Meanwhile, some horror movies were produced using this technique in the hope of providing added emotional stimulation for viewers. Los Angeles television station KTLA signed a contract to have certain public service messages—"Drive safely" and "Don't be a litterbug"—presented subliminally (Brean, 1958).

An appraisal of the effectiveness of this technique and of others with "hidden" messages will be provided later. The question here is whether they constitute persuasion as a form of influence. Clearly, the term "hidden" more fittingly applies to such devices of influence as subliminal stimulation and sleep teaching than to those evolved through motivation research as described by Packard. In subliminal stimulation, the receiver is unaware of a message's existence. He does not detect it, identify it, or, more importantly, perceive the message as a group of signs for meaning arousal—to indicate or represent something besides itself. In that no message is perceived, the receiver is unaware of any message source. He has no experience of choice in respect to the effort of a source. Thus, such means of influence, effective or not, are competitors to persuasion, not instances of it.

These devices, along with habit stimulation, signal response behavior, and the kind of suggestion involving uncritical acceptance, though not persuasion, typically use words and other types of signs. This fact has led some writers to include them all, along with persuasion, in one category. Usually, this grouping of techniques involving signs is called propaganda. Young (1956), for example, defines propaganda as "The more or less deliberately planned and systematic use of symbols, chiefly through suggestion and related psychological techniques, with a view to altering and controlling opinions, ideas, and values, and ultimately to changing overt actions along predetermined lines." In this sense, propaganda and persuasion are similar in two respects. Both use words and other signs, and both are employed instrumentally in bringing about intended action-goals. Persuasion, however, is distinctive in that the message is a major determinant of effect, the receiver sees himself stimulated by an external message-source, and he perceives choice and experiences the exercise of it. It is in these distinctive features that the potential and limitations of persuasion are to be found.

## interpersonal relations and persuasion

Earlier in this chapter it was implied that at times the relations between source and receiver may obviate choice. In a traffic jam, when a traffic officer directs a motorist to turn in a direction he does not care to go, he typically behaves as directed. The officer obtains the response he desires without obtaining the motorist's approval. When such a relationship between source and receiver exists, persuasive effects do not occur; indeed, the need to persuade is unnecessary. Examples such as this raise the question of what types of interpersonal relationships reduce the perception and exercise of choice, and consequently, the necessity to persuade.

Influence by one person on another may be based on power, authority, or persuasion (Blau and Scott, 1962). The stick-up man and the victorious army use power to influence. Power occurs when a social relationship is such that an individual [or group] is in a position to carry out his will despite resistance. In these relationships authority is not exercised. The latter is characterized by *voluntary* obedience to the directives of those in control. Those who respond to authority do so because they consider it *legitimate,* and even rewarding, for another to control their behavior in particular areas. Brown (1963) comments that the Prussian tradition in Germany has always involved an accepted "pecking order" such that the reward for being pecked by someone in authority was to peck in turn those over whom one had authority. In many business, educational, political, and military organizations, authority relationships are often found between members on one echelon and those on another. To contrast the two relationships, power generates forced compliance whereas authority produces voluntary compliance and often genuine acceptance. When either is the primary basis of influence, a persuasive effort though helpful is not necessary. Even though messages are involved, they are alternate types of influence, not forms of persuasion.

When an individual voluntarily accepts the influence of another, however, this is not necessarily evidence of an authority relationship between them. Acceptance also occurs as a result of persuasion. Blau and Scott (1962) point out that "Persuasion is distinguished from authority inasmuch as the latter involves an *a priori* suspension of the first person's judgment, obviating the need for persuasion." Unlike an authority relationship, a persuasive one arouses the perception and exercise of choice among alternatives.

Five bases of influence, rather than three, are described by French (1956). These are conceived as types of interpersonal power of a hypothetical person A over another person B. Person A may possess *attraction* power based on B's liking for A. Second, he may have *expert* power based on B's perception that A has superior knowledge and information. Third, he may have *reward* power based on A's ability to reward B. Fourth, he may have *coercive* power based on A's perceived ability to impose punishments on B. Finally, person A may have *legitimate* power based on B's acceptance of A's right to direct his behavior.

Several similarities between the two classifications can be noted. The principal point, however, is that various interpersonal relationships can generate an influence that becomes the major determinant of response. The effect is determined more by the relationship than by the message. When this happens, the effect has not been a persuasive one. The relationship has reduced the use of judgment and the perception of choice to an insignificant level. This implies that frequently the employer-employee, parent-child, physician-patient, friend-friend, leader-follower, and other relationships produce non-persuasive effects. The receiver may respond without perceiving himself the agent of effect, without exercising judgment, without the message being a major determinant of effect.

Of the bases of influence cited by these writers, that of *legitimate* influence involves more than so far suggested. Consider the typical relationship between the teacher and student. When we say that the teacher is in an authority relation to the student, we imply the student considers it legitimate for the teacher to direct his school behavior. But more than this is involved. He not only has notions of what behavior he expects from the teacher, but also notions of what is expected of him as a student. He knows he is expected to follow directions. Similarly, the teacher, in his role expects to direct the student, and has a set of expectations regarding what reciprocal behavior his own role calls for. Each person, then, in a social grouping has two sets of expectations: (1) what behavior his role legitimates and (2) what reciprocal behavior from others, in response to his role, is legitimate. This means that both the student and teacher can respond to the legitimate demands of either his own role or that of the other. In either case, the behavior is more determined by role expectations than messages. The student, for example, requests a conference and additional help with his studies. A teacher may see this request as legitimate student behavior. In response, he agrees to the conference and supplies the help. Does the student's request produce a persuasive effect? Not when the teacher is responding to what he considers is expected of his role; he may wish to turn down the request even though he fulfills it. The role expectation, not self, is the perceived determinant of response. The effect of role expectations on the behavior of each member of a social group reduces the number of effects that can be called persuasive even though messages are involved.

## GAMES, DEBATES, AND PERSUASION

In the last twenty years, a new theory of conflict has arisen, mathematical in approach, called the theory of games. In a "game," the kind of conflict involved is that which arises between individuals or groups, and not intrapersonal conflict. The word "game" is used in a sense that conveys much more than the Saturday night "penny ante" session or the antics of the bridge table. These games and many others, more properly called games of strategy, offer simplified models for this new theory. The theory, however, is being applied to warfare, labor-management bargaining, political bargaining, and similar non-playful situations. It could be applied to the conflict between integrationists and segregationists. These games of strategy provide a model of the behavior of people in many serious situations where "(1) there are conflicts of interest; (2) a number of alternatives are open at each phase of the situation; (3) people are in a position to estimate consequences of their choices, taking into consideration the very important circumstance that outcomes are determined not only by one's own choices but also by the choices of others, over whom one has no control" (Rapoport, 1960). Of concern here is the value of game theory in clarifying the role of persuasion in the many conflict situations arising in complex societies.

A major notion stressed by game theorists is that the participants behave often via messages, in such a way as to reduce or eliminate the perception of choice in others. In a political conflict between nations, the government of one may communicate an intention to use force if certain behavior from the other occurs or if specified activity is not stopped. This announced intention may be followed by statements and activity related to the mobilization and reassignment of military forces.

The Cuba crisis of 1962 exemplifies this kind of situation. This involved confronting Russia with evidence for believing that U.S. behavior would be determined by the behavior of Russia in this situation. To the game theorist, the U.S. as a participant employed a strategy to have Russia perceive its choices limited, or to perceive itself to have no choice. Moreover, a game of conflict involves the skillful non-use of force (Schelling, 1960). It is concerned with the exploitation of potential force, and seeks to influence other participants to avoid or discontinue certain behavior in their own interests. Games, then, tend to emphasize the goals of deterrence and discontinuance, although in particular instances they could seek the adoption or continuance of behavior in others.

Before the persuasive character of game behavior is appraised, it is well to examine the concept of a "move" in this theory. One's actions, including his messages, are moves. These are "moves" one makes as one makes a "move" in checkers or chess. Moves are selected and put together to carry out one's strategy for winning, obtaining the largest share of forthcoming damages or rewards. Moves, then, are provided to alter others' appraisal of one's strength, or of one's intent to behave or respond in particular ways, or to reduce their perception of choice. Messages are not used to persuade others of the rightness of one's goals. They are not designed to generate behavior in others in such a way that they act in harmony with their values, beliefs, and desires. Games, though involving messages, do not use persuasion as a form of influence to develop action in others. They use persuasion only in the limited sense of establishing beliefs. These help to create a situation in which possible rewards or punishments reduce the perception of choice and become the dominant determinants of behavior. Such effects, unlike those in persuasion, last only as long as these determinants are perceived to operate.

Regarding business games, March and Simon (1958) have observed, "Where bargaining is used, disagreement over goals is taken as fixed, and agreement without persuasion is sought." In the labor-management conflict, agreement may occur regarding compromise as a means of ending a mutually undesired situation, without genuine acceptance of the results specified in the settlement. Each side may immediately begin preparations to change that settlement in its own favor. March and Simon (1958) generalized their appraisal of the role of persuasion by concluding that it has little part in any type of intergroup conflict. The communicator's effort is more apt to be what Potter (1952) called gamesmanship rather than persuasion.

Still another viewpoint of relevance to persuasion is that decision, in a game, is in the hands of the participants involved. Decision or solution is not an act of a third party. Looked upon in this way, courtroom, political, and intercollegiate debates as well as cases of arbitration are not, strictly speaking, games. A non-participant, acting as a judge and decision-maker, affects the actions taken. These activities do, however, have the competitiveness and conflict of games. Participants design strategies and make moves to affect the game behavior of others. To the extent that a debater seeks to influence his opponent's choice of messages and judgments, he is not a persuader. His persuasive effort lies in generating a favorable decision in the judge.

Lastly, games of strategy are conceived to be of three types (Schelling, 1960). To identify them among the many events involving messages enables us to judge better which ones might effectively use persuasion to influence and which might require other means. The first type is the common-interest or coordination game. In this, the participants can be viewed as partners. The common-interest game involves the discovery of the optimal means of achieving a mutually accepted goal. One partner may persuade another to accept and act on a particular means of reaching a common goal. Conflict may arise over the division of labor in attaining the goal; to resolve this, persuasion is less apt to be attempted. The second type of game is that of pure conflict or the zero-sum game. Participants are viewed as opponents or adversaries. The goals sought by one are directly opposed to those sought by another. This is exemplified in checkers, chess, poker, and similar parlor games. One wins at the expense of opponents; the sum of gains and losses is zero. The philosophy of this type of game is an unreserved acceptance of competition. In this case, persuasion is not a useful means of influence. Opponents are not persuaded to act in each other's favor. The third type of game is the mixed motive or bargaining game. Participants are viewed as bargainers or negotiators. Of the term "mixed motive," Schelling points out that this does not refer "to an individual's lack of clarity about his own preferences but rather to the ambivalence of his relation to the other player—the mixture of mutual dependence and conflict, of partnership and competition." Labor and management, for example, may need each other yet compete for shares of the available profits. In such situations, persuasion has a limited role as a form of influence.

## summary

The determination-freedom issue was examined to suggest that choice may well be an illusion, but a necessary one for psychological health. The needed condition in persuasion, however, is the perception of choice rather than its actuality. When the receiver perceives himself to have choice, as he does in persuasion, there is a tendency toward harmony among his affective, cognitive, and overt components. This condition gives persuasion an advantage over other means of influence; effects tend to be more economically achieved and probably are more lasting. Among other means of influence, force is distinguished from persuasion in that the former does not involve the perception of choice. Additionally, persuasion is viewed as an effect involving the exercise of choice. On this basis, it is differentiated from habit behavior, signal responses, uncritical suggestiveness, subliminal stimulation, and sleep teaching. The uses of the term "suggestion" were examined with the conclusion that it is not needed for a perspective on persuasion. Finally, the effect of interpersonal relations on the use of persuasion was considered. Some relations favor the use of force or authority as a means of influence. The competitive relationships in "games" reduce the role of persuasion.

A concluding point that should be made to a consideration of choice and persuasion is that, in concrete situations, choice is difficult to verify. Not only does perception of a situation vary among individuals, but varies for the same individual from time to time. His view of a situation is dynamic rather than stable. For example, when one has been persuaded by another many times with rewarding results, he may begin to defer to the other's judgment. He seeks a dependent, submissive relationship. This new relationship, not message meaning, becomes the dominant determinant of effect. Choice is not exercised with respect to the message; only dependence is chosen. As a consequence, certain communicative events, in the abstract, cannot be firmly classified as persuasive events while others are typed as non-persuasive. This means that an individual in analyzing the available means of influence, should not assume that a particular kind of communicative event always or never dictates the use of persuasion as the most effective means of influence.

# Chapter 6

# Message and Effect: An Interpersonal Event

The specification that persuasion be viewed as an interpersonal event directs attention away from many events that involve or are presumed to involve the use of messages between other types of sources and receivers. Humans, animals, gods and other superhuman beings, machines and other inanimate objects have been considered sources and receivers of messages. These can be put in all sorts of interesting source-receiver combinations. And man has done just that! His belief in each potential combination is a fascinating story. Currently, in an age of computers, mechanical brains, and automation, men are conceiving of machines communicating with machines. Perhaps some are dreaming of machines persuading machines. Some illustrative source-receiver combinations will clarify the bases for rejecting machines as generators of persuasive effects, and for conceptualizing persuasion *as an event in which source and receiver are different persons.* Another justification for this restriction is interest. Professional students and practitioners of persuasion are overwhelmingly interested in person-to-other-person effects.

## *animals as sources and receivers*

In this combination of source and receiver, both are non-human organisms. It is often said that it is language or communication that distinguishes man from other animals. Much depends on what is meant by the terms language and communication. The evidence seems to indicate that there is here no strict dichotomy between humans and non-humans. Many other animals "communicate" and use "language." For example, remarkable communication occurs in bees. When a worker bee has found a food supply, he returns to the hive. Without leaving the hive he is able to give his fellows (receivers) not only the direction but also the distance to the food supply. He does this by means of a "wagging dance;" the farther the food the fewer the number of turns in the dance. The angle of the dance on the vertical comb, with respect to gravity, gives the direction to the food relative to the sun. If the sun is not shining, polarized light from the sky still provides the needed direction. Polarization appears to be the essential cue whether the sun shines or not. No communication, however, is possible if the sky is completely overcast (Hebb and Thompson, 1954).

The characteristics of language have been considered by many writers. Hockett (1960) employs a set of thirteen dimensions of language. The use of language by any organism, in his view, can be placed on a scale according to the number and quality of language features the organism uses to communicate. The dancing behavior of the worker bee has several of these characteristics. Its dance is significant, that is, likely to arouse meaning beyond itself; the movements and positions in the dance represent a distance and direction. In contrast, the mating or courtship dances of whooping cranes, birds of paradise, and the stickleback fish are not symbolic; they represent nothing other than what they are. The bee's communication also is characterized by capacity for displacement. This means the bee has capacity for sign storage; it has memory. Its communicative dancing can be displaced over considerable distance and time. It takes place away from the food supply and in another situation. Thus, it is said the bee's communication is not stimulus-bound, or more broadly, situation-bound.

Other writers (Bierans de Haan, 1929; Maier and Schneirla, 1935) restrict the term communication to "purposive" communication. It must be an act that is used with regard to the effect it has on other individuals. This has not been demonstrated for the worker bee. What happens when two bees report the same information, one following another? Does the second bee take into account the fact that the information has already been received? Apparently not. Communication with regard for effects, however, appears in other animals. The "broken wing" behavior of the grouse, for example, is of this character. It modified according to an enemy's behavior; it will vary in such a way as to draw the threat away from the hiding chicks. It is done with regard to the effect it has on others. The fact that the grouse's behavior varies as the situation changes shows that the bird has a degree of choice, if we use the term "choice" in the sense of response variability. This feature, of course, characterizes human communication and persuasion.

From instances of this kind Hebb and Thompson (1954) conclude, "It is important to recognize that purposeful communication occurs in animals, and just as important to recognize that language is something more." Rather than use a scale or continuum, these authors specify three classes of communication: (a) reflexive, (b) purposive but non-syntactic, and (c) syntactic and usually purposive. The last is considered true language. The authors continue and propose the minimum criteria of true language. First, it combines two or more signs (signals or symbols) purposefully, for a single effect. Second, these stimuli (movements, sounds, etc.) are grouped in different combinations for different effects. This is the syntactical feature. The combining of signs is exemplified when a child says "Daddy go," "Daddy come," Mommy go," or "Mommy come." The syntactical feature seems beyond any organism except man. This capacity to produce different combinations for different effects involves a degree of choice (response variability) not possessed by animals.

Though it may be granted that animals, to a degree, communicate, it is quite doubtful that they communicate to persuade. Such a goal would require that the animal communicate to produce instrumental effects. It would seek to arouse meaning which in turn would set in motion a chain of effects leading to its goal. The capacity, in animals, to visualize and understand such a chain of effects, each instrumental to the next, is to be doubted. Certainly, the ability to formulate a persuasive campaign, sustained over time, seems limited to humans. The effects sought by animals are dominantly consummatory, ends in themselves, not the means to further effects. The communication of animals is restricted to seeking effects which are immediately rewarding, and thus are time-bound. In this sense, persuasion is a kind of communication found only in humans.

## human sources and animal receivers

As receivers, animals appear to be limited to the use of signs as signals, never symbols. "But," protests an acquaintance of mine, "my dog understands many different things I say to it!" Possibly this is true, but the issue is how it understands. To a clever dog, the term "chow time" is used as a signal that its food is present. The words may have become associated with the presence of food just as Pavlov's dog associated the sound of a bell with food. The name of the dog's master is used as a signal of his presence; the dog perks up and looks for him. When the master says, "Sit!" or "Down" or "Heel" to the dog, its reaction is a signal response developed through successful associations in the past. It was previously noted that the signal response is much like a habit; that is, it is an immediate, highly probable response which is likely to continue upon stimulation even though it may not be rewarded. Such behavior, on the part of the dog, does not qualify as a persuasive effect. It is primarily consummatory, not instrumental to further behavior. Moreover, in that conditioning is involved, the experience of choice does not occur in the dog. My acquaintance has communicated with his dog, not persuaded it.

In the light of these viewpoints and examples it is not hard to see that those interested in persuasion have little interest in the source-receiver combination of non-human to non-human, or human to animal. If persuasion involves the seeking of instrumental effects, it implies a regard for message effect on another. Few non-human organisms appear to satisfy this requirement. Furthermore, the notion of instrumentality implies an ability to visualize a chain of effects in which one effect is the determinant of another. This ability has not been demonstrated in non-humans. Consequently, these source-receiver combinations are of more interest to the broader study of communication than the more specific use of communication for persuasive effect.

## *magic and persuasion*

Several explanations for the use of magic have been proposed. For Langer (1951), the direct motive for magic is the desire to symbolize great conceptions. Its function is to express. Magic "is not ignorance of causal relations, but the supervention of an interest stronger than his [the source's] practical interest, that holds him to magical rites. This stronger interest concerns the expressive value of such mystic acts." Langer grants, however, the use of magic for "practical" purposes. A second explanation, perhaps most commonly held, is that it is a method resting on a mistaken view of causality. Magic is employed to cause favorable effects. This viewpoint has led many to consider magic merely bad science. Magic is considererd an uncritical attempt to do what science does, but under mistaken notions that impersonal forces of nature are motivated by personal goals. Floods, tornadoes, famines, droughts, pestilences, and natural fires are evidence, in the view of animism, of the seeking of personal goals by such forces. These events call for counter-measures, namely, magic. Burke (1955) emphasizes a third explanation. For him, magic functions to persuade supernatural forces. The magical use of symbols in rituals and incantations is a mistaken use of a proper linguistic function—persuasion. Persuasion is applied to an area for which it is not fit. It addresses itself to receivers (inanimate objects or events) by nature incapable of sign stimulation. It is bad persuasion, not bad science.

Magic probably serves all three functions. The persuasive function, particularly, illustrates the source-receiver combination in which persons create messages to influence things or gods. Such a goal exists in more advanced religions. These postulate a personal God or gods. The source-receiver combination for persuasion becomes a person-source directing a message to a super-person receiver. Possible effects in the receiver for this combination are of marginal interest as events to be studied in persuasion. The issue is not the existence of a personal God and the possibility of producing persuasive effects through the prayer message. The point is that in this type of event the instrumentality of the prayer message is not demonstrable. There is no satisfactory way of analyzing effect on the audience. Because of this, the prayer message is of more interest as a form of self-influence in which the source is influenced by his own messages.

## self-influence

Another combination of source and receiver, often overlooked, occurs when both are the same person. The source, attending to his own messages, is influenced by them. He does more than simply comprehend or monitor what he has said. Message meaning generates *further* effects leading to the alteration of the source's beliefs, feelings, and actions. Do such effects constitute persuasion? Do they occur frequently enough to be significant?

Because we seldom seek to influence ourselves with our own messages, we tend to be unaware of the frequency and significance of these effects. In our typical efforts to influence others with our messages, the effect of these messages on ourselves gets little attention. This oversight is a major concern in Johnson's (1956) stimulating book. He notes that "we are usually far less attentive, however, to what goes on when the responses made by Mr. A, the speaker, are made by Mr. A himself, as his own listener. Yet it is the responses we make as our own listeners that are undoubtedly the most fateful of all. For every speaker —to say it again—is his own most affected eavesdropper, and that is why the art of talking to ourselves is one that we may not neglect save at the ever-present risk of growing self-distortion."

Johnson further points out that as we observe ourselves and others we begin to see that the source-receiver combination, wherein the source is his own receiver, is one we have overlooked and one in which significant influence often occurs.

> We come in time to realize that every speaker [persuader] is his own most captive listener [receiver]. And as we grasp the meaning of this more and more firmly, we are appalled by it. Because now we see something that had quite escaped our notice before. We had not thought of speakers [persuaders] as their own listeners [receivers].

Our oversight of message effects on selves is due, not only to the fact that we seldom seek such effects, but to an incomplete notion of feedback. We become quite aware of laughter, applause, restlessness, even silence in audiences. Newspaper editors note "Letters to the Editor" in response to their messages; radio and television executives take notice of telephone calls and program ratings as evidence of audience response. The persuader is looking for feedback from these intended receivers; he needs information on the success or failure of his effort. But feedback from self is apt to escape his notice; as an audience for his own messages, self is not an intended receiver. The feelings, beliefs, and actions generated in self, as a receiver, and their feedback effect on self as source is frequently left out of our notion of feedback.

What is more to the point in the study of persuasion is that message effects on self can be unintended or intended. Benito Mussolini has been cited as an example of the unintended effect of the self-reflexive feedback of one's messages. Frank Heller, the Swedish novelist (1944), saw this effect as Mussolini's great weakness. "If he did not become great it was because he let himself be drugged by a poison which is more dangerous than opium or hashish—by words. He talked so much and so often that at length he took his own words for reality and lost contact with the world." A similar unintended effect probably occurred and brought about the decline of Charles A. Lindbergh as a public hero. The adulation of the public and its readiness to be a Lindbergh audience likely tempted him to speak as a scientist and leader of men. When Lindbergh gave in to this temptation, he not only offended, but became his own best listener. His changes in beliefs, feelings, and actions were, at least partly, products of self-influence. His public pronouncements resulted in a reputation as a pro-Nazi and believer in racism. His acceptance of a decoration from Hitler suggests the impact of his messages on himself. These developments in Lindbergh, of course, led to public reaction. The "Lindbergh Beacon" atop a Chicago skyscraper was renamed the "Palmolive Beacon." The "Lindbergh Peak" in the Colorado Rockies, named shortly after his heroic flight, was renamed the less offensive "Lone Eagle Peak" (Boorstin, 1962).

Similar effects in other sources of persuasive effort, though less dramatic and publicized, suggest the generality of self-influence. Those who frequently function as message-sources in persuasion, more often than not influence themselves. A Presidential nominee, in his intensive effort to persuade others, comes to believe in the "reality" his messages depict and in his capacity to serve as President. The political columnist finds himself believing what he writes for others. The professor, hesitantly offering what he thinks is wisdom, gradually comes to feel wise. The preacher increasingly believes what he preaches. The salesman ends up his own most "sold" customer.

It is frequently claimed, particularly by those who are threatened by a persuader's messages, that he is insincere, malicious, a deliberate liar. It is also common for many professional persuaders—advertisers, publicists, press agents—to claim they are not taken in or influenced by their own messages. Part of their self-image as "pros" is to be too sophisticated to be influenced. Especially in politics and advertising, they seem to feel that the ethics of their fields permit and necessitate insincerity on their part as sources. Doubtless, instances exist in which self-influence does not occur, particularly where message production is not sustained over time. In contrast, however, such writers as Goffman (1959) and Berger (1963) take quite a different view. The latter points out that

> Most people are sincere, because this is the easiest course psychologically. That is, they believe in their own act [message], conveniently forget the act [or message] that preceded it, and happily go through life in the conviction of being responsible in all its demands. Sincerity

> is the consciousness of the man who is taken in [influenced] by his own act [message]. Or as it has been put by David Riesman, the sincere man is the one who believes in his own propaganda.

The effort and tension required to lie deliberately, over a sustained period, is probably beyond most of us. By definition, the liar knows he is lying. This requires a consciousness that his message is an action in conflict with his beliefs. As a result, the consciousness of conflict creates tension, a condition the individual seeks to reduce. It is easier to influence oneself. When this occurs, harmony is established between action and belief; tension is reduced.

In addition to deliberate lying and self-influence as explanations of untrue messages, there is a further accounting for them in terms of game theory. The used-car or art dealer may not perceive himself a liar, nor is he taken in by his own messages. He may view the sales situation as a competitive game. His goals and those of the customer are in conflict. They are competitors; the customer's loss is his gain. The dealer's messages are moves in a strategy to win at the other's expense. In a game, it is not necessary to believe in the truth of one's messages, but only to believe that these moves will result in winning. In this case, however, the difference from other games is that the customer often does not fully realize it is a game and is unaware of its thorough competitive nature. Doubtlessly, many so-called liars, swindlers, and hucksters play this game. Yet to play it without the psychological discomfort of tension requires acceptance of an extremely competitive view of life and a set of values most people find unacceptable. Few of us are comfortable seeing ourselves as the devil's disciple. The contrasting view of a persuader's response to his own messages holds that for most people self-influence is the easier resolution of conflict between message and belief.

Self-influence, when unintended, is a phenomenon worthy of study because it deals with an unsought effect of the persuasive process. In that the speaker is often his own most responsive listener, the effect he produces in himself is often excessive. He responds in excess of any effects he sought to produce in his intended receivers. Such malfunctioning of the persuasive process warrants study. Yet, the unintended effect of a message on the source should not be labeled a persuasive effect. Effects on self are not instrumental to the persuader's goals. The source does not see himself as part of his intended audience; from his view, he himself is an irrelevant receiver. Effects in himself are no more relevant to his intentions than in irrelevant receivers such as typesetters, cameramen, and other technicians necessary to the production and transmission of messages.

There are, on the other hand, instances in which a source intentionally seeks to persuade himself. Such effects are instrumental to the goals of the source as well as relevant. When the frightened speaker gives himself the advice, "If I just tell myself to be confident and believe it, I know I'll have no trouble," he seeks to produce an instrumental effect. Various advocates of self-suggestion exemplify similar interest in self-produced effects. The Coué School of the last century recommended that the individual daily repeat to himself, "Everyday in every way I feel better and get better." The wife of Tam, in Burns' poem Tam O'Shanter, "nurses her wrath to keep it warm." She no doubt talked to herself to produce a condition instrumental to her goal of adequately reprimanding her husband.

In spite of the fact that some self-produced effects are intentional, they are generally of marginal interest to the scholar or professional persuader. The politician, preacher, advertiser, and public relations expert are much more concerned with persuasive effects among other persons as receivers. It is for this reason that a concept is proposed which would direct observation toward this larger and more pertinent group of receivers.

## THE USE OF SELF-INFLUENCE IN PERSUASION

Harvey and Beverly (1961) conducted an experiment in which receivers produced their own messages and thus influenced themselves. The study was done in a small church-related college containing a large proportion of students with attitudes opposing the sale and use of alcohol. Attitudes toward alcohol were tested and 137 students opposing the sale and use of alcohol were obtained for the remainder of the experiment. These students were then divided into two groups. Both groups were asked to listen carefully to a 2500 word tape-recorded speech favoring the sale and use of alcohol. Following the speech, students in the first group were asked to reproduce the main arguments presented by the speaker. This procedure did not require listeners to produce messages of their own, but only to reproduce those they heard and remembered. The second group, however, was asked to write the best reasons they could in favor of the sale and use of alcohol and to make believe that these pro-alcohol arguments were to be used in an intercollegiate debate. In both groups, changes of opinion toward alcohol were tested by means of a 27 item graphic rating scale. The first group showed a mean change of opinion toward the sale and the use of alcohol of 13.31 while the second group averaged 36.34 scale points. The difference between these two means was significant at less than the .01 level of confidence. A good case exists for concluding that the second procedure was more effective in changing opinions.

It is, moreover, to be noted that the circumstances under which the second group produced their own messages were dominantly private rather than public. Students, when asked to write favorable arguments for use in a possible debate, likely considered the experimenter as the probable reader of these arguments. They were not asked to express themselves to the more public audience of other students. When a person is asked to verbalize an idea to others, to commit himself publicly, he is more inclined to accept it, than if he expresses it privately. He is influenced by a need to appear consistent to others in what he says and believes. This public commitment facilitates the effect of the message, and may even become a major determinant of effect. But, in this experiment, the self-produced messages appear to be the principal determiners of changes in opinion. Students were influenced, not by messages from outside sources, but by their own.

The use of the phenomenon of self-influence is available to the persuader as well as to persons using other forms of influence. The procedure involves persuading receivers to compose their own messages. In the field of advertising, it is employed when an advertiser sets up a contest for attractive prizes, and the buying public are encouraged to write in 25 words or less a message beginning, "I like ________ because . . ." The advertiser's task is to persuade the public to participate. It is hoped that in getting people to produce messages favorable to a product they will subsequently buy it. Self-influence is used in essay contests which offer cash or scholarship prizes. Usually, students are persuaded to write an essay favorable to Americanism or some other socially approved subject. The producers hope the participants, in writing their own essays, will increasingly accept those beliefs approved by the persuading agency.

The use of self-influence in support of a persuasive effort has not been used as extensively as its potential value would warrant. At least two conditions contribute to this oversight. First, our attention in persuasion has been on effects in receivers. Research on message effects, as is well known, has been almost totally concerned with effects in receivers. As a result, effects in sources from their own messages have been largely unnoticed. Second, the myths that meanings must be injected via messages into receivers and that audiences are essentially passive have worked against seeing the potential of self-influence. The contrary views that meaning arises in receivers and does not exist in messages, and that audiences can be highly active would promote a more favorable perspective on the value of self-influence.

Those using other forms of influence, of course, can employ self-influence in achieving their goals. In the experiment described above, it is possible that students participated because they perceived the experimenter as one having the legitimate right to direct their classroom work. In this case, the experimenter used authority as the means of bringing about self-influencing activity. On the other hand, he may have persuaded students to become experimental subjects by offering them a fee for participation. It would be interesting to know which of these two conditions best facilitates self-influence. Another instance of self-influence, often unintentional, results from taking the typical classroom examination. Through authority, the instructor directs that students answer examination questions. Students are influenced by the prize of a good grade to produce messages the instructor will approve. In producing these messages, they are inclined to accept the opinions they express. Self-influence can occur, and does occur, in any business, political, or other organization in which someone in authority directs others to prepare reports or other messages in support of organization policy. Self-influence was intentionally used, with the support of public commitment, in the self-analyses required by the Red Chinese in their so-called "brainwashing" of American prisoners of war (Schein, Schneier, and Barker, 1961). The use of the same phenomenon is found in the confessions required from "students" in the Chinese Revolutionary Colleges (Lifton, 1960).

## summary

Various source-receiver combinations are eliminated by the proposed concept of persuasion in that (1) they constitute an effort doomed to failure, (2) their effects cannot be demonstrated, or (3) the effects are simply not the kind of events that most interest the professional persuader. The source-receiver combination that avoids these three conditions is interpersonal. Self-influence, thus, is not persuasion, but can be a valuable supplement to a persuasive effort.

# Chapter 7

## Persuasive and Non-Persuasive Uses of Signs

The story is told of a couple whose child did not talk. When the child was two years old, the parents became concerned and sought the advice of the family doctor. He could find no explanation except to suggest the child would outgrow the problem. At the age of three, the child was taken to a speech and hearing clinic. No organic defects. Hearing was normal. Therapy did not get the child to talk. At the age of four, he was taken to a psychiatrist. No progress was made. Then, one morning at the breakfast table the child suddenly and clearly said, "Damn it! This oatmeal is lumpy!" The mother was surprised and delighted; she immediately called her husband home from the office. In the husband's presence she said to the boy, "Tell Daddy what you told me." The boy replied, "I said this oatmeal is lumpy." Overjoyed and puzzled, the father asked, "Son, you talk so well now, why didn't you talk before?" "Well," said the boy, "because everything was all right up to now."

The story implies that the *raison d'être* of language is a practical one—to communicate. It is a social tool used to affect the behavior of others, consummatorily or instrumentally. Only a part, however—though a very important part—of language behavior involves the practical goal of affecting others by our messages. Only sometimes are motives for the use of signs such that they are satisfied by the arousal of effects in others. Only some, not all, of our uses of signs result in overt expression—words, gestures, pictures, other acts used as signs.

Whorf (1956) observed that "Speech is the best show man puts on." If all the uses of signs are included in the show, nothing else that man does can compare with this performance in creativity, foolishness, in recklessness for the dangers involved, and in power displayed. The performance has all the elements for "the greatest show on earth." Our problem as an audience is one of being able to appreciate the show. Of more particular interest to careerists in persuasion, the noting of distinctions among the human uses of signs is of value to the understanding and use of persuasion as a form of influence. These distinctions clarify what language events we are going to classify as persuasion, and increase awareness of other goals in events which appear to be persuasive. They aid the persuader to a consciousness of what goals operate in his efforts. To those ends, an attempt to portray the human uses of signs schematically is provided in Figure 9.

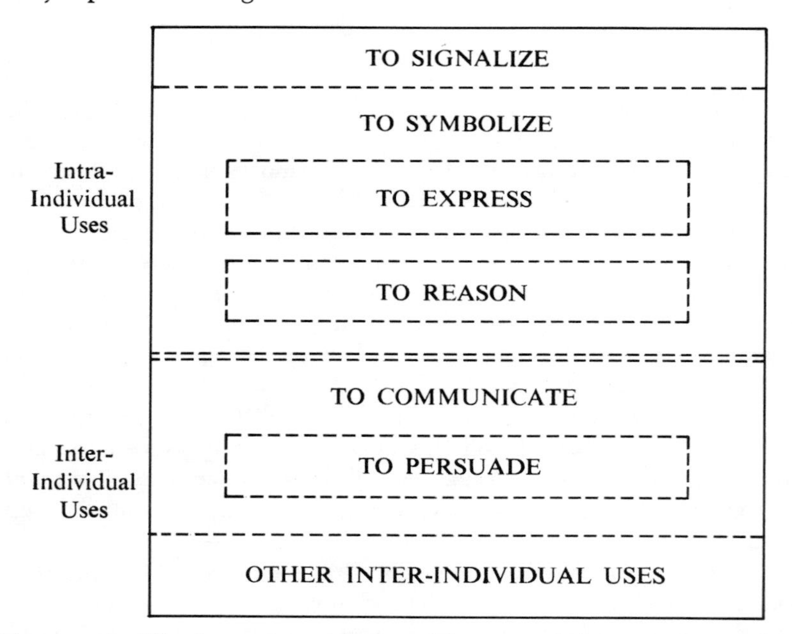


FIGURE 9. The human uses of signs. The sizes of the areas assigned to each use of signs is not meant to indicate the relative frequency of each use. The broken lines, however, are provided to suggest that a given sign-using event may involve more than one usage of signs.

In Figure 9, it is suggested that we can think of sign-usage in terms of two response systems: intra-individual and inter-individual. The first is a system of responses occurring in one individual; they function to satisfy needs different from those pertaining to other humans or animals. These responses enable a person to cope with his environment, to symbolize and express his experiences, and facilitate thinking. When we observe this system, the show we watch has only one star performer. The second is a system of responses involving more than one individual. Such a show has no less than two major performers and may involve millions. This system enables the individual or organization of individuals to arouse responses in others through the use of signs. More extensively for humans than animals, it makes communication, persuasion, and other inter-individual uses of signs possible.

## intra-individual uses

### TO SIGNALIZE

In Chapter Four, the human and animal use of signs as signals was discussed. There it was noted that of all the stimuli that impinge on us, some are used as signals; that is, they serve to indicate something beyond themselves—the presence of an object, event, or condition. When the gasoline gauge in one's car registers empty, it is used as a signal of a condition in the gasoline tank. For one of Pavlov's conditioned dogs, the sound of a bell is used to signalize the presence of food. For the untrained dog who has not learned this signal-object association, the bell is merely a stimulus indicating nothing beyond itself.

Man, we observe, puts on a spectacular show in the development and use of signs as signals to indicate conditions in his environment. Even a casual inspection of a dictionary reveals something of his vast array of signal-producing instruments. He develops meters—galvanometers, barometers, tachometers, sphygnometers, audiometers—and graphs—polygraphs, electroencephalographs, cardiographs, odontographs—and scopes—telescopes, orthoscopes, oscilloscopes, decibeloscopes. In the field of psychological measurement, more than 2500 sign-producing tests have been published. From a language perspective, tests of human abilities, achievement, attitudes, and other psychological dimensions constitute sign-producing instruments. Responses to an intelligence test, for example, serve as indicators or signals to the psychologist of the intelligence of the test-taker. Moreover, all substantive departments of a university provide instruction in the signal-producing instruments of relevance to the phenomena studied in those departments. For example, a speech department is likely to instruct students in the interpretation of the signals produced by an oscilloscope in response to speech sounds. And finally, many business corporations are formed exclusively to produce and market devices to produce signals of phenomena that concern man in coping with his environment.

In addition to developing and using instruments which expose to his senses indicators of objects, events, or conditions, man has a tremendous capacity to use available stimuli, including words, as signals of things he wishes them to indicate. He learns, through association, to treat a bell as an indication that a classroom period is at an end, in much the same fashion that Pavlov's dog learned it was an indicator of food. Man learns through association that the word "exit" signalizes the existence of a way out of a building. The array of bells, chimes, buzzers, lights, colors, and words and phrases like those we see while driving—entrance, rest area, detour, Philadelphia 30, and route 40 east—that man can learn to use signally seems limitless. Without considering his other uses of signs, this use of stimuli as indicators of objects, events, or conditions surely results in one of the largest sets of different learned responses in human behavior.

## TO SYMBOLIZE

The use of signs to signalize serves the practical end of more effectively sizing up one's environment, of becoming more aware of its threats to and provisions for the needs of the organism. Both humans and other animals use signs a great deal to this end. In comparing human and animal signal-usage, one is apt to conclude that man's superiority in the race for self-preservation is largely the result of his much greater repertoire of signals, his capacity to develop signal-producing instruments, his talent for creating artificial signals and using them to indicate conditions in his environment, and his superior ability to learn these signal-object associations. But the gap between humans and other animals in the use of signs as symbols is much greater, and contributes even more importantly to his superiority. It is from the use of signs as symbols that man develops his instruments and thinks about ways to cope with his environment. Furthermore, the utilization of signs to stand for concepts enables man to categorize objects, events, or conditions, to think of an attribute a set of phenomena have in common, and thus talk or think about them collectively. Although animals, as in the bee's wagging dance, may use "artificial" signs to stand for objects or conditions not immediately present, it is doubtful that they can use signs to represent attributes (concepts) of a set of phenomena.

At the same time, men who can use symbols to promote practical goals also use them in a way that results in fantastic foolishness, in behavior that warps and prevents effectively dealing with one's environment, in acts that make him the most dangerous and unpredictable of animals. As we observe man's "show" with signs, it is this latter use of symbols that arouses in us fright, amusement, outright laughter, tears, sorrow, and awe. Our impractical symbol-usage provides many of the dramatic elements that make for "the greatest show on earth."

A common experience in symbolization, serving no practical need, occurs in dream activity. If the process of ideation carried on in dreaming were instrumental, the activity presumably would produce remembrances, plans, decisions, and other mental products useful to purposive thinking. In this view of dreaming, if the mind were not providing these responses, it should at least be quiescent while the rest of the organism slept, or at most be dealing with digestive stimuli, reacting to muscular or temperature discomfort, or responding to after-images on the retina of the day's experiences. Instead of that, dreams present us with ideas we do not want to think about, ideas that warp and inhibit practical thinking. The brain produces a tumult of disconnected, illogical, unrealistic ideas that the sleeper is not using to think about anything practical. But, as Langer (1951) notes, "The brain is following its own law; it is actively translating experiences into symbols, in fulfillment of a basic need to do so." This need to symbolize is an end in itself, not instrumental in the service of more practical needs.

Dement (*Time*, February 14, 1964) provided some evidence of the need to dream, to symbolically process experiences. He designed an experiment to find out what happens when a person is permitted to sleep his normal number of hours, but is not allowed to dream. He made use of a finding that rapid eye movements, detected by an electroencephalograph, were associated with the onset of dreaming. Dement thus awakened his subjects whenever these rapid eye movements indicated the beginning of a dream. They were then allowed to fall asleep again. By the third night, most of the experimental subjects became increasingly on edge and began to behave not like themselves. In the final phase of the experiment, subjects were allowed to sleep as long as they wished; EEG records showed they dreamed twice as much as usual. Dement concluded that dreaming may serve a more important need than being, as Freud called it, the guardian of sleep. It may be the guardian of sanity itself. Behavior, when dreaming is denied, suggests that a fundamental need to symbolize experience is not being satisfied.

Man's special interest, as a receiver or viewer of artistic productions, in painting, music, architecture, and sculptoring, in rituals associated with marriage, death, and religious conceptions of communion and resurrection, in great conceptions enunciated in poems, essays, and speeches, all testify to his need, through a symbolizing process, to achieve satisfying conceptions of his human experiences. The four days from November 22 to 25, 1963, following the assassination of President John F. Kennedy, exemplified this need. Most Americans found themselves, somewhat to their surprise, spending many hours watching the funeral ritual of a head of state, listening to poetry and prose helping them to conceptualize this experience, and talking almost exclusively about this significant set of events. Concern for practical affairs—the stock market, the weather, department store sales, even the preparation of food—dwindled. Television programming was quickly and completely reconstructed to satisfy this different need. In one case, however, a local station misjudged the public need and presented a pre-scheduled film of a bowling tournament on November 23. The flood of telephone calls to the station made it apparent that this program was not in the public interest *at that time.*

Our love of humor, the use of symbols in magical practices, the universal development of ritual, the symbolism in art, and the symbolic activity found in dreaming are too extensive to permit the view that man uses symbols solely for practical ends. Moreover, as Langer (1951) suggests, man differs importantly from animals in that he has a unique need to symbolize his experience. This need is fundamental and an end in itself; only part of the time are symbols used to further the practical biological needs of food-getting, avoiding harm, and sex satisfaction. She says, "I believe there is a primary need in man, which other creatures probably do not have, and which actuates all his apparently unzoological aims, his wistful fancies, his consciousness of value, his utterly impractical enthusiasms, and his awareness of a 'Beyond' filled with holiness." Symbolization is both a need in its own right and an instrument in the satisfaction of other practical needs. As an end in itself it appears overtly in ritual, art, and dreams—as expression. As a practical process it functions intra-individually in thinking, and inter-individually in communication. It is only in this latter usage that persuasive effects occur.

## TO EXPRESS

Symbolization is covert; this processing of experience is, in itself, not observable. In general, however, covert mental activity tends to terminate in action. What we believe we tend to act on accordingly; what we think is apt to be the matter on which we take action; what we symbolize is apt to be expressed. Moreover, if symbolization is a unique human reaction to experience, it might well terminate in a peculiarly human form of overt activity. And, as Langer notes, "That is just what we find in the sheer expression of ideas. This is the activity of which beasts appear to have no need." The human need to express ideas seems to account for those behaviors in man not found in other animals—ritual, humor, laughter, art, crying, invention, and speech.

Expressive acts account for a substantial portion of the intra-individual use of signs. Though other persons may attach meaning to these acts, they serve a need that is satisfied within the individual. As such, expressive acts are not designed to communicate, and in particular, to persuade. Often, however, the need to express accompanies an intent to communicate. For example, Eisenson, Auer, and Irwin (1963) note that

> Sometimes the speaker may engage in a pseudo-communicative effort and seem to be trying to inform, direct, or persuade a listener by what he says. Actually, or perhaps better, unconsciously, the speaker may be using an alleged listener as an opportunity to "sound off," to express his feeling sweet, tender, bitter, angry, or whatever it may happen to be at the moment of evocation.

Not only does the individual use signs to express himself, but groups and organizations can engage in similar activity. Their efforts may be dominantly expressive though appearing to be communicative both to themselves and to others. White (1961), for example, appraises the production of a political platform as essentially an expressive act.

> In the hard life of politics it is well known that no platform nor any program advanced by either major American party has any purpose beyond expressing emotion. Platforms are a ritual with a history of their own and, after being written, they are useful chiefly to scholars who dissect them as archeological political remains.

Other expressive acts involving the use of language, and less disguised as or confounded with an intent to persuade, can be observed in our largely private, and sometimes public, behavior. Adults often talk to infants knowing they are incapable of understanding. There is no intent to communicate, only to express oneself. Many of us talk to animal pets in a similar usage of signs. At a football game, we cheer and urge the team to "fight." The effort is more to satisfy an expressive need than to communicate with the team. Even while watching televised football, basketball, horse races, and sometimes speakers or newscasters, we react in the privacy of our homes more to express than to communicate. We sing under the shower or in the tub. In the arms of someone we love, our talk is often more an expression of feeling than a communication. In any situation in which people are emotionally stimulated, as in a mob or riot, the shouting and exclamations generally serve an expressive function.

Expressive acts, it is well known, have cathartic value. The procedures of the counselor, psycho-therapist, and psychiatrist are designed to encourage talk for its value as a way back from anxiety and tension. In less clinical settings, the cathartic value of sign usage is found in mimicry and role-playing. They permit an expression of one's feelings. Goffman (1959) reports such a usage from Donovan's *The Saleslady*. He describes the behavior of saleswomen backstage and out of sight of customers.

> At every opportunity they play the game of "customer," a game which they have invented and of which they never seem to tire—a game which for caricature and comedy, I have never seen surpassed on any stage. One girl takes the part of the saleswoman, another that of a customer in search of a dress, and together they put on an act that would delight the heart of a vaudeville audience.

Moreover, this impromptu show delights the hearts of the participants. No audience is really necessary. The expressive value of the act—a symbolic aggression against the customer and her expectations—provides the major reward. Tension is reduced and the task of coping with difficult customers becomes more tolerable. Similarly, students will mimic a professor in his absence; employees caricature the role of the boss when opportunity arises. In each case, it may occur without the presence of others, purely as an expressive use of signs.

Several observations can be made regarding the human use of signs to express oneself. It seems clear that this use is a major function of signs. Secondly, this function is often confounded with the use of signs to communicate or persuade. The motivation energizing the use of signs may be multiple rather than singular. This suggests, for the persuader, that his effort may involve more than a desire to persuade others. When this occurs the persuader is apt to be less clear about his goals, and consequently less effective. Finally, the expressive use of signs, as in "sounding off," may not be used to affect others, but may affect them as well as self.

### TO REASON

A major use of signs occurs in the process of thinking. The term "thinking," borrowed from the vernacular of society, is not a very scientific term in the sense of arousing a precise concept among users. This term, and its varied meanings, do not allow behavioral events to be consistently classified as thinking or not-thinking events. Examples of the use of the term suggest the wide variety of meanings it yields—I think this plan is the best . . . I'm not ready to decide; I'm still thinking about it . . . I was thinking about our trip last year . . . What do you think about the election? . . . Somehow, I can't think of his name . . . I think it will rain soon . . . I think he's telling the truth. . . .

Carroll (1964) notes that such uses of the term, in part, refer to our beliefs, remembrances, mental discoveries, and expectations. These uses of the term, however, have in common the notion that thinking is "some kind of covert (unobservable) behavior in response to stimuli that may be absent, not immediately present to the senses." This is Carroll's concept of thinking. He further points out that from an early age, humans develop these internal (covert) processes and often become aware of them. When they learn language they are likely to call them by such a term as thinking. For Carroll, "thinking is the conscious or unconscious manipulation of internal processes for oneself, usually in some particular direction such as the solution of a problem."

Reflection on this concept of thinking suggests several additional notions. First, thinking involves an intra-individual use of signs; it is for oneself; it is an unobservable show in which one person is the only performer, the only user of the signs involved. Second, unlike the use of signs to express in fulfillment of a need to process experience symbolically, thinking is conceived as a practical use of signs. It is an activity for oneself, in coping with one's environment. We often state its goals in such terms as: to effectively write a particular paragraph, book, or letter, to solve the problem of whether to accept a job offer or not, to devise and select a plan for remodeling one's home, or to decide how best to persuade another. In each case, thinking serves practical goals; the activity is instrumental in the service of these goals, not an end in itself.

Third, if thinking is viewed as an internal processing in response to stimuli which may be present or absent, it may be that this processing is of many sorts, that there are many kinds of thinking. It is with this in mind that Carroll (1964) states

> Many kinds of "thinking" are non-linguistic. Some musicians report being able to "listen" to the music they are composing, before writing it down on paper or even playing it on an instrument; this sort of activity would qualify as a non-linguistic kind of thinking, and there are parallels in other spheres of activity—for instance, thinking through a planned aerial maneuver, a swimming stroke, or a dance step.

This means that thought units and their processing can be viewed, at least, as being both linguistic and non-linguistic. As we watch a diver, gymnast, or golfer pause and "think" about a maneuver he is planning to execute, his thought units appear to be more on the order of kinesthetic images than linguistic units. In fact until our present century, most theoretical discussions of thought hypothesized that thinking involved some kind of images—visual, auditory, kinesthetic, or otherwise. In order to draw a distinction between thinking in different types of thought units, Carroll (1964) prefers to view thinking aided by language as reasoning. For him, "The ability to reason depends largely on the ability to formulate steps in an inferential process in terms of language." The distinction is of value to a consideration of the human uses of signs. It is this type of thinking, done with the aid of linguistic units, that is important as an instrumental, intra-individual use of signs. Furthermore, thinking obviously is an activity necessary to the success of all persuasive efforts. The persuader reasons about his task before, during, and after its execution. The effects, however, of this use of signs are not effects in another person, not an interpersonal event. For this reason, such intra-individual effects are not conceived as persuasion.

## inter-individual uses

An inter-individual use of signs can occur without the attempts, abilities, or effects commonly associated with communication or persuasion. The critical difference between intra- and inter-individual uses will suggest why. An intra-individual use of signs is characterized by an individual's use of a stimulus, present or absent, as a sign. The stimulus, moreover, is something other than the sign-usage of another. Furthermore, an individual's response to his own sign-usage does not become a source of stimulation and sign-usage to other individuals. As a sign-user, the individual puts on a one-man show. This particular kind of behavior is not stimulated by nor does it serve as a stimulus for such behavior in others. In contrast, an inter-individual use involves a set of responses to signs in which the responses in one individual are used as signs by another. It is no longer a one-man show. Not only is more than one person a sign-user, but this behavior in one individual becomes the source of stimulation for sign-usage in another.

The implications of the response relationship, characteristic of an inter-individual use of signs, warrant attention. They aid in further differentiating the intra- and inter-individual uses of signs. They clarify the distinctions between communication or persuasion and other events involving the same response relationship.

First, when the responses to signs in one person become the source of stimulation to another, those responses must be observable. Such a condition is requisite to an inter-individual response system, but not to an intra-individual response system. In symbolization and reasoning, for example, an individual's responses may be entirely covert, not readily observable to others. Once the "show" involves two or more individuals, some of the responses to signs become overt. This fact is important. It makes inter-individual uses of signs more accessible to study and analysis; it is essential to the phenomenon we call a message; and in some circumstances, as in communication and persuasion, it creates a special problem of encoding.

Second, a one-person show does not involve the use of messages; an interpersonal event may or may not. A message is viewed as a set of overt responses by a source designed to arouse a particular meaning in another person. It is not difficult to see that messages, so conceived, are not essential to an inter-individual use of signs. For example, an individual may frown in response to a thought without any message to another being intended. Yet another person may observe the frown, assign meaning to it, and respond. An inter-individual use of signs has occurred. Thus, it is not the existence of a message that is critical to the functioning of an interpersonal system of sign usage. When messages are used, the interpersonal system is energized in order to communicate or persuade.

Third, both the individual and multi-individual response systems may or may not involve encoding—the deliberate couching of meaning in language or other code. Encoding occurs when the individual writes in a diary, talks to himself, or jots down a reminder of a future luncheon on his desk calendar. Encoding also occurs in the messages of advertisers, politicians, preachers, and psychiatrists to their audiences. There is, however, a big difference. The inter-individual system, when used to communicate or persuade, involves encoding with regard to the meaning it may arouse in another. Encoding for meaning arousal in another is clearly a more difficult task than encoding for oneself. The task of arousing an intended meaning through encoding for others is one of special concern to those who would communicate or persuade.

## COMMUNICATION

If words had feelings, the term "communication" might well be disturbed. It has experienced the cost of popularity; it gets man-handled, is used in surprising ways, and is thrown in with unexpected companions in strange sentences. One might imagine it developing a neurosis, no longer sure of its own identity. Consider a few of the sentences in which the term is used: the cigar ash on my coat communicates a meaning to others; our office furnishings communicate messages about us; the family room communicates with the kitchen; the reflexive crying of an infant, when someone responds, is its first communicative act; the frightened hen's clucking that sets her brood in flight is communication; the fly's struggle is communicated to the spider through the web; satellites communicate weather information back to earth; scatran is a language by which man communicates to a computer.

As a reader, you have surmised that the point in discussing the critical requirement of an inter-individual use of signs as well as the multiple uses of the term "communication" has been to suggest the need for a more precise and useful concept of communication. It should be more useful in two ways. It should enable distinctions to be made between the communication event and other events involving inter-individual sign usage. Those events thus identified as communication should be the sort of events most interesting to scholars and practitioners.

With this need in mind, communication, as I view it, occurs when an individual or individuals intentionally generate relevant effects in others by arousing meanings. Communication is a word, then, that identifies *effects* as well as the *process* that creates them. The concept implies more than assigning meaning to cigar ash on my coat. The stimulus in communication is intentionally transmitted to arouse meaning. The meaning generated is relevant to the communicator's goals; when other meanings and consequent effects occur, we speak of a communication breakdown. Communication is more than a satellite producing signs from its space environment. Such a process is an intra-individual use of signs; the satellite is an instrument employed by its user to convey signals not otherwise perceivable. It performs the same function as a microscope; simply because the distance between the instrument and its user is great does not make its signal emission an act of communication.

## PERSUASION AND COMMUNICATION

Some messages are transmitted to receivers to arouse meanings that are not intended to be persuasive. Some messages arouse the desired meanings; these can be communicative effects without being persuasive effects. This is a way of saying that communication is a much larger concept than persuasion; it includes persuasion.

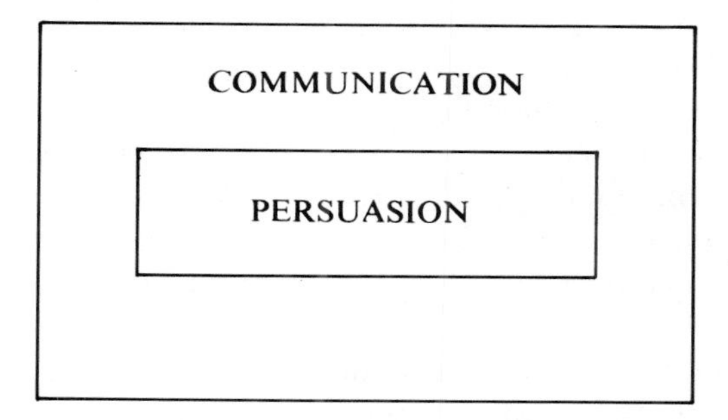


FIGURE 10. The relation of persuasion to communication.

What do communication and persuasion have in common? What is distinctive about persuasion that is not involved in other kinds of communication?

All communication, including persuasion, involves messages—the intentional use of signs to arouse meanings. All communication is characterized by the occurrence of relevant effects. All communication is interpersonal. This broad view of communication is reflected in Ross' (1965) concept. He views communication as "a process involving the sorting, selecting, and sending of symbols in such a way as to help a listener perceive and recreate in his own mind the meaning contained in the mind of the communicator." Such a viewpoint does not set forth several restrictions that seem to characterize persuasion. As a particular use of communication, persuasion is concerned with bringing about action in receivers. Effects such as comprehension, amusement, or acquisition of knowledge are sought only as instruments in the development of action. Persuasion, thus, stresses message effects for their instrumental rather than consummatory value. In persuasion the message is a major determinant of subsequent action; in other uses of communication, message effect may not be a major factor. In persuasion, the perception and exercise of choice by a receiver is a necessary condition, but not in other uses of communication.

A few examples of non-persuasive communications will clarify the distinction between persuasion and other uses of communication. One example of a non-persuasive communication would be a command or order given by a head to a subordinate. The military officer issuing a command communicates but does not persuade. When he adds, "And that's an order," he makes it clear that he expects to achieve his goal whether or not the receiver is persuaded. The boss assigning work to his subordinate does so via a communication. When the subordinate does that work because he considers it the boss's legitimate right to direct his behavior, a persuasive effect has not occurred. Even friendship often excludes the occurrence of a persuasive effect. When a friend asks a favor, the friendship relation rather than the message is often the major determinant of the response. One may lend a friend money, yet not be satisfied the request has merit. Such non-persuasive communications, however, have in common with persuasive events the intentional use of messages to affect the receiver. The difference is that the effect of what is said may not satisfy other criteria of persuasion—instrumentality, significant message effect, and choice.

## other inter-individual uses

The use of words and other stimuli common to communication events may serve to satisfy an individual's or organization's needs without being designed to produce effects by *what* is said. Such events entail non-communicative, yet interpersonal, uses of "signs." A vivid example of this is a U.S. Senate filibuster. In the 1960-62 congressional session there were three filibusters. In each, the objective was not to influence others by means of messages—by what was said. Influence was achieved by holding the Senate floor to prevent others from doing business. Talk, under Senate rules, accomplishes about the same effect as a lock-out; work ceases. Many senators may not even be present to hear the speaker; it's unimportant that they do. A filibuster is an event designed for bargaining, not persuasion. If there is communication, it is the event that arouses meaning, not what is said. The words are "signs" in appearance, not in function.

Other examples would include any situation in which the results sought by the sign-user do not involve message effects on receivers—the student gives a speech or writes a theme to fulfill an assignment, the teacher concentrates on covering the material he had planned with little concern for the effect of his lecture on students, the announcer reads a commercial to fulfill a job requirement, the speaker gives his speech to earn his fee, the congressman gives an eulogy in order to have it printed in the *Congressional Record,* the newspaper fills the white spaces around the advertisements with informative items, the effects of such "messages" being of little concern to the newspaper staff.

The use of words and other signs having the appearance of messages without being primarily used to function as messages accounts for a great deal of inter-individual sign usage. We often use speech more to satisfy a need for social contact with others than to communicate with particular message effects in mind. The long distance telephone call to friends or members of the family often serves a need for social contact. The effect of the experience on oneself may be more important than arousing meanings and relevant effects in others. In contrast, the business long distance call is likely to be motivated more by an intent to communicate or persuade. Telephone companies, in their advertising, recognize the value of the long distance call in serving both needs. Meerloo (1960) observes that the techniques of the brainwasher include the blackmailing of man's need for relatedness to others. "The need to talk . . . in days of loneliness and great boredom gradually becomes a need to confess." Fromm (1955) sees relatedness as a peculiarly human and basic need. And speech, message-like in form, is a peculiarly human and major way of satisfying it. Such sign-usage is inter-personal, but not, however, communication.

A sociological view of party behavior, non-communicative and non-persuasive in spirit, is given by Berger (1963). At parties, people typically "play society." They engage in a great deal of sign-using behavior and interact socially without seeking the serious goals of communication. "Sociability," he points out, "changes serious communication to noncommittal conversation, eros to coquetry, ethics to manners, aesthetics to taste." The party situation is an artificial, theatrical creation that quickly can be spoiled by anyone who fails to recognize its stage-like quality. The guest or host who stops "playing society" and launches a passionate debate or persuasive sales effort threatens the party. Others usually attempt to divert him from this serious effort at communication. It seems people at parties are more engaged in satisfying a need to play than a need to arouse serious meanings through communication.

In man's tremendous "show with words" other instances of non-communicative but interpersonal sign-usage can be observed. In them, the words (signs) are not used primarily for their meaning-arousal value. This occurs in ceremonies such as marriage and death. It occurs in our efforts to avoid silence in the presence of others. "Often we speak to prevent silence or to overcome its effects because a wordless relationship may not be comfortable or even bearable" (Eisenson, Auer, and Irwin, 1963). It occurs when we are expected to say something, because of our social roles, but wish to say nothing. Our "messages" are not used to function as messages. In this connection, Goffman (1959) cites a publication for civil servants in Great Britain. In it, advice is given to high ranking civil servants on how to speak for the purpose of saying nothing.

Two objections against the extensive study of these uses of signs can be made. First, the outcome sought may not involve developing any effects in receivers. A secretary, reading the minutes of the last meeting, is fulfilling a role expectation and usually has little interest in their effects on receivers. Her preference may be that no response develops. Second, receiver effects may be sought, but not by means of the messages presented. Extended interrogation of prisoners involves the use of talk to create fatigue and lower resistance; message effects may be incidental. In such an instance, the interrogator is neither communicating or persuading. Hence these uses of words do not involve an intent that listeners use them as signs, and consequently are not critical to this book or to persuaders.

## *implications*

The study of persuasion, in the past, has entailed little interest in man's spectacular show with words, his multitudinous uses of signs. After all, it is said, the goals in persuasion are quite different from those involved in sounding-off, in talking to achieve social contact, in fulfilling a role expectation, in the sheer expression of ideas. Such uses of signs are interesting, but . . . To say, however, that they do not belong to an effective persuasive effort is not to say that they are irrelevant. The study of persuasion could ignore other uses of signs except for one reason—an important one. It is quite possible to go through the motions of persuading while actually in the pursuit of other goals, and not be aware of it. More than one goal can operate in a supposedly persuasive effort. Study of various sign-uses increases awareness of their occurrence, and contributes to effectiveness through knowing what one is up to in his efforts. This is particularly needed when one's goals are either self- or socially disapproved. Such goals we seem inclined to deny to ourselves or misperceive.

The results of a class demonstration reveal the likelihood of a speaker or writer's misperceiving what goals he seeks. Students were given a list of socially disapproved goals sought through sign-usage. The list included such items as: (1) talking to get something "off my chest," (2) talking to put another person in an unfavorable light, (3) talking to hurt another person, (4) talking to gain sympathy for myself, (5) talking to "show off" new knowledge I had acquired, and (6) talking to get "in good" with influential persons. Ten such items were on the list; students were asked to check, on a five-point scale, how frequently or infrequently they spoke for these reasons. The mid-point of the scale was described by the words, "about as frequently as other college students."

Following this, the students were asked to fill out the Crowne and Marlowe (1960) social desirability scale. This scale was designed to measure the need for social approval. Two hypotheses were formulated: (1) that students would claim they spoke to achieve these socially unacceptable goals less than their peers, and (2) that students with high need for social approval would claim relatively infrequent efforts to obtain such outcomes. Both hypotheses were confirmed. "Less frequent" responses significantly outnumbered "average" and "more frequent" responses combined. The mean frequency rating was 2.1 instead of the average value of 3.0. The correlation between scores for frequency and social desirability scale scores was −.42, tending to confirm the second hypothesis.

In interpreting the results an assumption was made. It held that students did not perceive the demonstration as a threatening public exposure of the goals they sought through sign usage. If the assumption was valid, a minimum of contrived answers (deliberate distortions) was expected. Consequently, the results were viewed as a need to sustain an acceptable self concept. In his need to see himself as a person who sought ethical goals, the student misperceived his tendency to seek unacceptable ones. His self-concept and the list of goals presented to him were in conflict; reduction of the conflict presumably was achieved through defensive misperception.

Instances of motives or desired outcomes of sign-usage that cannot very well be admitted, even to oneself, are not hard to find. They commonly occur in conjunction with more acceptable sign-usage. Hoffer (1964), for example, observes that "the unattached intellectual's unceasing search for a recognized status and a useful role has brought him to the forefront of every movement of change since the Reformation." For some, the use of words may be more an act of aggression than an effort to persuade. Some celebrities, appearing before groups to promote their "favorite" charity, may be more concerned with adulation than persuasion. Some college commencement speakers may not be trying chiefly to affect their audiences; they may be doing what is expected to earn their fees. Some business and labor officials are not trying primarily to move their organizations closer to desired goals; they are more concerned with holding on to their jobs. Some "persuaders" writing letters to the editor, or editorials, or articles for the opinion magazines may seek catharsis more than the persuasion of readers.

The point of this is not the ethics of persuasion, or the goals for which persuasion ought to be used. Neither is it implied that the persuader must choose among the goals of sign-usage, that only a persuasive use of signs should operate. The persuader legitimately may seek persuasive and non-persuasive outcomes from his behavior. The problem is one of awareness. When multiple goals exist, and awareness of them does not, the result is confusion, uncertainty, and vagueness in the effective use of signs. When persuasion is one of the goals, its effective use is hindered by the simultaneous and unknowing use of signs for other ends.

## summary

The human uses of signs provide a complex and spectacular show. They may be divided into two broad categories—intra-individual and inter-individual uses. In both categories, man displays a facility with signs far superior, more varied and complex than that of any animal or machine. Among intra-individual uses, signaling, symbolizing, expressing and reasoning seem to be the dominant types. None of these constitutes a use of signs to communicate or persuade. Such goals are among those involved in an inter-individual use of signs. In this category, communication and persuasion account for only some of the uses of signs. Numerous other outcomes–social contact, catharsis, avoiding silence, filling a role, to name a few–from inter-individual uses of signs are sought. Because persuasion is confounded with other uses of signs, an increased awareness of the distinctions between these uses should improve effectiveness in persuasion.

# PART TWO

## THE POTENTIAL AND LIMITATIONS OF PERSUASION

# Chapter 8

# The Potential of Persuasion

"Actions speak louder than words!"

"My words were a waste of breath for all the good they did!"

"Talk is futile!"

"Sticks and stones may break my bones but names can never hurt me!"

"When all is said and done, more is said than done!"

"The pen is mightier than the sword!"

"If you give me the right word and the right accent in which to speak it, I can move the world."

"He who can phrase it can lead it."

"You can fool some of the people all of the time, and all of the people some of the time . . ."

"The depth manipulators are . . . starting to acquire a power of persuasion that is becoming a matter of justifiable public scrutiny and concern."

Such remarks on the ineffectiveness or power of talk are familiar to most of us. It seems particularly current today that we comment in superlatives. "It's the greatest!" "It's for the birds!" The practice, of course, represents more of an intellectual shooting from the hip than a considered appraisal. This chapter will attempt to identify some of these excessive evaluations of persuasion and to provide a basis for a more realistic appraisal.

## *deprecative evaluations*

Particularly in the industrialized democracy, it is not fashionable to underrate either communication or persuasion. Most of us are told in school that power leads to abuses, and examples of dictators typically illustrate the point. Persuasion is the approved form of influence; we are taught to have confidence in it. It is a proper way of getting things changed. Such was not always the case. At one time, we as a nation were largely occupied with handling things—clearing land, building homes for ourselves, securing food through hunting and farming, generally doing those things required in occupying a vast undeveloped land. Even in the nineteenth century, our major occupations were those which dealt with things. Among people so employed, there was less reason to consider speaking and writing important. Actions were more necessary than words. In such a culture, it was probably not an under-evaluation to consider persuasion a less important way to change things. Deprecative evaluations of persuasion develop in such a setting.

In spite of the fact that we profess preference for and confidence in persuasion, there is evidence that this method is undervalued and rejected. Emery and Katz (1953) surveyed preferences for solutions to discrimination against Jews. Among Jewish respondents, programs to assimilate Jews or action to strengthen the Jewish group were favored over efforts to persuade gentiles. Similarly, verbal persuasion has been increasingly rejected in the U.S. Civil Rights crisis as a means of change. Verbal persuasion is commonly considered a failure in this area. A widely-held view is that if overt discrimination is put down and legally punished, the attitudes of segregationists will eventually conform. Again, many who advocate "get tough" policies with juvenile offenders discredit the potency of persuasion. For them, the soft, persuasion-oriented practices of guidance, counseling, rehabilitation, and therapy simply do not get results. Such means, they say, are a waste of time and money.

Finally, revolutionary groups typically discredit the value of persuasion. Nomad (1961), in his analysis of revolutionary groups, noted that frequently the theorists in such groups advocated violence, not persuasion. A testament to violence as well as a deprecation of persuasion is found in a rhyme quoted by Minick (1957).

> With this commonplace
> Pistol I erase
> All who scoff, dissent, revile, complain;
> For nothing will persuade
> Reluctant man or maid
> As thoroughly as a bullet in the brain.

## *excessive evaluations*

The availability of and belief in persuasion seem to be cultural variables. It was not in violence-oriented Sparta, but in Athens, that persuasion theory developed and its practice flourished. The Athenians had persuaders, good and bad, wherever an audience could be obtained. They gave us the word, sought to distinguish it from other forms of influence and to understand its value. "The true theatre of a demagogue is a democracy," wrote James Fenimore Cooper in *The American Democrat*. It is also the setting in which persuasion abounds and in which it frequently is excessively evaluated. In such a culture, because of the sanction of persuasion, it is more necessary to appraise its potential and limitations for those to whom it has been made available.

In the present century, modern societies have considerably altered their evaluation of persuasion. Mills (1956) suggests a reason for the change. In analyzing occupational shifts in this country since the Civil War, he concluded that the most significant change was from the handling of *things* to the handling of *people* and *symbols*. For the first time, in 1957, the white collar workers in this country were in the majority. Increasingly, more workers find themselves employed to deal with other people. A much larger proportion of people are occupationally involved in communicating and persuading. Their own communicative behavior, now a major part of the occupational environment, provides observation of its importance. Appraisal is altered.

This alteration is revealed in the heroes and VIP's we approve today in contrast with former generations. Lowenthal (1943) selected two popular magazines—*Colliers* and *The Saturday Evening Post*—and studied the subjects of biographies for sample years covering the period 1900 to 1940. Among his findings, one of interest here was that men of "production" dominated the earlier period. Their achievements consisted in making or inventing things, building personal empires, and in the arts producing serious works of art. During the latter period, the principal shift was to successes in the entertainment field. These people were chiefly engaged in handling and pleasing audiences. Their achievements were not in productive enterprises. Perhaps this shift reflects a recognition, among a much larger proportion of people, of the relevance of handling people and symbols.

Furthermore, in non-democratic societies in which persuasion is not given the same degree of sanction, it has become valued, often excessively, as a form of influence. When the conditions of literacy and available mass media exist, those in power are apt to include persuasion as a technique of social control. Under such conditions public opinion and consequent behavior can be influenced. Possibly the outstanding example of excessive faith in persuasion occurred among leaders of the Nazi movement. Their fanaticism and unbounded confidence in the irresistibility of their movement rested on faith in two instruments: propaganda and the blitzkreig (Hoffer, 1951). Like modern Joshuas, they confidently expected to blow down the walls of resistance with the sounds of their persuasion. The Nazi bookburnings likewise reflected a conviction of persuasion's potency.

Though not fanatics, a group of contemporary writers also express what seems to me an immoderate confidence in or fear of persuasion and other techniques. We read of "hidden persuaders" using motivational research and the "coercive persuasion" of brainwashing, and of drugs designed to produce awesome behavioral effects, radios implanted in the brain to receive messages, sleep teaching, subliminal stimulation, mass hypnosis, and conditioning. These techniques tend to be pictured as irresistible threats. Even book titles suggest the threat: *The Engineering of Consent, Hidden Persuaders, The Battle for the Mind.* The implications of these viewpoints are that we are witnessing the control and ultimate domestication of man! Good-bye freedom! Supposedly, those in power now have the means to freeze a society! One wonders, along with Rosenberg (1960), if many of these writers are not more inclined to be novelists than social scientists.

These views, particularly the notion of freezing a society by persuasion or any other means, have been appraised by Bauer (1960). The gist of his argument is that "the system that has the least capacity or disposition to change is the one which is most subject to violent change (or to atrophy)." And atrophy is a form of change. One doesn't have to look beyond U.S. borders to observe the failure of attempts to stabilize a society. The State of Mississippi, in its literacy tests, economic coercion, legal barriers, and persuasive efforts is apparently failing to prevent change. Other political units, with much more power, have similarly failed. Moreover, the attempt to control large groups of people does not include the social cost of control, even if that control is achieved through the more economical techniques of propaganda and persuasion.

One writer, concerned about the power of persuasive messages, reconsidered the remark: some men are born to greatness; some achieve greatness; and some have greatness thrust upon them. He added a fourth possibility; some men hire a press agent. The champion believer in the power of words was possibly the publisher of the now defunct *Literary Digest*. In 1936, this magazine conducted a naive poll with regard to the Landon-Roosevelt election. Though the reverse happened, the poll predicted a landslide for Landon. According to Carter (1960), "When Morton Savell, who was one of the editors, went to the publisher to warn that the poll was in error, the answer was that as soon as the people read the *Digest* forecast, they would turn around and vote accordingly."

The extravagance in appraising the potency of persuasion is by no means limited to selected individuals or a small group of writers. It appears widely throughout the population. It is a commonly-held assumption that people are highly persuasible and can be manipulated into any viewpoint desired by those who command the persuasion agencies. This, of course, is the working assumption of the advertising industry, political propagandists, public relations counselors, public administrators, the press, mass entertainers, and some educators. An unfortunate result of this belief is the development and use of stock formulas in persuasion and the ineffectiveness they lead to. Examples are the politician's stock formula of "praising motherhood and damning sin," and the advertiser's notion that if you tell people something often enough they will believe it. The critical weakness of the stock formula is not that it never works, but that it involves rigid, fixed behavior in the persuader. It prevents a search for messages adapted to particular audiences at particular times.

Several hypotheses can be formulated to explain unrealistic appraisals of persuasion. Our anxiety about being manipulated or under the control of others may make us overestimate its danger. Lack of knowledge of the process involved leads to irrational fears of its potency. Certainly, such overestimation has occurred with other forms of influence when knowledge about their processes was lacking. Consider man's responses to such techniques as hypnosis, conditioning, brainwashing, and subliminal stimulation before he learned something of what they required to be effective. In regard to underestimating persuasion, it is probable that our desire for immediate results leads to downgrading its power. Persuasion often takes time; other forms of influence seem to get the job done quicker.

## effectiveness of non-persuasive methods

Persuasion is intimately bound up with other forms of influence. Its relative usefulness is better understood through identifying the strengths and weaknesses of other instruments of influence. In fact, the need for persuasion results from the shortcomings in other methods. This is most clearly seen in the varied means used by a society to achieve social control.

The widely accepted concept of social control refers to the various means used by a society to achieve deterrence or discontinuance of deviate behavior. More accurately, the reference is to groups of methods —legal, political, economic, primary group methods, persuasion, and so forth. Their interrelationship and simultaneous use is noted by Berger (1963).

> It is possible, then, to perceive oneself as standing at the center . . . of a set of concentric circles, each representing a system of social control. The outer ring might well represent the legal and political system under which one is obligated to live. This is the system that, quite against one's will, will tax one, draft one into the military, make one obey its innumerable rules and regulations, if need be put one in prison, and in the last resort will kill one.
>
> . . . . . . . . . . . . . . . . . . . . . . . . . . . . . . . . . . . . . . . . . . . . .
>
> Next in line after the political and legal controls one should probably place economic pressure. Few means of coercion are as effective as those that threaten one's livelihood or profit.
>
> . . . . . . . . . . . . . . . . . . . . . . . . . . . . . . . . . . . . . . . . . . . . .
>
> Very potent and simultaneously very subtle mechanisms of control are constantly brought to bear upon the actual or potential deviant. These are the mechanisms of persuasion, ridicule, gossip and opprobrium.

It goes without saying that a society is not the only agency seeking to influence, nor is the social control of the deviant the only objective. Organizations—business, labor, agricultural, religious, educational—as well as individuals seek to affect others. The behavior they seek from others differs considerably according to what they want adopted, not adopted, continued, or discontinued. To the extent that a society, organization, or individual has more than one means available, these are apt to be used simultaneously and present a choice or question of emphasis. It is well to gain some perspective on the various processes of influence as a basis for choice or emphasis.

### FORCE AND AUTHORITY

Power and authority, as means of influence, require the support of persuasion to be effective. Walter (1960) notes that power, even that of police and armies, is dependent on persuasion.

> Ultimately, power depends on voluntary obedience which is based on persuasion, and persuasion, in turn, depends on convictions, ideals, and respect. Certainly, force may be used in a domain of power to guarantee prescribed actions and to safeguard the limits of permitted behavior; nevertheless, sanctions, penalties, and the fear of punishment are merely braces and not foundations. As Rousseau put it, "the severity of penalties is only a vain resource, invented by little minds in order to substitute terror for that respect which they have no means of obtaining."

An analysis of the kinds of influence available to the President reveals the need for persuasion as a supplement, and often a better alternative, to force and authority. Such an analysis was the objective of Neustadt's (1964) work. In some detail he examined the Truman and Eisenhower administrations. He concluded

> The President of the United States has an extraordinary range of formal powers, of authority in statute law and in the Constitution. Here is testimony that despite his "powers" he does not obtain results by giving orders—or not, at any rate, merely by giving orders. He also has extraordinary status, ex officio, according to the customs of our government and politics. Here is testimony that despite his status he does not get action without argument. Presidential power is the power to persuade.

In the Presidential exercise of authority, Neustadt specifies five conditions that must exist for this kind of influence to be effective. Too often one or more of these is not operating. For a President to use authority effectively (1) his involvement in a situation must be unambiguous, (2) his words specifying his order must also be clear, (3) his order needs to be widely publicized, (4) the men who receive his order must have control of all that is needed to execute it, and (5) there must be no doubt of his authority to issue the order to those receiving it. Following his analysis of the conditions requisite to the effective use of authority, Neustadt concluded that "lacking any one of them, the chances are that mere command will not produce compliance."

The exercise of force, within political or other organizations, is evidence of the failure of power to effectively influence. In those communities, institutions, and organizations considered to possess extensive power, it is most likely accompanied by well developed sets of rules and regulations along with extensive control and use of the means of persuasion. In a dictatorship, for example, the limitations of power are recognized in the extensive use of regulatory agencies and propaganda efforts. Power, though possessed, is not meant for daily use, but as a last resort when voluntary compliance with authority or acceptance through persuasion have failed.

Moreover, even delegated authority requires the support of persuasion to be effective. There is no certainty that orders will be carried out simply because they seem legitimate to those who receive them. President Truman in 1952, contemplating the problems General Eisenhower would have should he be elected, is reported to have said, "He'll sit here and he'll say, 'Do this! Do that!' And nothing will happen. Poor Ike—it won't be a bit like the Army. He'll find it very frustrating" (Neustadt, 1964). One might also doubt the certainty and exact fulfillment of orders in military organizations. Moreover, our experiences with prohibition, speed limits on highways and illegal gambling are evidence that voluntary compliance with authority cannot be sustained without the support of beliefs established by persuasion.

The fact that most of us most of the time act in accord with external controls becomes incredible if these influences are presumed to operate without support. Only the certainty of penalty would deter behavior that might be socially unacceptable but individually advantageous. Enforcement of external dictates would be an unending, extensive practice. To explain why such enforcement is unnecessary, sociologists have constructed a concept—internalization—to refer to a process which supports external influence. Essentially, the notion points to a process by which we come, not only to comply with society's demands, but to accept them as legitimate and even desirable. Through internalization, we resolve our conflict with social demands. Through this process, social requirements no longer are resisted at the surface of our skins; they become internal determiners of our behavior. What is important is that persuasion assists and accelerates the internalization process. It is because of persuasion's value in bringing about internalization that unpopular dictatorships, contrary to widespread belief, may become greater users of persuasion than democracies. They have more need to gain acceptance for initially disliked rules. Perhaps this explains why Communist party organizations in Russia see to it that at least one pro-government lecture a month is given in every collective, village, and brigade (Butler, 1964).

Not only do power and authority require the support of persuasion, but the latter as a form of influence is more widely distributed and available for use. The availability of force and authority is limited. This is the case even for those agencies possessing these means. They simply cannot very well be invoked in many sectors of life. Evidence of this is to be found in the innumerable counseling, guidance, therapy and other "advice" programs used to influence behavior. Ultimately, power rests on popular support for its use. Some of the things we do are by long practice and tradition not to be forcibly denied; others are not to be forcibly required.

To some extent persuasion seems to be available to every man, whereas power and authority are not. It has been thought of as the weapon of the powerless. Those that have no other choice have opportunities, however limited, to persuade. This recourse to persuasion is exemplified in a study of the powerless, "coolcat" type of Negro by Finestone (1960). He observes that

> Despite the location of his social world in the "asphalt jungle" of the "blackbelt" he strictly eschewed the use of force and violence as a technique of achieving his ends. . . . He achieved his goals by indirection, relying, rather, on persuasion and on a repertoire of manipulative techniques . . . to be able to confront such contingencies [as police, jilted "chicks," and victims of his past behavior] with adequacy and without resort to violence was to be "cool." His idea was to get what he wanted through persuasion. . . . Indeed, he regarded himself as immeasurably superior to the "gorilla," a person who resorted to force.

In this case, the use of persuasion is the result of extreme powerlessness. Finestone found, in contrast, that the Negro's white counterpart typically used force and violence to achieve his ends.

At another level, Hoffer (1951) notes that mass movements begin with persuasion. Such movements do not "usually rise until the prevailing order has been discredited. The discrediting is not an automatic result of the blunders and abuses of those in power, but the deliberate work of men of words. . . . Moreover, the authorities, even when feeble and tolerant, are likely to react violently against the activist tactics of the fanatic." Thus, persuasion has an availability not accorded to other means of influence. While it may be granted that power and authority can produce more immediate and dependable effects, there are many occasions in which the powerful as well as the powerless find persuasion the only available means of influence.

The effectiveness of force is in greatest jeopardy when its imposition is relaxed or reduced. Once adopted as a means of influence, force becomes its own prisoner. In his discussion of force, its power and shortcomings, Hoffer (1964) comments

> One of the most remarkable things about the popular upheavals which have taken place in Communist countries since the death of Stalin is that hardly anyone in the West expected them. . . . We seem convinced that it [force] has a boundless power to shape and crush men's souls. It can make proud and brave men crawl on their bellies and confess the most fantastic and absurd crimes, and it can evoke in a population crushed by terror and stripped of all self-respect and integrity an almost religious dedication to fatherland and nation, and a readiness to die for their abusers and exploiters. We have witnessed again and again this miracle of perversion: The terrorized millions . . . proclaiming themselves in the vanguard of humanity, chanting the praises of their oppressors and hissing defiance at the outside world.

Hoffer, however, points to a major flaw in this exaggerated view of the power of force.

> We are told that an absolutist Communist leadership can change its attitudes and policies from one extreme to another without the least regard to the reaction of the populace. Still there is one thing it cannot do without risk, and that is to relent and reform. De Tocqueville puts it rather strongly when he says that "nothing short of great political genius can save a sovereign who undertakes to relieve his subjects after a long period of oppression."

The same author notes that the French and Bolshevik revolutions arose, not in periods of great oppression, but when it had been relaxed.

One area of the human experience in which force compares quite unfavorably with persuasion is in the tampering with meanings. When force is used to interfere with and violate the symbols and rituals that contribute to an individual's "reality," the effort to influence is endangered. To force a pacifist to bear arms, a patriot to insult his flag or honor another, an atheist to swear on the Bible, a scientist to doctor his data to support an approved conclusion, or a segregationist to serve a Negro in his restaurant is to generate a threat to his perception of reality. No matter how "immoral" or "unrealistic" are the beliefs a person holds sacred, or how much his symbolic rites conflict with the will or convenience of society, it is never a light matter to enforce their violation. What is required is a restructuring of meaning for economical and effective influence, and this means the use and support of persuasion. In the case of segregation, one observes that men will fight passionately against even lip-service to alien acts, because even the mechanical performance of alien behavior constitutes, to some degree, assent to its meaning. Such assent, incompatible with one's own perception of "fact and reality," works to corrupt and threaten that reality. As a result, when one is required to perform, confess, teach, or acclaim what he considers false, his response is apt to exceed that which ridicule, abuse, or rejection can arouse.

To say (1) that force and authority need the support of persuasion, (2) that their availability is limited, and (3) that their use requires behavior in violation of a man's "reality" is not the same as saying they are impotent forms of influence.

> There is evidence that the coerced convert is often as fanatical in his adherence to the new faith as the persuaded convert, and sometimes even more so. It is not always true that "He who complies against his will is of his own opinion still." Islam imposed its faith by force, yet the coerced Muslims displayed a devotion to the new faith more ardent than that of the first Arabs engaged in the movement (Hoffer, 1951).

The notion that an idea or a mass movement generated by an idea cannot be stopped by force is not literally true. Persistent and excessive coercion has an unmatched influence. It can stop, as in the Hungarian revolt, a movement of great vigor and popularity. It can change the ideas a man accepts, not only among the ignorant but among trained intellects. "When an arbitrary decree from the Kremlin forces scientists, writers, and artists to recant their convictions and confess their errors, the chances are that such recantations and confessions represent genuine conversions rather than lip service" (Hoffer, 1951). Genuine acceptance becomes a means of rationalizing and nullifying cowardice. Similarly, Bettelheim (1943) reported that some internees in Nazi concentration camps, after having been forced to behave in accordance with the opinions and values of their captors, eventually came to accept those opinions and values.

Of course, authority as a form of influence cannot be ruthlessly imposed. It implies an acceptance of another's legitimate right to direct one's behavior. Yet, in discussing the power of authority in an organization, March and Simon (1958) believe that "Acceptance of authority by the employee gives the organization a powerful means for influencing him—more powerful than persuasion." More broadly, in any situation where unquestioned acceptance of authority can be developed, it becomes an extremely effective form of influence. Where there is a good prospect of high acceptance of authority, persuasion is perhaps most useful in developing that acceptance, not substituting for it.

## OTHER FORMS OF INFLUENCE

A few observations regarding other forms of influence will suggest their shortcomings as competitors of persuasion. One of these is subliminal stimulation. In 1957, when substantial claims were made for its effectiveness, the research literature was investigated for additional information. Although the phenomenon has been demonstrated to exist, research findings do not support the extravagant claims made for it. As a technique of conveying complex "hidden" messages to influence, it is simply not effective. Its applicability as a practical means of influence, something more than restricted laboratory effects, is questionable. Such was the appraisal of the research evidence. For example, Blackwell (1958), and McConnell, Cutler, and McNeil (1958) examined more than one hundred studies of subliminal stimulation. Both sources conclude that experimentation provides no convincing evidence "that subliminal projections offer possibilities or threats of especially effective control of human behavior." Similarly, the British Institute of Practitioners in Advertising (1958) conclude that "present evidence shows little if any effect from subliminal communication in the fields of selling and persuasion. The dangers of this method of communication—which have given rise to public comment—are therefore not justified by any evidence submitted."

Another device, also involving presumably an uncritical acceptance and response from the receiver is that of sleep-learning or sleep-influence. Simon and Emmons (1955) examined the research evidence on this technique. They doubted that any acceptable evidence was available that influence by communication during sleep is possible. This would reject it as a significant technique in the promotion of the kinds of actions men seek to develop in others.

As alternatives to persuasion, habit stimulation and signal response stimulation (see Chapter 5) warrant appraisal. Unlike subliminal stimulation and sleep-learning, their use in generating relevant actions is indisputable. Habits and signal responses account for much voting behavior, cigarette smoking, stopping on "red" and proceeding on "green," and a host of actions sought by those who seek to influence. They have, however, limitations. Learning experiments involving habit building underscore the necessity of repeated stimulation. This, needless to say, requires extensive access to an audience in whom habit responses are sought. Furthermore, these techniques, due to the nature of habit, are limited in usefulness to actions of a repetitive nature. When the goal is to get others to adopt an action once only, habit is of little use.

Then, too, stimulus generalization is apt to occur in habit behavior. Much of our knowledge of this phenomenon comes from laboratory studies. Here it is observed under more controlled conditions. It has been shown, for example, that subjects conditioned to respond to light of a particular color will give the same response to light of a similar but not identical color. Outside the laboratory, this tendency is found in the same response to the various greens of different traffic lights. The stimulus for the response has been generalized. Small differences apparently are ignored. Similarly, a habit response built to sell one brand of cigarettes is apt in time to sell other brands. The result is "switching" brands. The name "Kodak," originally associated with a particular product (Eastman cameras), in time suggests all cameras. The implications of this tendency for influencing others by habit stimulation seems clear. Habit stimuli begin to vary, producting actions not sought and even detrimental.

## successful persuasive efforts

During World War II, one of the best known respected radio and movie personalities was singer Kate Smith. On two occasions, she conducted marathon broadcasts over CBS radio, the first for 18 hours and the second for 18½ hours. Working on behalf of the war bond drive, her goal was to obtain pledges and sell war bonds. During each marathon she made persuasive appeals every few minutes. In the first effort, she obtained pledges for roughly $39 million worth of U.S. Government bonds; in the second, a year later, she sold bonds worth $112 million. Both efforts were remarkable demonstrations of the power of persuasion (Wright, 1959). The relationship between Miss Smith and her audience warrants attributing the effort to persuasion without the help of force or authority.

The influence of force, authority and persuasion so frequently are intermeshed that evidence of relatively pure persuasive efforts is limited. Hoffer (1951), for example, notes that "there is hardly an example of a mass movement achieving vast proportions and a durable organization solely by persuasion." Whether the movement be judged good or bad, Christianity or Nazism, this applies. The civil rights movement of the present decade similarly intermeshes various kinds of influence—court decisions, publicity, picketing, boycott, parades, and a host of sit-ins including swim-ins at segregated pools, wade-ins at beaches, pray-ins at churches, park-ins at restaurant parking lots, stand-ins at theatre ticket windows, and lie-ins at construction sites in the path of approaching trucks.

Three areas in which the effect of persuasion can be studied in a more isolated form are advertising, experimental research, and studies of innovations. Success stories of persuasion in advertising are common. Pepsi-Cola was once considered a cheap drink. Persuasive messages stressed the theme of how much you get for a nickel. It is now advertised as a drink "for those who think young." This message change is considered the major factor in Pepsi-Cola's significant increase in sales. When Marlboro cigarettes switched its appeal to men, its sales soared 120 per cent in one year. The appeal for Brylcreme hair dressing was switched to sex. The new appeal was epitomized in the ditty, "Brylcreme—A little dab will do you, Brylcreme—the girls will all pursue you." The appeal helped to lift that hair tonic from fourth to first place in sales in less than three years (*Time,* October 12, 1962).

The evidence from experiments on the effects of persuasion similarly, and more consistently, supports its successfulness. These experiments typically present a message via a speaker or writer whose relationship to receivers is such that the influence of authority or power is minimal. When effects in experimental groups are compared with those in control groups, the former are quite consistently significant. Studies by Knower (1935; 1936) exemplify the usual finding. These dealt with a relevant issue (prohibition) to the audiences involved. He reported on subjects who listened to speeches opposing their views, subjects who read the speeches in printed form, and control subjects who did neither. In all experimental groups—those to whom messages were presented—significant changes in attitude occurred. These findings are presented in Table 2.

## TABLE 2

### Attitude Changes in Control and Experimental Groups Listening to or Reading Communications Opposed to Their Views

| Group | N | Mean before | Mean after | CR | Per cent shifting −.5 SM | Per cent shifting +.5 SM | Per cent shifting +1.5 SM |
|---|---|---|---|---|---|---|---|
| Controls | | | | | | | |
| (dry) | 111 | 6.97 | 6.97 | .00 | 31 | 32 | 4 |
| (wet) | 189 | 4.01 | 4.16 | 1.88 | 25 | 32 | 5 |
| Listening | | | | | | | |
| Exp. (dry) | 267 | 6.92 | 6.32 | 6.66 | 19 | 58 | 25 |
| Exp. (wet) | 340 | 4.02 | 4.77 | 9.38 | 15 | 61 | 27 |
| Reading | | | | | | | |
| Exp. (dry) | 85 | 6.83 | 6.39 | 3.14 | 24 | 56 | 20 |
| Exp. (wet) | 136 | 4.03 | 4.70 | 5.58 | 12 | 56 | 23 |

In the third area, the field studies of the adoption of innovations, impressive evidence is provided of persuasion's success. Inspection of Table 3 (Rogers, 1962) reveals the generally high percentages of adoption of innovations which were chiefly dependent on persuasion as the dominant means of influence.

## TABLE 3

### Percentages of Adoption of Innovations

| Innovation | Per cent adopted | Respondents |
|---|---|---|
| 1. Hybrid seed corn | 99 | 259 Iowa farmers |
| 2. Contour farming for soil conservation | — | 110 Illinois farmers |
| 3. Improved pasture | 94 | 100 N. Carolina farmers |
| 4. Growing alfalfa | 26 | 100 N. Carolina farmers |
| 5. Ten farm innovations | — | 493 Virginia farmers |
| 6. Antibiotic swine supplements | 71 | 148 Iowa farmers |
| 7. 2, 4-D weed spray | 87 | 148 Iowa farmers |

TABLE 3 (*Continued*)

| Innovation | Per cent adopted | Respondents |
|---|---|---|
| 8. "Miracle" fabrics | 91 | 148 Iowa farm homemakers |
| 9. 2, 4-D weed spray | 78 | 104 Ohio farmers |
| 10. Warfarin rat poison | 78 | 104 Ohio farmers |
| 11. "Miracle" fabrics | 79 | 88 Ohio farm homemakers |
| 12. Stilbestrol | 77 | 44 Ohio county extension agents* |
| 13. Bulk milk tanks | 89 | 44 Ohio county extension agents* |
| 14. Irrigation | 1 | 105 Ohio farmers using irrigation |
| 15. Line sowing of paddy | 59 | 63 Pakistani farmers |
| 16. Insecticides | 22 | 63 Pakistani farmers |
| 17. Fertilizers | 57 | 63 Pakistani farmers |
| 18. Revised Standard Version of the Bible | 27 | 117 Iowa church members |
| 19. Language laboratories | 1 | 51 U.S. high schools |

* Note: County extension agents become aware of an innovation much as farmers do, but "adoption" for county extension agents amounts to recommending the innovation to farmers in their county.

## summary

Campaigns to influence large groups of people generally involve more than one form of influence. Such efforts reveal the interdependence of these means in achieving goals. Force and authority, in particular, require the supporting effects of persuasion. Moreover, the alternatives to persuasion have serious limitations, especially in respect to availability, cost, and applicability to the various goals of adoption, deterrence, continuance, and discontinuance. "Hidden" techniques such as subliminal stimulation and sleep-learning have little to recommend them, on the basis of research findings, as effective means of influence. In appraising the success and potency of persuasion, the most independent uses of this means seem to occur in advertising, experiments, and in the promotion of innovations. In these areas, the effectiveness of persuasion is verifiable.

# Chapter 9

# General Limitations

For a balanced perspective, the next three chapters require an orientation to their objective. They concern the limitations of persuasion as a form of influence—those that are internal to the process, those that are external, and those specific unintended effects of persuasive effort that limit its value. These pages will provide a more detailed look at the shortcomings of persuasion than was done, in Chapter 8, for other forms of influence. This is not because it has more or greater weaknesses; the increased detail is a response to a more central interest in persuasion. The objective is not to deprecate persuasion, but to provide a perspective on what to expect from such efforts and to increase awareness of what might be done to mitigate these limitations.

## *the process of persuasion*

Implicit in a discussion of persuasion is the question, what explains change or continuance of behavior following the presentation of a message? What critical determinant warrants special emphasis? Answers are diverse. It almost seems that theorists are people who characteristically think otherwise. It is more probable, however, that persuasion, like any other field expanding in knowledge and interest, generates in the beginning a diversity of explanations. These gradually, through testing of their usefulness, reduce or converge into one or a few more inclusive views of greater predictive value. Yet, it contributes to one's perspective to note the principal approaches in the search for determinants of persuasive effects. Their recognition reduces the likelihood of a too limited view. They furthermore provide a background against which to appraise the focus of a particular discussion.

Briefly, the main trends in the search for explanations of persuasive effects have been those that stressed (1) stimulus characteristics of the message, (2) correlations of receiver traits with their behavior, (3) demographic approaches in which pollsters looked for the relationships of opinions, feelings, and behavior to social characteristics, (4) motivational factors in effects, (5) the study of cognitive activity involving consideration of matters such as set, perception, frame of reference, and memory, (6) the psychoanalytic view emphasizing the unconscious inner dynamics of the receiver rather than message or contextual factors, (7) the contribution of culture to behavior, (8) learning theory, (9) contextual elements surrounding a message, and (10) the sociological stress on the role of group relationships in determining an individual's or group's behavior.

Out of approaches such as these a variety of what have come to be called models have appeared. Models can be mathematical, mechanical, diagrammatic, or verbal, each seeking to provide a description and explanation which abstracts from the reality it represents certain features for emphasis. For example, a model of a new aircraft prepared for wind tunnel testing may emphasize shape and pay little attention to such features as size, construction materials, or weight. Examples of several communication models are presented and discussed in readings compiled by Campbell and Hepler (1965).

Communication models can be classified into four groups each having values peculiar to its basic emphasis. Their differing values suggest the kind of model most useful in understanding persuasion. The first group, the static models, is most useful to those concerned with the construction or maintenance of a system. A blueprint of an intercom system exemplifies the static model. The second group, the mechanical or working models, aids those most in need to know the normal functioning and malfunctioning of parts of a system. Speech clinicians, as expected, are more apt to study mechanical models of speech production because of their need to identify malfunctioning. The third group, the thermostatic or homeostatic models, serves those most interested in feedback, interaction, and in predicting immediate response. To focus on the thermostat-furnace interaction in a home heating system is to engage in this kind of emphasis. The thermostat model overlooks growth and permanent change in parts of a system. The last group, the human or open-system models, is most useful to those concerned with accounting for change and growth. These models emphasize a communication process in which sources and receivers continually change. It is this feature which seems to me most useful to emphasize in a model of persuasion.

## FOCUS ON MEANING AROUSAL IN PERSUASION

Meaning arousal is critical to the process of persuasion. This response to messages is the genesis of those subsequent behaviors sought by the persuader. Meaning is an instrument that generates further effects. A meaning arousal model rests on the principle that humans, particularly, assign meaning to impinging stimuli and that the meaning given is a major determinant of their subsequent behavior. This principle makes it requisite for students and users of persuasion to investigate the nature and effects of meaning arousal by means of messages. In this model of the persuasion process, the reader is asked to focus on the message-receiver. It is his responses that are emphasized, beginning with response to a message-stimulus.

Contu (1962) developed a general model of meaning arousal. His model was adapted and applied to the process of persuasion, and is represented by Figure 11.

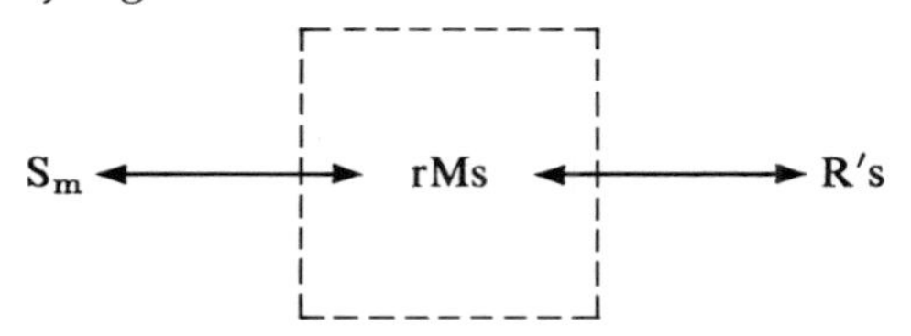


FIGURE 11. The symbol "$S_m$" refers to a message-stimulus intentionally directed to a receiver to arouse a desired meaning. In that persuasion is interpersonal, the stimulus is external to the receiver. The message-stimulus is reacted to signally or symbolically. The term "r" refers to such a response. This response is viewed as a mediation process in which a stimulus is used signally or symbolically. The term "M" stands for the meaning, signal or symbol, that results from the "r" response. The letter "s" indicates that the aroused meaning becomes a stimulus for further responses symbolized by "R." The two-way arrows "⟷" suggest that the receiver is not only stimulated, but in turn works on the message-stimulus to explore its meaning potential. Similarly, the individual responds "R" to a meaning stimulus "s," and in turn interprets and is affected by that response. That part of the process indicated by "rMs" is enclosed to suggest a central process, one that culminates in a meaning.

A model stressing the importance of meaning arousal in the persuasion process alters conceptions of the receiver and the role of the message-stimulus. The receiver is viewed as an interpreter, an active participant in the process. The term "receiver" is erroneously apt to suggest passivity on his part. It was Fearing (1953) who insightfully first spoke of the receiver as the "interpreter," thus stressing his active role. A person responding to persuasion is more than a knee-jerk receiver, more than a person whose overt behavior directly follows from a message-stimulus. Secondly, the message, in the light of this model, becomes a much more limited determiner of subsequent effects. An interpreting individual processes a message, contributing to and creating its meaning, responds to *his* meaning, and thus reduces the prediction of response from the message only.

When this model and these notions are applied to persuasion, the following process emerges: (1) a message-stimulus, designed to arouse a desired meaning, is directed to an interpreter; (2) the message is perceived in the sense of detection and identification; (3) the interpreter explores the probable meanings of the message and assigns a meaning; (4) this meaning, not the external message, becomes a stimulus for further effects; these are affective, cognitive, and overt in character; and (5) these effects may, in turn, generate the action (the goal) sought by the persuader. Thus, the politician's speech does not produce votes directly; it arouses meanings which generate feelings, beliefs, and actions relevant to those meanings; these in turn are instrumental in bringing about votes. The TV commercial, similarly, does not produce purchases of the sponsor's product. The newspaper editorial does not create, directly, favorable attitudes toward a civic improvement or a charitable enterprise. A magazine exposé of corruption does not directly alter public belief. The direct power of a message-stimulus is limited to arousing meaning. The meaning aroused and its effects are significantly determined by the processing activity of the interpreter.

Thus, the pertinent questions for the persuader to ask are: What meaning do I seek to arouse, not what do I want this person to do? What evidence supports a connection between this meaning and the action desired? Is this meaning a proven determiner of the desired further effects? For example, are meanings that arouse fear and discontent the kinds of meanings that lead receivers to participate in a movement to change the *status quo*? In their analyses of social revolts, Hoffer (1951) and Nomad (1959) conclude that a more proven determiner of such action is hope.

## FURTHER EFFECTS OF MEANING

The meaning aroused by a message is instrumental in generating further effects. The list of these effects is long and varied. *Messages,* for example, are accepted, rejected, remembered, forgotten, comprehended, misunderstood, passed on to others or diffused, not diffused, acted on, not acted on. Similarly, the persuader gains or loses popularity, is followed or rejected, is attacked, laughed at, praised, damned.

*Groups and organizations* with whom a persuader is perceived to be associated are affected. In August 1962, farmers in Iowa demonstrated in front of a Sears, Roebuck and Company store. They piled Sears catalogues in front of the store in protest against a report of the Government Committee on Economic Development. One member of this committee, T. V. Houser, was also a member of the Board of Directors of Sears. The report stated, among other conclusions, that many small-scale farmers should be encouraged to move off the farm. Another recent instance involving effects on organizations occurred shortly after the election of President Kennedy. His administration ruled that speeches or other communications, relevant to U.S. policies, by government personnel had to be approved before transmission. The rule recognized the impact of the individual's message on the group of which he is a part.

*Media* are affected by the messages they carry. Newspaper and magazine circulations, radio and TV ratings rise and fall with the messages they provide. Magazines and other mass media reject those advertising messages considered harmful to the image of the media.

These effects illustrate how varied the further effects of meaning arousal can be. To attempt a complete list would involve citing all behavior on the part of receivers in response to meanings aroused by messages. Such would not be helpful. Rather, it is more useful to seek basic classifications or dimensions of effect. Rosenberg *et al.* (1960) provide a classification of the components of attitude which with further generalization can be useful in classifying effects generated by message meanings. Three broad types of effect are proposed: affective, cognitive, and behavioral responses.

## AFFECTIVE RESPONSES

The first class, affective responses, involves the development of feelings of like or dislike, approval or disapproval, love or hate. We observe these feelings in ourselves in response to the presence of a lover, a job promotion, a kindness from another, or to the death of a friend, a crippling accident, a betrayal by another. Such internal responses may be inferred from measures of physiological variables such as blood pressure, pulse rate, or galvanic skin responses. More generally, affective responses to meaning are inferred from direct statements of like or dislike. The like or dislike responses, of course, may be directed to an indefinite variety of objects including the message, the persuader, the medium, and others.

### COGNITIVE RESPONSES

The second class, cognitive responses, involves any knowledge, opinion, or belief about one's environment, about oneself, or about one's behavior. To alter beliefs, opinions, and knowledge is a common instrument to the persuader's goal. This view of cognition is similar to that of Festinger (1957). In speaking of his concept of cognition he notes that his use of the term "knowledge" includes more than is usually implied, for example, it includes opinions. He makes the point that a person does not hold an opinion unless he thinks it is correct. Psychologically then, an opinion is not different from knowledge. An opinion one holds, in this sense, is a subjective "fact," part of the "knowledge" that constitutes reality for an individual. The same is true of beliefs, values, or attitudes which function as subjective "facts" for the individual. They are part of what he "knows." Cognitive effects of messages are generally measured by paper and pencil tests.

A look at the advertising of product-producing companies will reveal examples of cognitive effects. Messages are presented to potential customers to increase familiarity with a company name, a brand name, a trade mark, or a company symbol, to establish a belief in the company's leadership in the industry, to increase knowledge of the company's activities, to provide knowledge of a new use for a product, to establish a belief that the company is a good place to work, to increase recognition of the package containing a product, to provide knowledge of the company's achievements in research, and to increase knowledge of unique features of a product. Similarly, the preacher, politician, pressure group, and other persuaders seek a wide variety of cognitive effects.

### OVERT BEHAVIORAL EFFECTS

The third class, behavioral effects, involves a receiver's acts or overt behavior. Examples from the world of advertising are such acts as a potential customer's sending in a coupon, visiting a showroom, entering a contest, contacting a dealer, or visiting a display at a fair. Frequently, it is possible to observe or measure these effects directly. Lewin (1947), for example, in studying the effects of lecture and discussion on housewives in respect to changing food habits, followed up the persuasion with visits to homes to observe if the recommended practices were carried out. In other studies, such as Rosen (1961), the receiver's behavior is predicted from what he says he will do or plans to do.

The notion of "possible further effects from affective, cognitive, or overt responses" is the thesis of the work of Rosenberg and others (1960). These authors present a theoretical discussion accompanied by research evidence that a principle of consistency operates to create further effects from the initial effect generated by message meaning. Their contention is that a change, for example, in belief, brings on changes in affective and overt behavior. The receiver's tension is reduced by a consistent relationship among his affective, cognitive, and overt responses. Much of their work examines the hypothesis "that affective and behavioral changes will result from exposure to verbal stimuli which change one's conception and perception of the object of the communication."

Other behavioral processes, such as inference and stimulus generalization, produce further effects of interest to the persuader. When the candidate's message, for instance, arouses a belief that the nation's economy is stagnant, receivers are apt to infer that the incumbent administration is at fault. Likewise, when messages generate approval for a company's product, the approval is apt to be generalized for other products of the company. A whole class of stimuli now produce the approval. The word "kodak" originally specified a particular make of camera; this word has now been generalized to include all makes of cameras. What matters more in the understanding of persuasion is not a listing of behavioral processes that lead to further effects, but the fact that further effects of the message-meaning, favorable or unfavorable, are likely to occur.

## VARIABILITY OF MEANINGS

A major internal limitation of persuasion results from the varied meanings a message may arouse.

One way of thinking about what a persuader is up to is to note that he seeks low variability among meanings aroused. If the action he seeks in others is to be generated by the arousal of a particular meaning, then that meaning and no other becomes the direct objective of his message.

Perhaps the jury trial illustrates this objective as well as any effort to influence by persuasion. The attorney, in quest of a unanimous decision, begins by presenting messages to his audience of twelve jurymen to create meanings similar to the ones he has in mind. One suspects this often is not the result and that other sources of influence operate to bring about a unanimous verdict.

The variety of meanings generated by an event or message is vividly illustrated in a study by Hastorf and Cantril (1954). The event was a football game played Saturday, November 23, 1951, between Dartmouth College and Princeton University. Two conditions made this game unusual. To begin with, Princeton had won all its games, and this was the last game. Princeton's star, Dick Kazmaier, was a strong candidate for All-American and had just appeared on the cover of *Time* magazine. He was playing his last college game. Its importance to Princeton made it something of a special game.

Shortly after the opening kick-off, players, officials, and spectators realized this was going to be a rough game. The whistles of the referees frequently interrupted the game; numerous penalties were stepped off. In the second quarter, Kazmaier's nose was broken, forcing him to leave the game. Later, a Dartmouth player's leg was broken. Tempers flared on and off the playing field.

The game immediately created a flood of accusations from both campuses. Campus publications printed numerous indictments of the opposing team. As a result, the incident and subsequent messages generated by it fanned the interest of players, students, coaches, faculty and administration officials. Probably few persons on the two campuses remained unaware of the game.

The second condition that added to the uniqueness of this game was the fact that two behavioral scientists set about to study the difference in how students on the two campuses reacted to the game. Their procedure involved two steps. The first consisted of answers to a questionnaire; this sought opinions about the game and who was responsible for the way it was played. These were given to undergraduates in introductory and intermediate psychology courses. The second step involved showing the same motion picture of the game to undergraduate fraternity members at both schools. These students were instructed to watch the film and check all infractions of the rules they saw, and note which team was responsible.

Of interest are the answers of those who were present at the game, or viewed it on television, or later saw a film of the game. These results are presented in Table 4.

TABLE 4

OPINIONS OF THE GAME BY THOSE WHO SAW IT

| Question: From your observations of what went on at the game, do you believe the game was clean and fairly played, or that it was unnecessarily rough and dirty? | Per cent of Dartmouth students | Per cent of Princeton students |
|---|---|---|
| Clean and fair | 6 | 0 |
| Rough and dirty | 24 | 69 |
| Rough and fair | 25 | 2 |
| No answer | 45 | 29 |

Also of interest are the number of infractions of rules observed by students while watching a film of the game. These results are contained in Table 5.

TABLE 5

AVERAGE NUMBER OF INFRACTIONS CHECKED BY OBSERVING A FILM OF THE GAME

| Group | N | Average checked against Dartmouth team | Average checked against Princeton team |
|---|---|---|---|
| Dartmouth students | 48 | 4.3 | 4.4 |
| Princeton students | 49 | 9.8 | 4.2 |

From these and other data the authors conclude

It seems clear that the "game" actually was many different games and that each version of the events that transpired was just as "real" to a particular person as other versions were to other people.

In brief, the data indicate that there is no such "thing" as a "game" existing "out there" in its own right which people merely "observe." The "game" exists for a person and is experienced by him only in so far as certain happenings have significances in terms of his purpose.

. . . It is inaccurate and misleading to say that different people have different "attitudes" concerning the same "thing." For the "thing"

> simply is not the same for different people whether the "thing" is a football game, a presidential candidate, communism, or spinach.

Similarly, messages that make up lectures, TV commercials, films, plays, magazine articles, and letters are interpreted differently by each listener or reader. Schramm (1956), noting the variability of meanings that reading of the same material can produce, commented, "In effect, two individuals reading the same page may actually be reading different materials, so different are their perceptions of the material." Though the aroused meanings differ widely, each individual's version is "real" to him. Likewise, it is misleading to think of a message as something existing "out there" which people hear or see mechanically as a tape recorder or camera would. People do not react to the same message; they react to the individualized meaning the message arouses. The message "exists" for the receiver as he interprets it.

Another example of the variability of images people acquire from the same event is found in the studies of the first Nixon-Kennedy television debate in 1960. Eight audience studies of this debate are reviewed by Katz and Feldman (1962). People were asked who made the better impression, who did the best job of stating his case, who won the most votes and similar questions. Among Republicans, Democrats, and Independents, there was little agreement on what happened.

Still further evidence of meaning variability aroused by messages is found in the responses to the Semantic Differential, an instrument for the measurement of meaning developed by Osgood, Suci, and Tannenbaum (1957). This instrument makes use of what people do when they distinguish between things or concepts. Take, for example, two words frequently used in this book: *persuasion* and *force*. Ask several individuals in what ways these two concepts (forms of influence) differ. Distinctions that are apt to be made are: persuasion is ethical, but force is not; persuasion is good while force is bad; persuasion is slower than force; persuasion is considerate while force is cruel. Thus, in distinguishing only two concepts, people react in terms of dimensions or characteristics on which they differ. Moreover, people perceive these characteristics to exist in varying degrees, rather than as either- or categories. For example, a "goodness" characteristic may vary from very good to very bad with gradations in between these extremes.

Osgood, using this tendency of people to distinguish concepts by comparing them on various dimensions, designed a rating procedure in which he asked subjects to rate concepts on a series of scales bounded at the ends by opposite characteristics such as good-bad, slow-fast, cruel-kind. For example, on the good-bad scale, a person might assign *persuasion* and *force* the following positions:

persuasion force

good /____/____/↓____/____/↓____/____/____/ bad

The general form of the Semantic Differential contains 20 such scales, selected following a study to determine what and how many scales would provide the best map or profile of a person's meaning of any concepts so measured. Generally, however, this instrument has been given to groups of persons and the ratings averaged for each scale. Used this way, Jenkins (1958) has published an *Atlas of Semantic Profiles for 360 Words*. He reports, for instance, the average values on the good-bad scale for such concepts as *scientist* (2.20), *politician* (3.90), *minister* (1.97), *doctor* (1.60), and *ditch-digger* (5.53).

Note that averaging ratings over many individuals does not expose the important fact that ratings vary. This is our concern here. The meanings that a word or other stimulus may arouse often will vary considerably, thus limiting the certainty of desired effects from persuasion. As a classroom project, 26 students responded, using the semantic differential, to the concepts: persuading, motivating, selling, manipulating, and propagandizing. The distributions of their ratings, reflecting the variability of meanings these words arouse, are illustrated by those ratings obtained on the cruel-kind scale. Note, for instance, the varied ratings assigned to the term "persuading" in Table 6.

TABLE 6

DISTRIBUTIONS OF RATINGS ON THE CRUEL-KIND OF THE SEMANTIC DIFFERENTIAL FOR SELECTED CONCEPTS

| | Cruel | | Ratings | | | Kind | | Mean |
|---|---|---|---|---|---|---|---|---|
| Concepts | 1 | 2 | 3 | 4 | 5 | 6 | 7 | rating |
| Persuading | 1 | 3 | 6 | 6 | 7 | 1 | 2 | 4.00 |
| Motivating | 0 | 0 | 2 | 11 | 4 | 8 | 1 | 4.82 |
| Selling | 0 | 5 | 6 | 8 | 2 | 4 | 1 | 3.88 |
| Manipulating | 0 | 4 | 10 | 10 | 2 | 0 | 0 | 3.38 |
| Propagandizing | 2 | 12 | 10 | 2 | 0 | 0 | 0 | 2.46 |

## DIFFICULTY IN MODIFYING MEANINGS

Look at the figure below and decide what you see—what it means. Many people see an attractive young woman with her head slightly turned away from them. Others see an ugly, old woman, witch-like in appearance.

FIGURE 12. The young lady and the old witch—an illustration of an ambiguous figure. Reproduced by permission of E. G. Boring and the *American Journal of Psychology*.

Such a "trick" drawing seems to contain two pictures, two legitimate meanings. It illustrates an important concept, that of selective perception. First, you may notice that you see one of the women but not the other. You may have difficulty in seeing the other woman and actually need the help of someone to point her out. Once you've seen both women, generally you can see either as desired. It is, however, difficult to see both women at once; the two meanings seem to compete with each other and one or the other tends to dominate at a given moment. To obtain meaning we seem to select and organize those stimuli which support a particular meaning and to censor those contrary to that meaning. As Rapoport (1960) notes, "Since we *must* select, we must be blind to what we have left out." It is this blindness to contrary stimuli that makes persuasion difficult. When we present messages to modify the meaning another holds, it is not an easy thing to overcome his rejection of signs contrary to his own meaning.

FIGURE 13. The vase and the profiles.

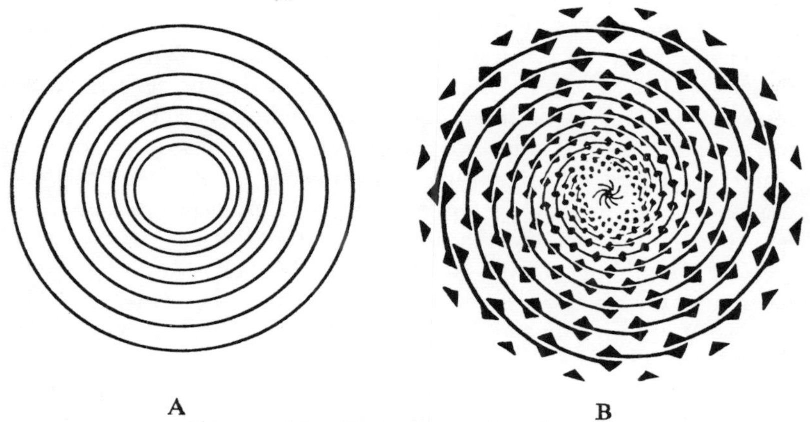


FIGURE 14. The spiral and circles.

There are many "trick" drawings, some designed to be merely illustrative of perceptual phenomena, while others, as in contemporary optical art, provide the viewer with an interesting experience in perceiving. Of Figures 13 and 14, the first illustrates an instance in which most people find it easy to shift back and forth from the "vase" meaning to the "profiles" meaning. The second generates one dominant meaning, that of a "spiral." You may learn to see the "circles," but this meaning keeps slipping away and the dominant spiral returns. Careful inspection of Figure 13 will reveal that there is no spiral; the figure is constructed of a series of jagged circles. Yet the less "real" meaning is the dominant one. This latter drawing demonstrates that meanings, generated by stimuli selected from the same pool of objective stimuli, do not have equal stability even when both meanings have been pointed out to us.

With regard to persuasion, if its process begins with the arousal of a meaning it becomes important that the meaning be sustained. This is necessary to the development of further effects and ultimately the action sought. If the persuader's immediate task is to establish another meaning, merely doing this is no evidence that it will be sustained long enough to be useful. Such a limitation restricts the influencing power of persuasion. There is evidence that meanings are not sustained. In studies of attitude change by persuasion, it is generally found that the percentage of persuaded persons declines with time. Measures of effect, immediately following a message and those made at a later date, favor immediate over delayed effect. Such results, though not measures of meaning, do imply a regression toward original meanings.

It is a major thesis of this chapter that the persuader's messages are perceived by receivers in the same fashion as the messages in "trick" drawings. The receiver's meaning, in defense of his reality, creates resistance to the different meaning desired by the persuader. In the case of the ambiguous drawing, it is relatively easy to enlist the receiver in searching out the other meaning. Once told he is examining a "trick" drawing, he accepts the existence of another legitimate meaning. Such is generally not the case in the practical persuasive situation; the receiver's meaning to him is apt to be the only legitimate, "real" meaning. He refuses to give equal credence to another viewpoint. This defense of one's reality adds to the difficulty in modifying meaning, the difficulty in persuading.

Several methods for dealing with the receiver's "defense of his reality" appear in the literature on persuasion. Two of these were discussed in Chapter 3: The message organization used in psychotherapy and the two-sided structure for persuasion. Others include the implicative method (Minick, 1957) and the congruent method (Ewing, 1942). The implicative method employs an inductive arrangement of messages. The conclusion, which presents a viewpoint different from that originally held by receivers, is placed at the end of the series. The receiver's viewpoint is not directly challenged until acceptable evidence has built a foundation for the conclusion. In the congruent method, the persuader begins by declaring his position to be similar to that of the receiver even though he realizes his view and that of the receiver differ. He then presents evidence in support of the meaning he seeks to establish.

## limitation by regulation

An Associated Press item (February 20, 1963) contained the following:

> Los Angeles—A Superior Court judge has permanently barred a group from placing cards in merchandise protesting the sale of Communist-made goods by a Southern California department store chain. The cards advised patrons: "Always buy your Communist imports at Bullock's."

After the action by Judge Kenneth Chantry, attorneys for Bullock's, Inc., announced the chain would drop a four million dollar damage suit against the Committee to Publicize the Sale of Communist Goods on the Local Business Scene.

This limitation on persuasion is *external* rather than internal to the process. Many such regulatory limitations exist on persuasive messages.

We recognize that when we speak of "freedom of speech" and everyman's right to persuade we are speaking of a limited right. One limitation is that imposed by the regulatory agencies of society, one of which is the judiciary. Instances of its restrictive power over messages occur constantly in the news. In an Associated Press report (August 20, 1963), one reads of a $3.06 million award to Wally Butts, a former University of Georgia coach and athletic director, in a libel action against the Curtis Publishing Company. In its magazine, *The Saturday Evening Post,* it had charged Butts was involved in fixing an Alabama-Georgia football game. In another Associated Press item (May 22, 1962), it was reported that Charles E. Chapel was found guilty by a Sacramento Superior Court jury of violating California's bomb hoax law. He had remarked, aboard an airline, that there was nitro-glycerine in his briefcase. Chapel maintained that his remark was only a joke, which prompted Asst. District Attorney Tocher to comment that the law "makes no exception for jokers." Incidentally, Mr. Chapel was a California assemblyman who on two occasions had voted for the statute.

In the eyes of the society, Mr. Chapel's "crime" was excessive emotional stimulation of others through communication, against which the law was designed to protect them.

The restriction of messages by the courts is also found in the rules of admissability. The kind of messages to be presented to juries is regulated by rules regarding the use of hearsay evidence, the opinions of unqualified witnesses, the opinions of experts, the right of cross-examination, the use of hypothetical comparisons, the use of legally irrelevant material, and the requirement that the "best" evidence be used (McKelvey, 1944). The philosophy of courtroom procedure is that persuasion needs to be regulated, and particularly that juries of untrained receivers should not be exposed to unrestricted persuasion. The shift to this view is found in the early history of the use of juries (Wigmore, 1942).

> When the Norman judges organized the jury to assist them in their investigations, the jurors were at first left to their own discretion in the use of evidence (except for a few rules about documents). They might use their own impressions . . . and they might even go about among the neighbors asking for information out of court. In the earliest period, witnesses in court were not commonly heard—due chiefly to a scruple about "maintenance" (or officious intermeddling to influence the jury). But as this feature gradually disappeared, and witnesses in court became a usual means of information (later 1500's), the jury's own "knowledge" played a minor part. Finally, by the end of the 1600's, the jury were deemed and allowed to have no information except what was offered in court—a complete reversal of function.

Other agencies, public and private, exercise a regulatory function over persuasion and thus limit its use. Among public agencies are the Federal Communications Commission, the Food and Drug Administration, and the Securities Exchange Commission. Examples of private agencies set up by communication industries to provide self regulation are the National Association of Broadcasters and the Motion Picture Association of America. The NAB, for instance, publishes a Television Code which lists 103 rules governing and limiting messages presented via television (NAB, 1965). Illustrative rules include

> Attacks on religion and religious faith are not allowed.
>
> Respect is maintained for the sanctity of marriage and the value of the home. Divorce is not treated casually nor justified as a solution for marital problems.

A television broadcaster should exercise particular discrimination in the acceptance, placement and presentation of advertising in news programs so that such advertising should be clearly distinguishable from the news content.

A television broadcaster should not present fictional events or other non-news material as authentic news telecasts or announcements, nor should he permit dramatizations in any program which would give the false impression that the dramatized material constitutes news. Expletives . . . such as "flash" or "bulletin" and statements such as "we interrupt this program to bring you . . ." should be reserved specifically for news room use.

The use of the television medium to transmit information of any kind by the use of the process called "subliminal perception" . . . is not permitted.

Advertising copy should contain no claims dealing unfairly with competitors, competing products, or other industries, professions or institutions.

The advertising of "fortune-telling, occultism, astrology, phrenology, palm-reading, numerology, mind reading, character reading or subjects of a like nature is not permitted.

Because of the personal nature of the advertising of medical products, claims that the product will effect a cure and the indiscriminate use of such words as "safe," "without risk," "harmless," or terms of similar meaning should not be accepted. . . .

## contextual limitations

A group of limitations, also external to the process of persuasion, can arise from unfavorable contextual factors accompanying the message. In Chapter 4, these factors were discussed in more general terms. What concerns us here is their role as limiters of message effect. In this light, *what* is said can be limited by *who* says it, *who* sponsors the message, by *unfavorable relationships* between the source and message receivers, by negative reactions of *groups relevant to the receivers,* by the *media* carrying the message, by the *presence of competing messages,* and so on. Without the aid of a favorable context surrounding the message, a severe limitation is imposed on the potential of persuasion.

Messages, for example, can be made more effective by eliminating competing messages. The seeking of a monopoly or near monopoly to enhance the effect of non-competitive messages is particularly observed in the study of "total" institutions. This would include such institutions as prisons, POW camps, homes for the aged or mentally ill, and totalitarian states in which communication along with other aspects of living are highly regulated. The U.S.S.R. handling of messages, for example, reflects an intent to control messages available to receivers. Details of the control mechanisms are discussed by Wright (1959). Similarly, in Poland, government observers are used to check on the messages produced by the church in its religion classes. This pressure for monopoly was revealed in a United Press report (January 8, 1963). "Stefan Cardinal Wyszynski told a congregation in St. John's Basilica Sunday that the Roman Catholic Church will pay the fines of priests who are penalized for barring government observers from religious classes." The desire for monopoly in POW camps and its use in "brainwashing" has been reported on by Schein (1956) and Brown (1963). Writing of total institutions generally, Goffman (1960) describes their monopolistic conditions which result in the elimination of competing persuasion. All aspects of life tend to be conducted in the same place and under the same authority. The life of the "inmate" is carried out in the presence and company of many similar others. Activities are tightly scheduled. Activities, including reception of messages, are part of a single overall plan, the goals of the institutional authorities.

In settings where a free market in persuasion is held to be the ideal, substantially monopolistic conditions develop. Competing messages are, in terms of practical effect, eliminated. The impact of the remaining messages, so favored, is heightened. Merton (1946), for instance, notes that the mass media in this country may in effect constitute a monopoly when they produce messages essentially saying the same thing. Receivers become a captive audience through their inability to gain other exposure. When it is argued that receivers have opportunity, if they exert themselves, for other exposure, the argument as a program for reducing monopoly is unconvincing. The point here, however, is not the morality of an effective free market, but the fact that persuaders recognize the value of monopoly and the reduction of competing stimuli. Advertisers, financially able to dominate the major message channels, achieve greater effect through elimination of exposure to competitive messages. Newspapers, unchallenged locally, find their power to persuade enhanced by their near-monopoly whether they have sought that condition or not. In this connection, Smith (1962) presented figures on the death rate of newspapers and the consequent greater monopoly of those that survive. Back in 1920 there were 500 cities with competing newspapers; today only 60 remain. The value to the persuader in eliminating competition also is recognized in efforts to ban certain types of speakers from college campuses.

## summary

Diverse explanations of persuasive effects are apt to produce different models of the process involved. Various models abstract different features for emphasis. The perspective favored in this discussion is to focus on meaning arousal as the genesis of those subsequent behaviors desired by the persuader. The further effects of meaning arousal are grouped in three categories—affective, cognitive, and overt responses. These, of course, are not consistent among receivers. This inconsistency is attributable, to a considerable extent, to the fact that the same external message generates variable meanings and consequently various further effects. Moreover, the meanings elicited by messages are difficult to modify. Receivers tend to view their own meanings as real and legitimate; in defense of that reality they resist changing them. Finally, two other factors impose external limitations on persuasion. One of these arises from the extensive social regulation of persuasive efforts, and the other the impact of the message context.

# Chapter 10

# Unsought Preliminary Effects

In the preceding chapter, attention was called to that segment of the persuasion process beginning with a persuader's directing a message to an interpreter-receiver. The message hopefully energizes a set of interrelated responses—meaning arousal, cognitive, affective, and overt responses to meaning—culminating in action which constitutes the persuader's goal. These interrelated responses and subsequent actions vary a great deal between individuals and for the same individual at different times. It is well to size up the extent of this variance, the problems it exposes for the persuader. Though reflexive behavior, such as the eye-blink, also varies between individuals and for the same individuals on different occasions, for most people, a stimulus capable of producing an eye-blink generally results in the expected behavior. Response variance is relatively low; thus, response prediction is high. Similarly, I might vary in response to a stop-sign and certainly individuals vary, but for the most part, we respond by stopping our cars. In persuasion, however, response variance is high, ranging from belief to disbelief, approval to disapproval, favorable action to completely contrary action. Some of these responses, of course, are inimical to the persuader's goals.

It is high response variance that increases the necessity for analysis of specific audiences in particular situations. It is high response variance that increases the likelihood of unsought or unexpected message effects, especially to those expecting or assuming too much uniformity among responses. It is because of highly variable responses to messages that a science of persuasion, or advertising, or political campaigning is an overpowering term if we mean by science the capacity to predict effect with some certainty. This, however, does not mean that the methods of scientific investigation along with others cannot contribute to greater prediction of effects, identify those contrary, unsought effects of messages, identify when and among whom they are likely to occur, and suggest means of reducing such undesired responses. This is our concern here, to bring to bear some of the findings of research and observation that promote these ends. To organize this material, the unsought effects of persuasion are put into two groups: (1) those earlier responses in the persuasive process that serve as determinants of undesired subsequent action, and (2) the kinds of receiver-actions highly deviate from those sought by the persuader.

## selective exposure: defense by avoidance

Festinger (1957) published *A Theory of Cognitive Dissonance* which provides some theoretical background on selective exposure. His work stresses the effects of inconsistencies between facts we have. He summarizes his theory: (1) there may exist inconsistencies among "facts" we believe are correct; (2) this dissonance (inconsistency) generates pressure to reduce the disharmony or *to avoid increasing it;* and (3) the operation of these pressures leads to cognitive and behavioral changes. It follows from Festinger's observation that if receivers avoid increasing dissonance, then a persuasive effort may have unfavorable effects before the message itself is presented. If the receiver has an expectation that the message opposes his view or is otherwise disturbing, he will defend himself by avoiding it. Such defense-by-avoidance is implied in a line the comic, Dick Gregory, used, "I have been reading so much about cigarettes and cancer, I quit reading." Cohen, Brehm, and Latané (1959) speak of selective exposure as a type of strategy to deal with tension and dissonance.

In his research, Rosen (1961) asked students to choose between taking an objective or essay examination. They were then given a contrived annotated list of six articles, three supporting objective examinations and three supporting essay tests. Students were asked which they preferred to read by ranking all six in order of preference. The results showed students significantly chose articles favorable to their examination decision and avoided articles opposing their decision ($p < .001$). More than two-thirds of the students displayed this tendency. Mills, Aronson, and Robinson (1959), in a very similar study, obtained similar results.

Brodbeck (1956) told small groups of a proposed law to legalize wire-tapping. Opinions of the subjects were then measured. This was followed by a tape-recorded speech on wire-tapping. Measures of opinion followed and the subjects were asked to reveal their positions on the issue. Then each subject was asked to write down the names of others in the group with whom he would prefer discussing the issue. Those subjects whose opinions were shaken but not changed from disapproval to approval chose persons who also disapproved of the position taken in the speech. Those subjects who changed and accepted the viewpoint of the speech chose persons who held similar opinions. In each case there was an effort to seek out support for their opinions.

Lazarsfeld, Berelson, and Gaudet (1944), in studying voting behavior, found that people read and listen to those sources that support their own viewpoints and avoid those which do not. Ehrlich, Guttman, Schonbach, and Mills (1957) found that new car owners read advertisements for their own make of car more than for any other make. Star and Hughes (1950) studied a plan, conducted in Cincinnati, Ohio, to inform people through the mass media about the United Nations. The plan was a failure; among people studied the percentage of those who remained uninformed about the United Nations' main purpose remained about the same. The authors felt that the uninformed simply didn't expose themselves to the information. Similarly, Cartwright (1949) studied those who attended a wartime documentary film. It was widely advertised and offered free admission in order to inform civilians on how to best help the war effort. The audiences were largely composed of persons already doing more of the practices which the film encouraged. The desired audience simply did not expose itsslf to the message.

One group of persons who presumably expose themselves to divergent views are the independent or uncommitted voters. Recent research, however, on voting behavior has all but dispelled the myth of the "independent voter" (Katz and Feldman, 1962). This mythical voter is pictured as the ideal citizen who seeks out and exposes himself to the persuasion of conflicting parties. He suspends judgment, does not make up his mind until election eve. At that time, he presumably weighs the arguments in the quiet of his study. The truth is that people who make up their minds late in the campaign are more likely to have little interest in the election and less likely to expose themselves to campaign persuasion. Even in the Nixon-Kennedy television debates, "independent voters" were far less likely to hear those debates.

Clearly, selective exposure characterizes the voluntary audience rather than the audience required to receive a message. It follows, then, that voluntary audiences often hold views similar to those they expose themselves to, and therefore have little stimulation for the adoption of different views. This is essentially what happens. Those whose views the persuader would like to change have avoided his message. McGuire and Papageorgis (1961) concluded, after studying captive audiences used in experiments and voluntary mass media audiences, that significantly greater adoption effects are obtained with the former. Their explanation is that voluntary audiences can and will defend themselves against dissonant views through avoidance. Similarly, Hovland (1959) reconciled the conflicting results of experimental and survey studies by distinguishing between captive and voluntary audiences, and noting the practice of selective exposure. It is this effect that a number of writers likely had in mind in noting that the mass media are useful in supporting existing behavior (continuance goal) and of limited value in changing behavior (adoption and discontinuance goals).

Another aspect of selective exposure, of relevance to the persuader seeking an audience, is the finding that many people emphasize the use of local and personal message sources and avoid non-local sources with whom they have no personal contact. Such selectivity, in contrast to the behavior of the person who extends his exposure to sources beyond his locality and personal contacts, has led some authors to label the former as a "localite" and the latter a "cosmopolite." Evidence of these differing emphases in the selection of message-sources is reviewed in Rogers (1962). To the extent that a persuader is perceived as an outsider to the "localite," avoidance of exposure to his message is likely to occur. This happens, not because the localite perceives the outside source to have differing views, but simply because impersonal, non-local sources are not used by such persons.

Kris and Leites (1947) suggest another facet of selective exposure. The term used by the authors is *privatization.* It implies generalized avoidance rather than selective. Too much news, for example, is said to produce privatization. The receiver, overwhelmed by the amount and variety of information directed to him, responds by turning his back on all of it. He concerns himself predominantly with his private life over which he has more control. Other matters are left to the "experts." Perhaps a generalized avoidance is operating in the substantial proportions of potential audiences who fail to expose themselves to the most prestigeful speakers on important occasions. On the evening of Monday, September 26, 1960—the evening of the first Nixon-Kennedy television debate—about one-third of homes contacted reported their TV sets not in use. In fact, studies of the sizes of the available audiences for presidential speeches over both radio and television characteristically report large percentages of people not tuned in.

Further evidence of privatization is time after time reflected in the surveys of what the American public knows. For example, one would suppose that, after more than a decade of extensive news coverage and frequent crises, few Americans would be unaware of the existence of Communist China and Nationalist China. Yet in 1964, a survey of 1501 people, conducted by the University of Michigan Survey Research Center, revealed an incredible 28 per cent of the sample indicated they did not know "if there is a Communist government in China now." Moreover, 39 per cent did not know of the existence of the Nationalist Chinese government. Perhaps the most valid interpretation is that large numbers of people simply avoid contact with sources and messages they perceive as unneeded in their private lives.

## SECURING AN AUDIENCE

The problems in dealing with the avoidance tendency in potential receivers have led to a number of practices in securing desired audiences. They are not equally applicable to all situations in which an audience is sought. The persuader's task is to identify specifically what audience he seeks, and what means of securing audiences can be adapted to his resources. Solutions are more apt to be the result of problem-solving activity than the application of some stock formula for obtaining audiences. The major practices can be conveniently grouped under the following headings: (1) rewards for attendance or punishments for non-attendance, (2) the use of intermediary sources to diffuse messages, (3) the promotion of group rather than individual attendance, (4) techniques of agitation, (5) procedures to monopolize communication channels, and (6) the purchase or free access to audiences developed by others.

When the anticipated message is disturbing, rewards establish for the potential audience an avoidance-approach set of alternatives. From the persuader's view, it is hoped the reward strength exceeds that associated with avoidance. In like manner, punishments establish two avoidance alternatives; the object is to make avoidance of the punishment more attractive than avoidance of exposure. In the case when there is not sufficient interest or motivation for exposure, rewards provide motivation and create a captive (motivated) audience. Illustrative of the great variety of rewards used by persuaders are free dinners, door prizes, a program which includes attractive entertainment along with the message, opportunity to see celebrities, free admission, and free transportation. The choice of reward or punishment varies with circumstances and the particular audience sought. Automobile dealers often provide a contest with tempting prizes and require participants to obtain entry blanks at the dealer's showroom. This gives the salesman a chance to present a sales message. In contrast, the author was recently offered $30 in books to attend a six hour seminar. The reward was well designed for the type of audience sought. In establishing an expectation of reward, publicity is an extensively used practice. It provides messages about a forthcoming event, typically stressing the rewards associated with attendance. Illustrations of the use of publicity in obtaining audiences can be found in books on public relations (e.g., Cutlip and Center, 1964).

The value and necessity of using intermediary sources to pass along messages arises from the fact that receivers, through selective exposure, make it difficult for the persuader to reach them directly. Others must be used to carry messages to them. For example, UCLA Market Researcher Charles R. Campbell concludes that teenagers aid in developing mass buying trends involving the adult market by being the carrier of the persuader's effort into the family circle. With many receivers, if the persuader's message is to reach them, he must recognize and make use of the limited sources to which many receivers attend. Studies of diffusion (Rogers, 1962) identify an important intermediary, the opinion leader, in the process of diffusing a persuasive message. These individuals are sought out by their neighbors and associates. Their opinions are valued. If these individuals are persuaded, they in turn persuade others who respond to their opinions. The role of the opinion leader as an intermediary source suggests that persuaders might be less concerned about the number of persons reached directly and more concerned with the particular persons reached directly. The "opinion leader," of course, may have wider influence than a few neighbors or work associates. Frequently, clergymen, professors, labor leaders, business leaders, politicians, and newsmen are looked to as opinion leaders by substantial numbers of people. Through them, receivers not directly accessible can be reached.

Sometimes, an audience can be secured more effectively by promoting group attendance rather than that of individuals. The Billy Graham organization, in securing audiences for religious meetings, exemplifies this practice. Lang and Lang (1960) studied the results of this procedure in the Billy Graham Crusade held in New York's Madison Square Garden. They report that their 43 observers were clearly able to identify the organized audience elements as well as the many individuals who found their own unshepherded way to the Crusade. The substantial majority of the audience had been secured in groups. Apparently, the same method was used in Columbus, Ohio in the Summer of 1964. Local church officials were interviewed and reported organizing bus loads of church members; these groups formed a significant part of the audience.

Still other methods of securing exposure can be grouped together under the heading of agitation. *Life* (March 19, 1965) compiled a list of attacks on U.S. embassies, consulates, and USIS libraries. Between October 24, 1964 and March 4, 1965, 25 attacks occurred from the Sudan to Moscow to Venezuela. On October 24, Sudanese students broke into the U.S. embassy in Khartoum and ransacked the USIS library; on March 4, 1965, students attacked the U.S. embassy in Moscow. Similarly, lists of civil rights demonstrations, rallies, and riots, and "freedom of speech" demonstrations on college campuses could be compiled. Frequently, these are referred to as agitation or the work of agitators. The typical connotations of both words are negative, and unfortunately mask the value of agitation in persuasion.

Agitators, we note, sometimes arouse people through speech making, other times through non-verbal acts. The acts may be violent or nonviolent; violence is not a necessary characteristic of agitation. In the Berkeley affair in 1964–65, students and non-students carried signs on which the world's best known four-letter word was printed, made speeches, and read excerpts from *Lady Chatterley's Lover.* They were thrown in jail. Whether this performance, or wrecking a USIS library is agitation depends, not on what is done, but on what objective is sought. Not all acts, however threatening or disturbing, are agitation. A boycott, a strike, a bombing of an enemy base are not instances of agitation. The objective of the agitator is to prepare people for subsequent persuasive messages. The act of agitation contains no specific message, is not designed to force compliance, and is not engaged in as a cathartic experience for the participants. Its role is to create uncertainty about what is going to happen, to unstructure the world as potential receivers view it. It is designed to make people wonder if "God *is* in His Heaven and all *is* right with the world." Thus, agitation seeks to motivate, not to inform; it energizes people to reduce the uncertainty and tension it has created, often by exposing themselves to messages about the disturbing event.

The technique of agitation is to violate the expected, to violate the norms of the onlookers. The agitator says or does those things which are typically not expected in orderly social behavior. In view of this, it follows that the audience, upset and uncertain, is likely to view agitation unfavorably. Despite this, agitation secures an audience for subsequent persuasion. People are disturbed enough to lift their eyes from their usual routine. People seek the resolution of uncertainty or chaos in their worlds. For many of us, at least on some issues, there seems to be no other effective way of getting our attention. The role of uncertainty in getting people to expose themselves to persuasion and engage in recommended actions is commented on by Hoffer (1964). He views agitation as an essential method in the art of government.

> To dispose a soul to action we must upset its equilibrium. And if, as Napoleon wrote to Carnot, "The art of government is not to let man go stale," then it is essentially an art of unbalancing.

Agitation, viewed as a method of getting attention, differs from traditional attention-getting techniques. It emphasizes the internal determiners rather than the characteristics of stimuli that attract attention. Pillsbury (1908) and writers on persuasion, following his lead, have tended to stress those stimulus characteristics useful in getting attention. These include such features as intensity, contrast, novelty, movement and change, and repetition. The usefulness of this emphasis has been discarded to a considerable extent by psychologists. No contemporary text in general psychology includes a chapter on attention. The emphasis has shifted to discussions of motivation and perception. The contemporary position seems to be that, to stimulate people to expose themselves to persuasion, it is more effective to alter their motivational level and their perceptions of the situation in which they find themselves. What this means for the persuader is that agitation and other devices for altering the motivational levels of potential receivers is a more fruitful consideration in getting attention than the use of novelty, contrast, or action verbs in messages.

Finally, a group of procedures to reduce selective exposure has as its objective the control or monopoly of message-sources used by receivers. These methods generally are more available to nations or other organizations capable of extensive control over the major media of communication. When monopoly is mentioned, the first thought apt to come to mind is the monopolistic control of communication sources found in totalitarian countries. It is the monolithic state, we note, that outlaws private media of communication, jams broadcasts from outside its borders, restricts importation of books, newspapers, and magazines, and rigidly censors newsmen, speakers, authors, and others permitted to use the available channels. We perceive people in such countries exposed to a single viewpoint, that of the state. In such a situation, it is easy to see that the state increases the chances that receivers will expose themselves to its persuasion; little or no selection exists. The alternative is to shut out relevant information about one's environment. Most persons, however, cannot leave unsatisfied a need to know what is going on or what might happen.

In contrast, we perceive ourselves to have choice among message-sources. A wide variety of books, magazines, newspapers, and speakers are available to us. Having choice, however, is not the only consideration. Is choice exercised? For many, the answer is no. For many, the use of limited sources gives these sources a receiver-imposed monopoly over messages received. Thus, without censorship or the forceful elimination of competitive sources, practices which encourage limited exposure increase the influence of those remaining.

Access to audiences can be purchased or achieved by acquiring free space or time to present messages to audiences developed by others. The first of these is most extensively used in advertising. The details of purchase and the available audiences for sale are generally discussed in any good standard text, for example, Wright and Warner (1962). The purchase of advertising space or time, of course, does not carry with it freedom to present any desired message. When purchase is achieved, however, it does assure a specified set of opportunities to present a message. The practice of obtaining free access to audiences characterizes the public relations field (Cutlip and Center, 1964). Often the PR specialist who wants his message exposed must get "free" help from the mass media. His message, to be used, must dovetail with the needs of the media contacted. To the extent the media editors judge the message will satisfy and retain their audiences it will be accepted. Without this harmony of goals, the PR message may end up in a wastebasket. Despite this requirement, success in placing a message is common.

## rejection: non-instrumentality of message

In one experiment after another, the reader cannot help but notice the large percentage of persons who apparently do not change, who reveal no significant affective, cognitive, or overt change in behavior. Even where the effect measured is information gained, many show no significant change. The kind of "no change" I have in mind is tensionless. For this type of response or lack of response I prefer the term "rejection" to distinguish it from "resistance," which implies tension. The principal explanation of tensionlessness is the lack of motivation. No unsatisfied need has been aroused. Generally, motivation is conceived as a state of tension brought on by some unsatisfied need. Another explanation of rejection is frustration. In the face of all the messages directed to him, the powerless person in our society perhaps feels he is not a protagonist in his own drama, but merely an unheard offstage voice. He reacts with rejection and indifference. Among many of the younger generation, the "cool cat" has become the ideal; why get "steamed up" over issues one has no part in resolving?

Unlike selective exposure, the rejected message reaches the receiver. He sees the advertisement on the highway billboard, looks at the TV commercial, or, as a captive audience, hears the political address, the Sunday morning sermon, or the experimental stimulus-message. Presumably, the message is perceived and assigned meaning; yet no further measurable response occurs. Relating this phenomenon to the model of the persuasion process presented in Chapter 9, it can be hypothesized that whatever meaning is aroused is an insufficient stimulus for further responses. This suggests that meaning does not automatically, necessarily, or invariably operate as a generative force for further behavior. It is not enough that a receiver be exposed to a message and perceive its meaning, or even repetitively be presented a message. To approve of, believe in, and act upon a message requires that it be relevant to or activate some need in the receiver.

Another possible explanation of rejection may lie in the nature of the needs that messages may arouse. Not all needs, even when activated, lead to action. A distinction can be drawn, as Deese (1964) has done, between manifest and latent needs. The former lead to action by the individual in attempting to satisfy them. Latent needs are met through responses such as dreaming, fantasy, escape experiences in reading, vicarious behavior in the lives of others, fictional or real. What is sought in persuasion is the activation of manifest needs, those that lead to action, hopefully in a form desired. When aroused need is satisfied by symbolic processing of experiences, the action-goals of persuasion are thwarted. Such symbolic processing, rather than action, may well lead to no change in the affective, cognitive, and action components of behavior. The result is rejection, the lack of need to respond with action.

The cost of rejection in a persuasive effort can be sizeable. For example, in *Fortune* (January, 1963) some of the casualties of rejection were discussed. The article concerned the tobacco industry and the launching of new brands of cigarettes. It noted that the promotion costs in introducing a new cigarette are approximately ten million dollars. Among the casualties were Hit Parade and Riviera, 1956 and 1959 introductions by the American Tobacco Company, and Kentucky Kings, a 1960 effort by the Brown and Williamson Company. Similarly, political persuasive campaigns commonly fail to penetrate an indifference which seems to insulate the receiver from stimulation. To the extent these failures reflect rejection, it becomes a limitation to be reckoned with.

Janis and Feshbach (1953) present findings which suggest another aspect of rejection. In this case, high school students were captive audiences without choice to avoid exposure. Their results suggest that the subjects avoided or rejected a disturbing message either by not thinking about it or by simply not accepting its seriousness. The experimenters developed three illustrated speeches each 15 minutes in length on the topic of dental hygiene. The principal difference in the speeches was the amount of fear-arousing material. Each speech contained the same set of recommendations on oral hygiene practices. All speeches were presented by the same speaker.

Speech I provided a strong fear appeal along with the use of personalized threat-references directed to the audience ("This can happen to you"). Speech II (moderate appeal) described fewer dangerous consequences of improper oral hygiene in a more factual way, using impersonal language. Speech III (minimal appeal) provided little reference to dangers and tended to deal with social effects such as appearance. A questionnaire was given to students one week after the speeches to determine changes in dental hygiene practices. These effects are presented in Table 7.

## TABLE 7

### Effects of Talks on Conformity to Dental Hygiene Recommendations

| Type of change | Strong fear % change N = 50 | Moderate fear % change N = 50 | Minimal fear % change N = 50 | Control group % change N = 50 |
|---|---|---|---|---|
| Increased conformity | 28 | 44 | 50 | 22 |
| Decreased conformity | 20 | 22 | 14 | 22 |
| No change | 52 | 34 | 36 | 56 |
| Net change | 8 | 22 | 36 | 0 |
| Significance of differences | | CR | P value | |
| Control vs minimal | | 2.54 | <.01 | |
| Control vs moderate | | 1.50 | <.07 | |
| Control vs strong | | 0.59 | <.28 | |

In terms of developing responses in the form of overt behavior, the strong use of fear was surprisingly ineffective. Such strong fear appeals are frequently found in the persuasive communications presented via the press, radio, television, and other mass media. Fear has been used with such topics as the H-bomb and civil defense, highway accidents, excessive speed, and safety belt campaigns, the problem of syphilis in military groups, and in an effort to frighten people into paying their proper income tax. The Bureau of Internal Revenue, about each February, seems to like a story well publicized of some income tax cheat getting his comeuppance.

The ineffectiveness of strong fear appeals is open to several interpretations. Among the reasons suggested are that the receiver has learned to minimize the threat, fails to pay attention to what is being said, or has developed a defense through rejection. People do not always cope with the external problem which they face. They may resort to defending themselves against their anxieties and neglect the situation confronting them. They reject consideration of messages relevant to that situation. With a situation such as the H-bomb and civil defense, Dollard and Miller (1950) suggest another explanation for the lack of recommended behavior. The receiver wishes to avoid disrupting his way of living and at the same time avoid death by the bomb. This is described as an avoidance-avoidance conflict. In this kind of conflict the receiver must choose between two undesirable alternatives. If he moves away from one of the choices toward the second, the avoidance tendency to the second becomes greater and the person moves back toward the first choice. This kind of situation Dollard and Miller call a stable equilibrium; the individual vacillates and does not take definite action, and may withdraw, or reject consideration of the problem.

## MOTIVATING THE RECEIVER

One approach in dealing with rejection involves the arousal of manifest needs, those that energize the individual to engage in action, those that are not to be satisfied through daydreaming, fantasy, or other symbolic experience. The techniques of agitation, discussed earlier, function to do this. They serve to unstructure or unfreeze the individual's perception of his environment. His view of reality is challenged. The disturbance becomes a matter to be satisfied, not by dreams, but by actions in coping with threats and changes implicit in the agitation. His environment becomes something no longer to be taken for granted, no longer a matter of indifference to him. The behavior of people in response to agitation further suggests that when it takes an action form it is more likely to generate a readiness for action in those exposed. A demonstration, for example, is more likely to evoke action than a printed editorial or a speech in conventional surroundings.

If motivation is the means of dealing with rejection, it should be clear that energizing an urge to act is not wholly satisfactory to the persuader. Deese (1964) points out that there are two basic problems in motivating others. One is the problem of activation; how is behavior to be energized? The other is the problem of direction, or what conditions determine the particular action that a motivated person will take? Both problems are relevant to the persuader. To successfully stimulate receivers to action is not enough to assure the achievement of the persuader's goal. In addition, a particular direction or form of the action must be promoted. It is for this reason that agitation, or other devices to activate, must be followed by subsequent messages. These provide direction for the action to take.

Murray (1938) has contributed a useful distinction to a perspective on the role of persuasive messages in motivating receivers. He distinguishes between what he calls a *press* and a *need*. A need is a condition within the individual; a press is an external condition requiring action, an external circumstance pressing from the outside. A persuader's message is designed to develop such a circumstance. Presses serve to activate needs. For example, if a person has a need for aggression, a frustrating work experience such as being refused a raise or promotion may activate that need. In the persuasive event, the message and the meaning it arouses operate as a press. The message does not create a need; it arouses an already existing need.

Finally, this discussion of motivation attempts no catalog of man's needs or to specify their order of importance. A list, for example, headed by self-preservation as the most potent motive is not provided. Such a list is of limited usefulness in assessing the needs that might be activated in a given situation. It serves best to suggest the variety of goals that may have, in various situations and with different people, motivational value. Some kind of record was established early in this century by the psychologist, E. L. Thorndike. He listed approximately one hundred motives. It was in following this practice that some of the older books in psychology and chapters in persuasion texts became tiresome to read and unrewarding in understanding human motivation. In contrast, contemporary motivation literature seems substantially agreed that no order of importance of the motives can be substantiated by evidence; self-preservation, for instance, in some circumstances is not the most impelling of motives. Furthermore, there is little or no evidence for secondary or derived motives, often implied by such lists, which are thought to function even though the biological motive upon which the secondary goal is based is satiated (Deese, 1964).

## distortion: cognitive restructuring

An unsought response in receivers, generative of unfavorable subsequent actions, is that of "cognitive restructuring." Although the objective of the persuader's message is to arouse a particular meaning, it frequently happens that his intention is distorted or restructured. The meaning assigned is more the result of receiver appraisal of source intention than the message. The same message, without the potent effect of source association, would arouse more of a face-value meaning. Thus, this effect tends to arise when the receiver has strong affective responses, likes or dislikes, toward the source.

We expect, for example, those we perceive as good men to say good messages; these two "facts" are congruent. But when the good man says or is reported to have said a bad message, we alter the meaning of the message to make it consistent with the source. We decide the good source intended a different meaning than the face-meaning of the message would suggest. Consider the reactions of many of those strongly favorable to Republican candidate Goldwater in the 1964 presidential election in response to his message, "Extremism in the defense of liberty is not a vice; moderation in the pursuit of justice is not a virtue." Many of his stanch supporters, including his campaign organization, offered explanations of what the message really meant. Those without strong feelings toward the nominee, took the message more at face-value and did not offer explanations of what he intended to say. This example is not meant to declare what was the nominee's meaning, but to illustrate that restructuring of meaning arises in those with emotional attachments to or animosities toward a message-source.

Similarly, a bad man (head of a rival, threatening nation) is expected to hold bad ideas and say bad messages. If he communicates a message, the face-value of which would suggest a good message, we are apt to react with "That's not what he really means," or "You can't believe a thing he says." This is the notion, as the American Indian is supposed to have said, that the enemy speaks with a forked tongue. The apparent message meaning is not considered the intended meaning. Thus, when a U.S. President declares we seek peace, not territory, in Asia, it is to be expected that Chinese Communists would distort the face-meaning of this message. Similarly, when Russian officials advocate peaceful coexistence, many Americans are sure that what is meant is that we may peacefully coexist as slaves. Again, this is not an argument that these Americans are wrong in their appraisal, but an illustration of our tendency to read into a message a meaning consistent with our feelings toward the source.

Cognitive restructuring is supported by research. Lewis' (1947) experiments involved assigning statements or messages to highly approved and highly disapproved sources. When the "good" source was reported to approve a "bad" message, interviews with subjects revealed their tendency to justify the approval by restructuring the meaning of the message. When the "bad" source approved a "good" message, he was called a hypocrite or liar who did not mean what the message should mean. The message was restructured to have a more congruent meaning.

Other conditions, similar to source-message incongruity, that bring about distortion and the restructuring of meaning are (1) dissonance between belief and behavior, and (2) inconsistencies with our established view of reality. When belief and behavior are dissonant, what frequently results is the restructuring of belief rather than behavioral changes. For example, a smoker may change "his facts" about the harm of smoking rather than give up the habit. A smoker may distort, upon hearing or reading a set of facts about smoking, the meaning of those facts. For the smoker, cognitive restructuring may be easier. Future health may be less motivating than the desire and habit of smoking. In any event, what he "knows" about smoking tends to be that which justifies his habit. In a survey of opinion about the relationship of cigarette smoking and lung cancer, only 7 per cent of heavy smokers versus 29 per cent of non-smokers believed that the relationship had been proved (Festinger, 1957).

The circumstances under which meaning distortion occurs suggest some of the means of reducing it. Clearly, when it is apparent that receivers feel unfavorably toward a source, the use of other more neutral or favorable sources is indicated. The practice is common. Other sources are enlisted in presenting the message. In cases where an individual's "facts" are distorted to be consistent with his behavior, one approach begins with a determination of what he considers to be the "facts." The fast automobile driver, for example, may have found it convenient to believe that speed is unrelated to accidents. Such a "fact" may be effectively discredited in further messages. In instances of meaning distortion to make them consistent with other beliefs, it seems desirable to spell out the implications of messages. Some message forms such as cartoons, pictures, and events generally leave the implications unspecified; these invite meaning distortion.

## *congruity effects*

Closely related to distortion, resulting from cognitive restructuring, is the unsought effect in which the persuader loses popularity by supporting unpopular ideas. Similarly, a popular idea may lose support because it is advocated by an unpopular source. Osgood and Tannenbaum (1955) postulated a "principle of congruity" to explain these effects. Although the principle would apply generally to the interaction of any attitudes held by an individual, most persuasion studies have focused on the interaction of attitudes toward source and idea held by the receiver.

In persuasion terms, the principle of congruity states that when a receiver's attitudes toward source and idea are different, *both* will change in such a way that greater harmony between the two attitudes is brought about. Such changes may be either cognitive or affective. Although Lewis (1947) discussed the individual's effort to make the elements in a situation congruous, she was concerned particularly with the change of message meaning as the means of achieving harmony. In this case, the means of achieving harmony involves changing responses to both source and idea.

The study of Berlo and Gulley (1957) illustrates the effect involved. They used 174 listeners. Two predictions were made for each listener; the first predicted attitude change with respect to the speaker, and the second attitude change with respect to the idea. Predictions were made in the direction of greater harmony between the two. Of 174 predictions of the direction of attitude change for the speaker, 117 were verified; for the idea, 112 predictions were confirmed. In both cases, the number of correct predictions significantly exceeded that which could be attributed solely to chance ($p < .0001$).

The authors further specify that (1) the greater the difference between a receiver's attitudes toward source and idea, the greater the pressure to change, and (2) of the two attitudes, that which is more extreme will exert greater pressure for change on the less extreme attitude. From these propositions predictions were made of the size as well as the direction of each change. Obtained change scores correlated significantly with predicted scores ($r=.63$ for speaker scores, and $r=.71$ for idea scores).

Bettinghaus (1961) also studied the operation of this principle. He used speeches on four different issues; drinking regulations, grading curves, parking regulations, and the eighteen-year-old vote. The speeches were presented by four different speakers to groups of undergraduates totaling 178. Bettinghaus concludes that receivers tended to shift attitudes about source and idea to more congruous positions, although his results were not as significant as those of Berlo and Gulley.

Byrne (1961) had subjects fill out attitude scales. Later he showed members of one group the same scale but presumably filled out by a "stranger." For each member of this group, the "stranger's" scale was filled out the same as his own. Members of the second group also received a "stranger's" scale but filled out to indicate dissimilar attitudes. Both groups were asked to appraise the "stranger" from his revealed attitudes. The results showed the first group indicated significantly more positive feelings toward the "stranger" than the group who received scales reflecting dissimilar attitudes. Moreover, the similar attitude group rated the "stranger" higher on intelligence, knowledge of current events, morality, and adjustment.

If the persuader proposes to espouse unpopular ideas, perhaps his first step in dealing with the consequent disapproval he will receive is to recognize the likelihood of this reaction. Knowing its probability, he is better able to judge his willingness to accept loss of personal popularity. In addition to experimental evidence, history is replete with instances of the price exacted for championing unpopular causes. This, of course, is no solution, only an appraisal of the costs involved. It is this cost which has promoted that persuasive behavior in leaders which has come to be called leadership-through-followership. The road to popularity and the retention of office is to support what is already approved and attack what is already widely disapproved.

Another approach to the handling of unpopular ideas, other than avoiding them, is the trial balloon method. Organizations engaged in persuasion, such as a government, sometimes find it useful to launch an idea without involving the organization's leaders. If the idea's reception is uncertain, it can be "leaked" to friends in the news services. Its reaction can be studied, and in turn overtly supported, altered, or denied. Another form of this method is to have the idea presented by someone not perceived as an official spokesman of the organization. In a sense, his popularity is expendable without threatening the popularity of the organization's leadership. Such methods are forms of pre-testing an idea prior to the main effort to persuade. Frequently, other sources such as the press find it consistent with their own goals to continue producing messages and serving more than a pre-testing function for the persuader. Political campaigns frequently furnish illustrations of other sources performing a dominant role in presenting messages which might harm a candidate's popularity if he were perceived as the source. For example, the 1964 Kerner-Percy gubernatorial campaign in Illinois exposed a conflict of interest scandal in the Kerner administration, involving his campaign manager. Kerner's opponent, Charles Percy, said nothing about the scandal in his effort to persuade the electorate. Newspapers and other mass media were saying all that needed to be said without his aid.

A "both sides" presentation of an issue is useful in handling unpopular ideas and in reducing loss of source-acceptance. This method was discussed earlier in Chapter 3; experimental evidence favored its use with audiences opposed to the speaker's position. What matters here is that the method avoids or reduces loss of source-popularity. By acknowledging those counter-beliefs held by the audience, the source is perceived as more fair and responsible in his treatment of the issue.

## *forgetting: selective recall*

The results of research and informal observation overwhelmingly verify that receivers forget cognitive elements in a communication event. Knower, Phillips, and Koeppel (1945), for instance, found that information gained from listening to or reading speeches decreased approximately 40 per cent between measures of immediate recall and delayed recall. Although studies generally have dealt with forgetting knowledge of content, forgetfulness of source, media or any other "knowledge" the receiver initially acquired from the message may occur.

Studies have used three different indices of retention. The first is *recognition;* the receiver is asked to identify the material or other cognitive elements presented. Recognition is frequently measured through the use of true-false or multiple-choice items in a test. The second measure of forgetting is *recall;* the receiver is asked to reproduce the information. Completion or fill-in questions are commonly used to indicate recall. The third measure of forgetting is *"relearning."* The receiver is asked to learn the material a second time; the economy in learning the second time is tested. Comparisons of these three measures, done by Luh (1922), show that the rate of forgetting is greatest for recall and least for recognition. More receivers can be expected to recognize, for a longer period of time, something presented in a message than can recall it. For this reason, it is to be expected that receivers are more likely to recognize a product name, a trademark, or a candidate's name than to recall why the product is superior or what the candidate advocates. In all three forms of retention, however, significant forgetting occurs.

In persuasion, which attempts to modify meanings as a means of generating further effects, the forgetting of material which disagrees with the receiver's beliefs is particularly pertinent. Studies confirm the conclusion that controversial material in messages is forgotten more rapidly than content consistent with the receiver's views. Among illustrative studies is that of Watson and Hartmann (1939). The authors studied the abilities of theistic and atheistic students to recall material which supported or opposed their position. They concluded that supporting messages were retained better. Edwards (1941) gave ten-minute speeches to college students. The speeches were pro-New Deal, neutral, and anti-New Deal. The relative amount forgotten was related to the degree of conflict between the message and the receiver's beliefs. Levine and Murphy (1947) used pro-Communist and anti-Communist receivers. These subjects read passages on Russia which supported or opposed their viewpoints. They were asked to reproduce the material read at various time intervals from fifteen minutes after initial exposure to nine weeks later. They were given the material to reread before each test period during the first four weeks, and then retested during the next five weeks without further exposure. The results were that these receivers learned the favorable material better and forgot it less. As the learning and forgetting periods increased the differences became greater. Wallen (1942) asked experimental subjects to check 40 adjectives; each person checked which adjectives described him and which did not. A week later each subject was shown a set of check marks presumably made by someone describing him. Half the checks agreed with the way the subject checked himself and half did not. Two days later, subjects were asked to recall the "fictitious" marks. Errors of recall on checks that disagreed with the subject's own evaluation were significantly greater than those checks with which he agreed. From such studies, this tendency to differentially forget has been called "selective recall." It implies that what is remembered or forgotten is more than a matter of chance. Studies of this tendency also reveal that forgetting is more of a handicap to the persuader than other communicators.

### REDUCTION OF FORGETTING

Evidence favoring the retention of non-controversial ideas warrants the development of methods to make use of this finding. One practice, already in use, might well be called the method of escalation. It involves the presentation of a series of ideas, beginning with those least different from receiver views, and as these become acceptable, escalate to those more provocative ideas for which greater readiness for acceptance has been developed. This has been employed recently in a campaign to persuade women to smoke cigars. The same procedure was used to introduce cigarettes to women. In the initial phases of the campaign, women are shown to be interested, curious, ready to light the male's cigar. The outright recommendation that they smoke cigars is not presented; it would violate their norms and be objectionable. Gradually, ideas that move closer and closer to the desired behavior are offered. The method would, of course, have other applications such as the acceptance of ideas on birth control or any new, provocative policy. When ideas are being established, persuasion becomes the art of the possible.

Ewing (1942) experimented with another method. He recognized that what is important in making an idea controversial is not the actual difference between an advocated view and that of the receiver, but the difference perceived by the receiver. He set about to alter that perception. The same message was given to two groups. To the first group, it was introduced as a controversial message, opposed in content to their beliefs. To the second group, it was declared to be consistent and supportive of their beliefs. Greater change of opinion, acceptance of the ideas, occurred in the second group. Altering perception to reduce the controversy gap is also promoted by the names given to programs or organizations. A Job Corps will be perceived more acceptably than a Youth Unemployment Program. The American Council for Civic Responsibility is perceived less controversially than a Committee to Expose Rightist Literature.

The point should not be overlooked that forgetting occurs with noncontroversial ideas. Themes used in advertising or in platforms of political candidates, though often in harmony with receiver views, face this effect. This seems particularly the result where there is low motivation for the ideas presented. For this reason, the method of repetition is used extensively in advertising, political campaigns, and public service campaigns such as conservation and safety. The ideas to be retained are repeated over and over. Additionally, the ideas to be established are formed into slogans, rhymes, or new lyrics to a familiar melody. This is done to aid retention.

## discontinuance of beliefs and feeling

Somewhat related to forgetting is the discontinuance of a belief or feeling. Both can represent the discontinuance of a desired effect, instrumental to a persuader's action-goal. Many studies, in which a delayed measure of belief or feeling is made, provide evidence of discontinuance. Thistlewaite and Kamenetsky (1955), for example, used four different types of speeches; effects were measured immediately after stimulus presentation and three weeks later. In all cases, the immediate effects in establishing beliefs wore off to a significant degree over the three week period. The need to re-establish belief through repetition or restatement is suggested by such findings. Methods of reducing the discontinuance of preliminary effects as well as action are brought together, because of their similarity, in Chapter 11.

## disassociation

With respect to persuasive goals, another unfavorable effect is that of disassociation of source and content. Though source and message are communicated together there exists a tendency for the receiver, after a period of time, to disassociate one from the other. He forgets the source but remembers the message; he remembers the source and not the message; he attaches a new source to the message, or new message to a source. In everyday observation we see the operation of this effect in gossip, rumor, and plagiarism. The gossip or rumor is repeated; its source is forgotten. This seems particularly the case if the message is desired but the source is unacceptable. In unintentional plagiarism, the actual source of a good idea is less important to us than the idea. We may unknowingly disassociate the actual author from the idea, thus making it ours. The disassociation effect is particularly relevant when, in persuasion, a highly approved source is used to help establish a belief. The benefit of such a source deteriorates because of disassociation. In contrast, ideas presented by a disapproved source are apt to benefit from this effect.

Hovland and Weiss (1951) prepared written messages on four topics of current interest. For each topic a high and a low credibility source was used. Immediately after students read the messages, measures of opinion change were made. Those students who read the material when it was associated with credible sources made significantly ($p < .01$) more changes in the direction of the messages than those students who thought they were reading from non-credible sources. Four weeks later, student opinion was measured again. The differences between the sources had virtually disappeared. And of most interest was the fact that students who read non-credible sources *increased* their approval of the content, while students who read highly approved sources *decreased* in acceptance of the ideas. These findings are provided in Table 8.

TABLE 8

NET PER CENT OF SUBJECTS CHANGING OPINION IN DIRECTION OF COMMUNICATION

| Source and time of measurements | Net per cent changing |
|---|---|
| High credibility source | |
| Immediately after communication | 23.0 |
| Four weeks after communication | 12.3 |
| Low credibility source | |
| Immediately after communication | 6.6 |
| Four weeks after communication | 14.0 |

One explanation of the increase in approval of the content of these messages is that the source and content became disassociated. In explaining this effect the authors point out that, "This may or may not require that the source be forgotten. But the individual must be less likely with the passage of time to associate spontaneously the content with source." For subjects reading low credibility sources, the authors found that those who showed increased belief forgot the source about as much as those who showed decreased belief.

Other evidence that appears to support the disassociation effect is found in Hovland, Lumsdaine, and Sheffield (1949) and Kelman and Hovland (1953). The message stimulus in the first study was a film, *The Battle of Britain.* Effects were measured five days and nine weeks after exposure. Opinion changes showed an average *increase* between the earlier and later measures. In the second study, it was confirmed again that the benefit of an approved source declined over time. The experiment, however, provided for the "reinstatement" of sources; that is, receivers were reminded of the sources of the messages presented. This apparently served to nullify the disassociation effect. Belief in the ideas, reinforced by approved sources, rose substantially. This suggests that subsequent effort to re-associate idea and source is called for to sustain belief.

## resistance: contrast effects

Resistance, unlike rejection, is conceived as a tension involving response. It is not an indifferent response to a message, occurring in an unmotivated person. On the contrary, it is a response expected among receivers who not only tend to have a pro or con position on a message-idea, but hold their position with some intensity. This group of receivers would also include that "neutral" individual who intensely maintains his neutrality. Two forms resistance may take are a "no change" or a change in opposition to that desired. The latter response has been called a contrast or boomerang effect in persuasion. It is with this second type of response that resistance can most validly be inferred.

Several experiments have been conducted to examine contrast effects. From these, several dimensions of contrast effects emerge. The first is an affective response. The response is less favorable to the position supported in the message *after* receiving it than *before*. The second is a cognitive response. The receiver perceives the persuader's position further away from his position than other evidence shows it to be. Presumably, a third response is possible, that of contrast or boomerang behavior. In this instance, the receiver would overtly behave more negatively after the message than before. Such behavior was discussed by Allport (1924) under what he called negativism. Contemporary thought tends to use the term "naysayer" to label those likely to respond in contrast to the effects desired. It is thought that some persons are characteristically naysayers while others are yessayers. Perhaps the most useful distinctions between these two response sets is that one involves stimulus resistance while the other is associated with a set for stimulus acceptance. The set of the naysayer results in resisting the admission of stimuli to consciousness without censorship or distortion.

An illustrative example of contrast effects is given in Hovland, Harvey, and Sherif (1957). Messages (tape recorded speeches about 15 minutes each) were developed to present two opposite extremes and one moderate position on the controversial issue of prohibition and repeal in a dry state (Oklahoma). The speeches were presented to receivers who had taken a public stand on the issue or belonged to a group (WTCU) known to have a position, as well as to unselected audiences. Their data on opinion change are reproduced in Table 9.

TABLE 9

OPINION CHANGE: PERCENTAGE OF SUBJECTS CHANGING IN THE DIRECTION OF THE COMMUNICATION OR IN AN OPPOSED DIRECTION

| Group and communication | N | % of change toward communication | % no change | % of change opposing communication | % net change |
|---|---|---|---|---|---|
| Wet communication | | | | | |
| Dry Ss | 69 | 27.5 | 49.3 | 23.2 | 4.5* |
| Unselected Ss | 92 | 52.2 | 23.9 | 23.9 | 28.3 |
| Dry communication | | | | | |
| Wet Ss | 25 | 24.0 | 56.0 | 20.0 | 4.0 |
| Unselected Ss | 87 | 40.2 | 33.4 | 26.4 | 13.8 |
| Mod. wet comm. | | | | | |
| Dry Ss | 114 | 31.6 | 49.1 | 19.3 | 12.3 |

* Diff. between net changes significant ($p < .04$ one tail).

The more committed "dry" and "wet" subjects, especially with the more opposing speeches, responded with significantly larger combined percentages of "no change" and "change opposing the communication." Following the strong wet speech, 72.5 per cent of dry subjects resisted change toward the position advocated while only 47.8 percent responded similarly among the unselected subjects. The comparable percentages for the dry speech were 76.0 and 59.8 per cent. Although some persons in all groups may have simply rejected rather than resisted the message, this was more likely to occur in the less committed, less involved groups. Thus, the inference of resistance may be more valid than the data suggest.

Affective responses specifically suggesting contrast with the communicator's position are the percentages of subjects whose change after the speech is in a "direction opposed to the communication." Cognitive responses were studied with respect to the moderately wet speech. The authors report "Those at the wet end judge(d) the communication advocated a drier position that it did and those at the dry end judge(d) that it was advocating a wetter position than it did."

Gibson (1962) compared the shifts of opposed subjects with control subjects in response to a speech on censorship. When control group shifts were used as a norm, he found that 36 per cent of his experimental subjects made significant changes in opposition to the speeches. Two studies, reported by Katz and Feldman (1962), suggest that the first Nixon-Kennedy debate produced unfavorable attitudes for both candidates in opposition party viewers; the Democrats became much more unfavorable to Mr. Nixon. In view of the goals of the candidates, these constitute contrast effects.

Manis (1960) found some evidence for cognitive contrast effects particularly among those most in opposition to the message. Undergraduate students wrote paragraphs about fraternities, and were tested for attitude toward fraternities. Four profraternity, four antifraternity, and four relatively neutral paragraphs were selected and presented to 70 undergraduates enrolled in a psychology class. They were asked to predict the attitudes held by the writers. Receiver attitudes were also measured before exposure. Antifraternity readers rated profraternity writers more pro than was found in measuring writers' attitudes, and profraternity readers displayed the same contrast effect for antifraternity writers.

## REDUCTION OF CONTRAST EFFECTS

Existing research provides a basis for hypothesizing, as was done by Hovland, Harvey and Sherif (1957), about one condition that will permit a prediction of those receivers who will resist a persuader's message. Their thinking suggests a useful method in reducing resistance. Three ideas are offered: first, each individual receiver has a region of acceptance and region of resistance with respect to an incoming message; second, persons who hold extreme attitudes toward an idea have smaller regions of acceptance and larger regions of resistance; third, if an idea is within an individual's region of acceptance he will tend to assimilate or approve it, and if not, it is predicted he will resist it or engage in contrast behavior. These notions are graphically presented in Figure 15.

In Figure 15, it can be seen that receivers holding moderate or neutral positions (3, 4, 5) have larger ranges of acceptance. For these receivers, ideas more removed from their own position still have a probability of being accepted. A person, for example, whose position is slightly unfavorable to an idea might find a slightly or moderately

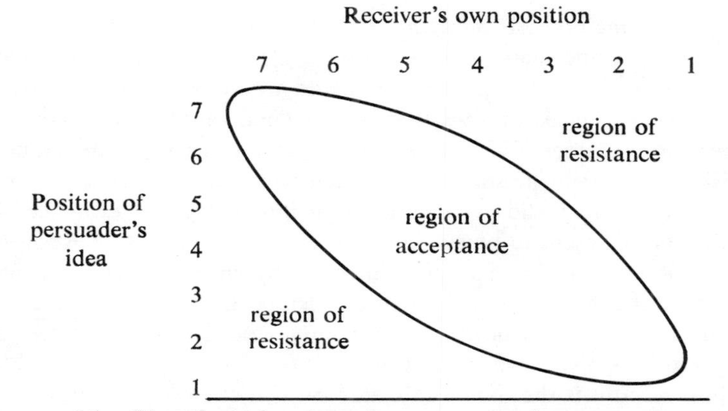


FIGURE 15. Hypothetical regions of acceptance and resistance for receivers holding various attitudes toward ideas of varying degrees of extremeness. The (1) and (7) positions represent extreme positions, pro or con toward an idea.

favorable message acceptable. In contrast, receivers with extreme attitudes (1, 7) are likely to accept only those ideas quite close to their position. For an extremely favorable receiver, a moderately favorable idea might still be resisted. Observations of extreme groups, Right or Left, seem to confirm this. Often such groups attack those with more moderate positions yet on the same side of the political fence as themselves.

These notions suggest that persuaders do well to predetermine the position held by prospective receivers. It is to be expected, of course, that greater acceptance is to be found among receivers not far removed from the position advocated. Such an audience provides the greatest probable yield from a persuasive effort. In presenting messages to groups holding extreme positions, it seems realistic for the persuader to seek acceptance for ideas only slightly different from the position of his receivers. Over time, it may be possible to escalate through a series of small changes to a substantial change from the original one. Finally, it seems a better expenditure of resources to reach those moderate or neutral receivers; more substantial changes in belief are predictable. Such a decision was made, for example, in The Ohio Right-to-Work campaign in 1958. The organizations opposing the issue concentrated successfully on those voters considered to hold moderate or uncommitted views.

Another method of reducing resistance is to decrease receiver perception of the persuader's intent to persuade. There is evidence that people resist an intent to persuade them, and are more influenced if that intent is not perceived. This was the experimental variable in a study by Walster and Festinger (1957). It was found that when receivers did not perceive an intent to persuade them, they were more influenced than another group which did perceive such an intent. Further evidence of resistance of an intent to persuade is suggested in a finding of Knower (1936). Of persons significantly influenced by speeches, 24 per cent, when asked if they had been influenced, denied that they had been so affected. This implies a need for autonomy, a need to resist perceived attempts to influence. One interesting practice which seems to take this need into account is the use of animated cartoon characters to present a persuasive message. Characters such as Smokey Bear, Mickey Mouse and Donald Duck probably evoke little need to resist this type of source.

A widely used practice in reducing the perceived intent to persuade involves the use of communication forms not typically associated with persuasion. Among these are: newspaper reports, TV newscasts, documentary films, comic books, research reports, textbooks, movies, novels, songs, lectures, and seminars. Smith (1965), in an unpublished study found significant differences in the perception of persuasive intent between such forms and the traditional ones—for example, newspaper editorials, TV commercials, and advertisements.

## summary

The substance of this chapter is that people vary a great deal in their responses to messages, more so than to many other kinds of stimuli. One determinant of this high variance is the fact that a particular set of words is not the same message to different people. Message meaning, even for the "same" message, is a highly individual and variable experience. Among the varied responses to messages are many that are unsought and detrimental to the persuader's goals. These effects can be grouped into two categories: (1) those, though not actions in themselves, which are generative of unsought subsequent actions, and (2) those actions which the persuader does not want. It is the first group that is considered in this chapter. Among those pre-action effects of messages which seem sufficiently identified and verified by research are:

selective exposure, rejection, distortion, congruity effects, selective recall, discontinuance of feelings and beliefs, disassociation of source and message, and resistance effects. For each of these unsought effects, methods applicable to its reduction or prevention have been discussed.

# Chapter 11

# Unsought Action Responses

The responses to messages discussed in the previous chapter are instrumental in bringing about behavior unsought by the persuader. These forms of behavior replace the desired goals of adoption, deterrence, continuance, and discontinuance; they represent failures of persuasion as a form of influence. Verification and appraisal of these unwanted actions contribute to a richer perspective on persuasion. Methods of lessening these forms of behavior more directly supplement those useful in reducing unsought meanings as well as the undesired cognitive and affective responses to those message meanings.

## *adoption delay*

The types of behavior people can be persuaded to adopt has no end. They have been persuaded to buy new products such as frozen foods, plastic dishes, contact lenses, outdoor rotisseries; to participate in a "free speech" demonstration, a picket line, sit-in; to use self-service laundromats, travel services, airplane travel, employment agencies; to become members of the Ku Klux Klan, The Congress of Racial Equality, churches, service clubs, front organizations; to use new methods of farming, manicuring grass, teaching students, processing data; to adopt the "new look," "old look," "casual look," beards, crew cuts, wigs; to vote for candidates, new taxes for schools, highways, and welfare, approve prohibition or repeal it; to sign a petition, write a letter to a senator, or contribute to a political campaign fund.

To obtain initial adoption of behavior, in response to persuasive stimulation, frequently involves a good deal of energy and money over a considerable period of time. The rate of adoption has not had extensive attention and measurement in persuasion. Again, this requires repeated measures of the same subjects or many samplings from the same population of subjects. Experimenters have concentrated more on immediate effects. Additionally, the message-stimulus has typically been a one-shot affair; much less is known that would be applicable to lengthy persuasive campaigns. Some evidence is found in the sales trends of products but frequently new customer adoption is confounded with repeat orders. Better evidence is found in studies of innovations and their diffusion. Rogers (1962) provides illustrative figures on the length of adoption periods—the time between awareness of a recommended action and its adoption. These appear in Table 10.

When adoption-times are arranged in frequency distributions, it has been found that most of the distributions are normal or "bell-shaped" in character (Rogers, 1962). If, however, these are cast into accumulative frequency distributions, a finding of significance for persuasion is more explicitly revealed. Figure 16 is designed to illustrate a typical distribution of this type.

S-shaped distributions have been produced for a number of studies of adoption rate. They typically show a slow rate of adoption early in a persuasive campaign, then the steep incline of the curve shows a rapid rate of adoption, and finally the rate slows again during the effort to persuade the "holdouts." The implications of this for one's perspective on persuasion are: it is to be expected that the adoption rate will be slow at first; it is probable that the best period to intensify persuasive efforts is during that time when adoption is accelerating most; the efficiency or profitability of persuasion is lowest when the rate decelerates; attention might well be turned to achieving continuance of the desired behavior among adopters rather than adoption by those who have refused to respond.

There are several ways by which adoption delays can be reduced. One is to reduce the risk involved. Such a method is applicable when the adoption proposal creates an approach-avoidance conflict. The risks involved threaten the individual, creating an avoidance or non-adoption tendency. Sometimes the recommended behavior can be put on a trial basis, thus reducing risk. Products are frequently marketed on a trial basis in which the right to return the merchandise reduces risk. Special prices and sales tend to reduce the perceived risk. Tax laws, proposed for a specified time, provide a trial period; the time limit could well accelerate adoption. On the other side of the coin, the balance of

## TABLE 10

### Length of the Adoption Period for Certain Innovations

| Innovation | Average length of adoption period (in years) | Respondents |
|---|---|---|
| 1. Hybrid seed corn | 9.0 | 259 Iowa farmers |
| 2. Contour farming for soil conservation | 5.0 | 110 Illinois farmers |
| 3. Improved pasture | 8.0 | 100 N. Carolina farmers |
| 4. Growing alfalfa | 5.0 | 100 N. Carolina farmers |
| 5. Ten farm innovations | 3.7 | 493 Virginia farmers |
| 6. Antibiotic swine supplements | 1.6 | 148 Iowa farmers |
| 7. 2, 4-D weed spray | 2.1 | 148 Iowa farmers |
| 8. "Miracle" fabrics | 1.6 | 148 Iowa farm homemakers |
| 9. 2, 4-D weed spray | 1.3 | 104 Ohio farmers |
| 10. Warfarin rat poison | 0.8 | 104 Ohio farmers |
| 11. "Miracle" fabrics | 0.5 | 88 Ohio farm homemakers |
| 12. Stilbestrol | 2.1 | 44 Ohio county extension agents* |
| 13. Bulk milk tanks | 2.4 | 44 Ohio county extension agents* |
| 14. Irrigation | 4.5 | 105 Ohio farmers using irrigation |
| 15. Line sowing of paddy | 2.5 | 63 Pakistani farmers |
| 16. Insecticides | 2.2 | 63 Pakistani farmers |
| 17. Fertilizers | 3.8 | 63 Pakistani farmers |
| 18. Revised Standard Version of the Bible | 3.4 | 117 Iowa church members |
| 19. Language laboratories | 2.0 | 51 U.S. high schools |

* Note: County extension agents become aware of an innovation much as farmers do, but "adoption" for county extension agents amounts to recommending the innovation to farmers in their county.

approach and avoidance tendencies can be tipped in favor of adoption by increasing the rewards perceived. In marketing products, additional rewards to bring about adoption are exemplified in offers of toys to

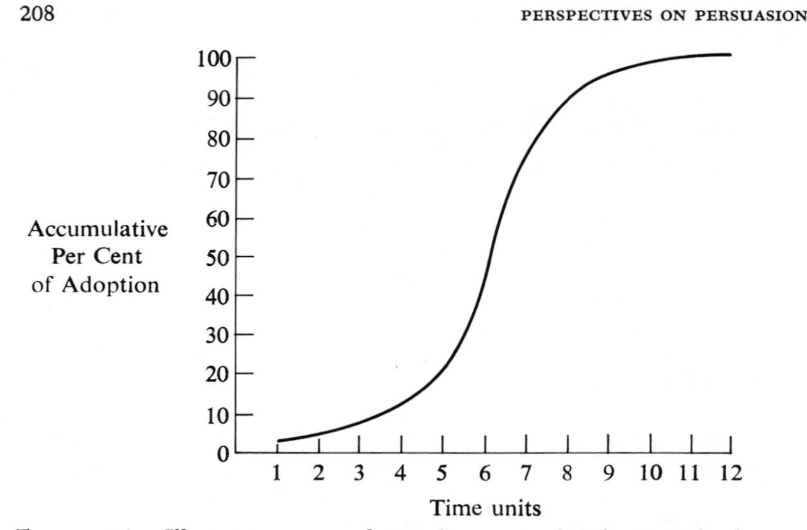


FIGURE 16. Illustrative accumulative frequency distribution of adoption times.

youngsters in exchange for box tops, silverware or glassware in exchange for coupons, and the giving of trading stamps as a reward for purchase.

In judging the two methods, there is a principle in conflict theory which favors reducing avoidance factors over emphasizing approach rewards. The principle holds that we more strongly seek to avoid an unpleasant circumstance the closer we are to it than we seek to engage in an attractive action the closer we are to it. At a distance from the adoption decision, the adoption tendency may be stronger than the avoidance tendency. But as the decision time is reached, the avoidance tendency may well produce delay in responding. Observation supports the principle; salesmen often find the tendency to avoid or delay increases as the time to act is approached.

In considering the use of risk reduction, a distinction should be drawn between adoption delay and non-adoption. Delay implies that the recommended action has appeal and that other factors interfere to delay its fulfillment. As further influence occurs, action, though delayed, has a reasonable probability of happening. Non-adoption, on the other hand, is conceived as an improbable action because it lacks appeal, is irrelevant to receiver needs. Many students, for example, may find no appeal in a proposal that they vote in a campus homecoming queen election. Their behavior is apt to be one of non-adoption rather than delay. Moreover, risk reduction is not always an effective solution for adoption delay. In some situations and for some individuals risk is courted, or at least is not a deterrent to action. The persuasive messages of Churchill to the people of wartime Britain, of Martin Luther King to potential participants in civil rights activities, and of the Peace Corps do not stress the reduction of risk. In such situations a potent reward is provided, as some receivers perceive it. This is the opportunity to make their lives meaningful.

## non-adoption

Like the rejection response discussed in Chapter 10, non-adoption is largely a motivational problem. The analysis and arousal of needs in receivers by pre-persuasion or by persuasive methods is called for. These include agitation and/or messages designed to activate manifest needs, those that can find their satiation in the recommended action. For example, the recruiting messages of the Peace Corps, in part, reflect a judgment that young people often have needs for achievement and meaningfulness in their lives. Messages in news releases and recruitment efforts seek to arouse these needs. It is anticipated that young men and women, thus motivated, will join the organization.

A form of non-adoption, often overlooked, occurs when the persuader seeks to have receivers diffuse messages to others. Repetition is the action sought. The receiver, in such a circumstance, must be motivated to diffuse the message. The act of passing along its content does not occur automatically, but in response to the satisfaction of need. For such an action, a need to make an impression on others, to excite or affect others, to achieve recognition from others seems the sort of need that would be satisfied through diffusing a message. Careful selection of its content by the source should lead to the activation of such a need. The Le Fleur and Larsen (1958) study illustrates this requirement. Their interest was in the potential use of air-dropped leaflets during wartime disruption of typical communication media. The diffusion of leaflet-messages was observed. They found that many persons ignored the leaflets, and that, among those who examined the messages, many did not diffuse the content to others.

A means of bringing about adoption that otherwise might not occur is to persuade a receiver to engage in an action he is willing to take, and which also is consistent with a subsequent action desired by the persuader. The principle involved hypothesizes that we have an impulse or need to keep our behavior consistent, and avoid contrary or dissonant actions. This was used by the Kennedy campaign organization in 1960. It led to new procedures, a new style in political campaigning (White, 1961). The new program, rather than set up a small, closely managed organization, provided for participation in the campaign from the largest number of persons possible. It was important to get persons to do whatever they were willing to do in the campaign, and not important to ask them to vote for Kennedy. If they were willing to help with luncheon arrangements or lick stamps, fine. Neither was it important that the actions be significant contributions to the campaign. What mattered was that the actions were consistent with subsequent voting for the candidate.

This consistent-actions principle applies even when the initial action is something said or written. Speech, of course, *is* action; writing a letter *is* action. Butler (1964) considers the common misconception that verbal expression is not an action. We have created, he notes, a misleading dichotomy between the use of language and other actions. It is reflected in the expression, "Your actions speak so loud I can't hear what you say." Yet, what a man says or writes is an action he has taken. It may be at odds with something else he does, but the tendency is toward consistency. Because of this, verbal behavior is used as an instrument for generating other consistent action. For example, in the clinical use of non-directive therapy, the therapist encourages the patient to analyze his own problem and, in his own words, specify what he ought to do. The presumption is that this verbal activity will aid in bringing about other correlated behavior. The discussion, in Chapter 6, of self-influence through self-produced verbal activity suggests possible methods of using what a receiver is willing to say as a means of generating desired subsequent actions.

## over-adoption

Adoption of recommended behavior can have unfavorable effects when it is extreme. This occurs most vividly in mob behavior; the persuader may find his proposal perceived as too mild by his audience; it over-reacts and responds with excessive behavior destructive of his desires. Rogers (1962) reports a number of instances in rural sociological studies of over-adoption of recommended practices by farmers.

An example of this occurred throughout the Midwest in 1949 and 1950. The weed-killer 2,4-D had had spectacular results since its introduction in 1946. Farmers used it on cornfields sometimes to excess and more frequently without regard for whether increased yields justified its use. Observers estimated that millions of dollars were wasted through over-adoption. This behavior seems to follow the notion that if a little of a good things helps, a lot will help much more. Similarly, over-adoption seemed to be an effect that disturbed integration leaders in the U.S. It was noted in Chapter 2 that the Negro followers pressed for activities not planned or sought by many of the Negro leaders. Over-adoption created a situation where the followers led and the leaders followed. Similarly, the history of labor strikes is replete with instances in which the labor force over-responded to persuasive messages from its leaders. Subsequent actions, unsought and detrimental to strike goals, have included throwing paint, wrecking automobiles, destroying equipment, smashing windows, and beating strike-breakers. Often the leaders' messages contained unrealistic strike demands voiced to arouse the members, but which the leaders were prepared to reduce during negotiations. When the more realistic strike settlement was achieved, it occasionally happened that the rank and file defied their leaders and refused the settlement.

Frequently, the over-adoption response is emotional (affective). Feelings of hate, rage, and anger are involved. Hebb and Thompson (1954) draw some interesting conclusions about the emotionality of man which are quite relevant to the over-adoption effect in persuasion. They examined numerous animal studies and compared the evidence of emotionality across species. They report that

> Evidence from species comparison suggests that emotional susceptibility increases with intellectual capacity. Man is the most emotional as well as the most rational animal. But this susceptibility is partly self-concealing: its possessor tends to seek the environment in which a too strong emotion is least likely to occur. . . . In man, this makes for the establishment of "civilized" societies, the chief characteristic of which (at least until recently) is not that they improve the economic lot of the average member, but that they provide an environment in which the frequency of acute fear, disgust, anger, and jealousy is decreased. The further a society has advanced along this path, the less subject to strong emotion its members [will] appear.

The protective function of a society conceals the emotionality of man, and we begin to think of adult man, particularly civilized man, as typically unemotional. This thinking carries over to our view of audiences; we are inclined to attribute passiveness, unresponsiveness, and orderliness to the civilized and unemotional character of adults and not reckon with the deliberate social effort to protect audiences from excessive stimulation. It may be nearer the truth that the more advanced societies simply have greater control over the environment and can provide greater protection from emotion-arousing stimuli. Hebb and Thompson suggest that education, and by implication persuasion, can serve this protective function. Typically, we think of education's impact on the individual and overlook the kind of environment it produces. We credit education with producing an emotionally stable adult and forget it also provides "a uniformity of appearance and behavior which reduces the frequency with which the individual member of the society encounters the causes of . . . emotion."

If we are so protected, what, then, explains the frequent emotional outbursts of our generation? There is no evidence that excessive fear, jealousy, anger, and rage in individuals have largely disappeared. The number of emotion-generated murders, muggings, rapes, and riots does not sustain this view. One wonders how many automobile accidents are the result of an emotionally aroused driver? Similarly, groups rioting over civil rights, throwing rocks at the floodlights on the East German side of the Berlin wall, and teenage gangs brutally beating innocent people are not evidence of successful protection against emotional overstimulation. If we explain these outbursts as the behavior of the uneducated and unintelligent (those who have not received the protective training education provides), other evidence casts doubt on this explanation. Students at the University of Mississippi, during its civil rights crisis found themselves shouting, "Two-four-six-eight! We don't wanna integrate!" In addition, their behavior included rock and Molotov-cocktail throwing (*Time,* October, 1962). In 1962, the writer attended a faculty meeting on the issue of faculty jurisdiction in the selection of campus speakers. Speeches supporting a presidential veto over faculty-approved speakers were responded to by hisses, boos, feet stamping, and profanity—by members of the faculty! Historical records provide instances of parliaments in similar emotional outbursts. In these instances, the lack of intelligence and education is an inadequate answer.

If lack of education as an explanation is supplemented by the view that man is a highly emotional creature quite capable of being stimulated to over-response, a useful contribution is made to a persuader's perspective. The question of what constitutes excessive stimulation becomes relevant to his effort. Doubtlessly, stimuli that are excessive vary from culture to culture, and group to group. What would arouse one group would not similarly affect another. Yet, as the persuader approaches an audience, one hypothesis that may be of value to him holds that the more uniform the group the greater its susceptibility to excessive stimulation. Small differences in behavior, appearance, and belief appear strange and intolerable. This thesis implies that differences from the group such as skin color, church membership, political affiliation, differences in belief and attitude, and differences in symbols approved, such as the eagle or the hammer and sickle, can and do become sufficient to generate emotional disturbances. Differences of this character commonly become the focal point of the persuader's messages. They carry the power of producing responses in excess of the persuader's goal.

From studies of humans and other animals, Hebb and Thompson note other evidence that helps to explain man's susceptibility to emotional disturbance. The evidence shows

> that mammals seek excitement, and this search has desirable possibilities in society as well as extremely undesirable ones. The animal [man] that is so vulnerable to emotional disturbance nevertheless seeks the situations that produce emotional disturbance in mild degree. . . . It appears empirically that for any one animal there is an optimal level of fear or frustration.

Seeking situations that are emotionally arousing is easily observed in man. It is found in his liking for dangerous sports: auto racing, skiing, and parachuting. It is found in the excitement of driving at dangerous speeds. It is found in the optimal level of frustration provided by bridge, or jigsaw and crossword puzzles. It is found in the risk of gambling on horses, dice, and cards. It is found in attendance at the theatre, movies, and football games, in the reading of detective stories and sex novels, and in the television viewing of serials, westerns, and horror shows. The Purdue Opinion Poll (1954) reported that someone was injured, threatened, or killed once every six minutes of program time. Over 7000 acts or threats of violence were counted during one week of TV programs presented in New York. And it is found in the desire to witness a civil rights demonstration, an America First rally, or a religious revival. These latter occasions are apt to have the additional feature of a persuasive effort to arouse further behavior. The result can be an emotional disturbance in excess of an optimal level.

Still another contributor to excessive emotional response lies in man's capacity and need for symbolization (see Chapter 7). Other animals predominantly use the signs in their environment as signals, as indicators of the presence of some object, condition, or event. Man, besides using signs as signals, also uses them very frequently as symbols. Symbols can generate conceptions or meanings in the mind, which for strangeness and threatening qualities, seem to exceed anything other animals experience. These may become the stimuli for emotional disturbances. The mutilations, human sacrifices, tortures, and emotional orgies of primitive rites are testimony to the power of symbols to generate emotion. In "civilized" man, the meaning he attaches to flags, the cross, the swastika, the hammer and sickle, a beard, a ducktail haircut, or the words Communist, rock and roll, right winger, and nigger are sufficient to disturb him emotionally beyond any optimal level. It is because of this that over-adoption becomes a possible, though unintended, effect of persuasion. The persuader's message can contain the kind of stimuli that generate excessive responses.

The thesis that man is the most emotional, and consequently the most dangerous, of animals is summarized by Hebb and Thompson by means of a hypothetical comparison.

> Picking a human society at random from all those that have existed, one might say that the risk taken by a stranger entering it—a member of another society, also chosen at random—would not be less than that taken by a chimpanzee or a wolf encountering a group of his fellows. It is not wholly fantastic, consequently, to suggest that man is more emotionally excited by what is strange than lower animals are, except after special training.

Neither is it wholly fantastic to suggest that the persuader's words can generate meanings which provoke man's emotionality. One would also suppose that special training in and understanding of the role of language in human behavior would reduce the likelihood of excessive response. From the persuader's view, such an understanding should enable him to reduce the risk of over-adoption.

Man's dangerousness was vividly portrayed in the Great Apes House of New York's Bronx Zoo. A mirror, with bars across it, was mounted on the wall between the orangutan and gorilla cages. A visitor, looking in the mirror, saw himself as if in a cage. Above this caged-in effect were the words, "THE MOST DANGEROUS ANIMAL IN THE WORLD." His emotionality, perhaps more than his weapons, make him this way.

### METHODOLOGICAL IMPLICATIONS OF OVER-ADOPTION

The persuader is by no means alone in his concern for the prevention of over-adoption responses. All societies are characterized by efforts to control over-stimulation by persuaders or others and over-response in receivers. The protection of members from excessive stimulation is a major function of the society; the more advanced the society the better its protective efforts. Thus, many of the means of dealing with over-adoption, especially in a highly organized, interdependent society, are not at the disposal of the persuader. Collectively, these are known as methods of social control, and include laws, punishments, enforcement agencies, as well as the controlling power of social norms. Particularly with respect to social norms, the persuader through his messages can become an agent of social control in the prevention of over-adoption. Martin Luther King, for example, in advocating non-violence, supports and utilizes social norms to direct behavior useful to his goals and to prevent excessive responses.

In addition, persuaders do well to recognize the over-response probabilities in the use of pre-persuasive agitation and the deliberate creation of events to serve as messages. If agitation is designed to violate the expected, to unstructure the environment, to break through the protective screen of social norms, over-stimulation is a reasonable expectation. The stimuli provided tend to be strange and disturbing, the type that activate man's emotionality. Similarly, manufactured events, used as messages, have a vividness that is double-edged; it adds to their attention-getting value, and, when perceived as threatening, has greater potential in generating excessive responses. This is one of the major reasons that few agitating incidents are provided spontaneously by volunteer groups. Persons trained in agitation or in producing an event-message are better disciplined, and better able to control or model the desired response. It is well known, in this connection, that members of picket lines, demonstrations, and sit-ins receive training. One of its objectives is to prevent excessive, unwanted responses.

The development and the use of methods to reduce over-adoption follow in part from an appreciation of the nature of this phenomenon. The persuader needs to appreciate that words and symbols as well as incidents have the power to arouse strange and threatening meanings. Also, he should be aware that people will seek to satisfy a need for emotional stimulation. When those who were present at a campus riot were interviewed, the most common reason they gave for being there was that it was "where the action was!" It should further be recognized that emotionality and excessive response are not limited to the young or immature; they exist potentially among the old and young, the educated and uneducated, the civilized and savage. And finally, when emotionality has been aroused, it is apt to be expressed in action. When a situation exists in which excessive response is to be prevented or reduced, various methods have been tried that are consistent with this goal. They are, of course, not the product of scientific experimentation; excessive stimulation, as an experimental variable, involves too many ethical and procedural problems. They appear in the descriptions of incidents of over-response. Among methods reported are the use of unemotional language, a low-key presentation, seated rather than standing audiences, reminders to audiences of social norms, the provision for acceptable rather than excessive action, and the sealing off of the audience from disruptive elements as well as from those simply seeking excitement. Turner and Killian (1957) observe in accounts of riots and mob behavior that onlookers seem to stimulate people to over-respond.

Related to the notion of audience composition is the effect of audience size on response tendencies, especially when the audience is a decision-making or decision-approving group. The general finding is that small groups tend to be less conservative than larger groups. If over-response is the concern, a larger decision-making group would be called for. If, for instance, a union's leadership wishes a more conservative decision approved, that desire is enhanced by obtaining a larger attendance at a meeting.

## action substitutes

**B**oth selective exposure and rejection are responses that are socially disapproved, particularly for persons whose positions carry an expectation of concern with issues beyond their private lives. Frequently, these individuals substitute "being informed" for becoming involved in an issue, and apparently make the assumption that the latter is equivalent to the former. In the University of Mississippi crisis, precipitated by the arrival of Negro James Meredith, some of the faculty appeared to behave as spectators, interested but not involved. This substitute effect, of course, can be detrimental to a persuader's goal. Another action substitute sometimes takes the form of appointing a committee to deal with a problem; the committee membership is sometimes such that no action is likely. On other occasions, a study group is formed to examine a problem and report at a later date. In both cases, the expectation of interest is fulfilled without the recommended action. Still another example occurs when the receiver offers to contribute money and thus dispose of any further obligation. The manner in which funds are solicited for charity and various medical research and aid programs invites action that frequently substitutes for more significant participation in welfare. Many contribute, then vote against hospital, welfare, and school taxes. One action nullifies the other. In the commercial world, substitute action takes the form of buying what is perceived as an equivalent, yet competitive product.

A key problem with unsought substitutes is to change the perceived equivalence of different actions; substitutes must not be viewed as acceptable alternatives. To this end, alternatives are analyzed to determine their differences. Characteristics of the desired action, not possessed by the alternative, are brought out in messages. This is a common practice in advertising competitive products or services. Often the results of tests on those characteristics favoring the advertised product are provided to increase the differentiation. The principle of differentiation applies to equivalent alternatives in the achievement of non-commercial goals.

## non-deterrence

Quite in contrast with seeking adoption, persuaders often seek to deter action, to prevent change. Deterrence may be defined as an effort to prevent the initial adoption of an action by individuals, groups, or nations. The term is distinguished from a discontinuance goal, or one in which the objective is to stop an action already adopted. Deterrence goals are common. It could be maintained that a society is more apt to have strong institutions functioning to deter change than to promote it. Certainly, those members of a society benefiting from the *status quo* have an interest in preventing change they may perceive as threatening.

Generally, they have the means to influence others. Prominent among the available means is persuasion.

Deterrence goals are common in regard to legislative proposals. Efforts to prevent bills to construct dams, highways, and parks, to provide medical care under government auspices, to finance mental health programs, to raise taxes for schools, hospitals, and welfare serve as illustrations. Robinson (1965), for example, reported on a successful effort to deter the passage of some twenty mental health measures in the Wisconsin legislature which seemed certain of passage. Deterrence is often the goal sought among individuals as well. Illustrative are those persuasive efforts to deter the young from smoking, drinking, and other behavior. An effort to deter action, of greater pertinence to persuasion than to other forms of influence, consists in preventing the diffusion of a message. In this case, the persuader considers certain particular receivers necessary to his goal, but others inimical to it. He wishes to prevent the diffusion of his message from intended to unintended receivers.

A critical task in deterrence by persuasion is to bring about the sort of circumstances in which no new action is apt to be undertaken. Among these are confusion, uncertainty, and conflict. These become the instruments, established by messages, which prevent action. It is thus possible, even common, that these become included in the process of persuasion. It is not, however, within the province of this writing to pass judgment on the ethical quality of a means of persuasion apart from the particular case in which it is used. Suffice it to say, for example, that bringing about confusion and uncertainty in the minds of others may be as defensible as enabling people to feel the opposite. Our jury system recognizes the validity of establishing uncertainty. A defense attorney may justifiably seek to deter a guilty verdict by providing a legitimate basis for uncertainty and "reasonable doubt." The same principle could apply to other efforts to deter action. The problem here is to gain perspective on the persuader's tasks and those means, potentially ethical, of accomplishing them.

## unsought discontinuance

**S**imilar in practical effect to forgetting is discontinuance. This effect occurs when a receiver adopts a persuader's recommended action and later discontinues it. Rogers (1962) reviews several field studies in rural sociology and education in which individuals had taken to farm or educational practices, materials, or equipment after receiving messages recommending them, only to discontinue at a later date. The two general findings of the studies were: (1) discontinuance is related to and predictable from other characteristics of the individuals involved, and (2) the percentage of persons who discontinue tends to be surprisingly high, generally more than 20 per cent, though this varies considerably with the nature of the idea or equipment adopted.

The discontinuance effect, of course, is important in many other fields besides agriculture and education. For the evangelist or mass movement persuader, the continued membership of those converted is a concern. The persuasion of persons not only to become members of political parties, pressure groups and other organizations, but also to continue active membership, is an important goal. Some service clubs, for example, lose through discontinuance as high as 40 per cent of their new members during the first year of club association. In the 1964 political campaigns, the Republican party was particularly concerned with the discontinuance of Republican voting. The typical manufacturer is concerned, after his product has been adopted, with the customer's continued use of it, and with those factors which bring about discontinuance. Any persuader desiring continuance of effects has interest in this problem.

Field studies and surveys have provided more information on the discontinuance effect than have experiments. In the latter type of study, immediate and relatively immediate effects have generally received the most attention. Certainly, one consideration for the experimenter has been the difficulty and expense of follow-up measures long after the initial experimental session. Frequent use of the same subjects, of course, introduces methodological problems: memory of previous responses, disinterest, unavailability, and sometimes fatigue.

An unintended effect which some claim produces discontinuance has come to be called overexposure. We read that entertainers, particularly those in television, sense this as a real problem. Statements by entertainers that they decline offers for fear of overexposure, of course, do not constitute evidence that such an effect takes place. On the other hand, politicians and their strategists are also said to consider this a problem. Mostly, overexposure is associated with changes in the receiver's image of a source rather than with ideas, products, things, events, or conditions. These apparently are thought to suffer less from overexposure. The term implies repetition though not necessarily of a verbal type. Generally, the evidence of experience and the research on repetition stress positive rather than negative effects. These findings, however, typically deal with repetition effects of slogans, trade-marks, product names. In any event, there appears to be little or no research to confirm the detrimental effects of repeated exposures.

## PREVENTION OF DISCONTINUANCE

If it can be justifiably assumed that discontinuance of belief leads to discontinuance of action, several methods of prevention warrant consideration. One of these is censorship and consequent monopoly over messages transmitted to receivers. This method was adopted by the Union of South Africa in June 1962 when it passed the General Law Amendment Act. The law prohibits quoting from the writings and speaking of those on the banned list. At that time, 102 persons were on the list. Furthermore, newspapers, magazines, and books published in South Africa or imported from abroad were not permitted if they contained anything these "subversives" had written or said (*Newsweek,* August 13, 1962). The objective was to prevent the discontinuance of beliefs and actions approved by the government. Monopoly not only aids in the adoption of beliefs, as previously noted, but promotes the continuance of accepted ideas and actions. One of its chief liabilities, however, lies in the inability to make the monopoly complete, or to prevent discontinuance in those from whom the protective screen is removed. This was the American soldier's experience in Korean POW camps. His belief in democracy had been supported by what amounted to, in practice, a monopoly; at least, he had been consistently exposed only to supporting messages. In Korea, removed from the shelter of this uniform support, he became vulnerable to counter-persuasion.

It was the American soldier's vulnerability to counter-persuasion and his inability to cope with it that led many to favor more monopoly to assure the continuance of democratic beliefs and actions. It was urged that discontinuance or doubt could be reduced if our schools would more extensively teach the reasons for having these beliefs. The notion was that the best defense for an attack on beliefs and consequent behavior was reinforcement. Several state boards of education and local school boards, following this method, added courses to further strengthen democratic beliefs.

In a set of studies (McGuire and Papageorgis, 1961; Papageorgis and McGuire, 1961; and McGuire, 1961) monopoly and reinforcement were challenged as effective methods of preventing discontinuance.

They proposed a third method, that of pre-exposing a person to counter-arguments to his beliefs, but in a context and form that weakened their impact. Because of a similarity to an immunizing procedure in medicine in which weakened forms of a disease are deliberately injected, it was designated an immunizing method. The principal finding was that this method was significantly more effective in developing resistance to attacks on culturally approved beliefs that tend to be accepted without challenge.

In their second experiment, for example, two widely held beliefs were used: (1) everyone should get an x-ray each year to detect any possible tuberculosis symptoms at an early stage, and (2) everyone should brush his teeth after every meal if at all possible. When agreement with these beliefs was measured on a 1-15 point scale, very high agreement was found (an average of 14.34). Different groups of subjects were used to provide comparisons of different methods of developing resistance to discontinuance. The results appear in Table 11.

It can be observed that those subjects whose highly approved beliefs were attacked, without immunization, were most affected by the attack. Their mean agreement with the beliefs fell to 5.73. It appears that these subjects, when under attack, lacked information and experience in countering the challenge to their beliefs. Their beliefs lacked the kind of cognitive depth and structure necessary to withstand attack. Subjects given prior immunization, whether attacked with the same counter-arguments or with others experienced less decline in their belief strength (9.25 and 8.70). Both these means are significantly higher than that of the first group. Finally, pre-exposure only without subsequent attack did not damage belief as a comparison with the control group reveals.

Another method of pre-exposure to contrary beliefs, under favorable conditions, is described by Tannenbaum (1962). In his history of the French rightist movement, the Action Française, he reported on their use of a "contradictor" in their meetings. The organization invited a speaker known to hold views contrary to the beliefs of the organization. He provided an attack on what the organization's leaders had said or written. The contradictor was not merely a devil's advocate but a legitimate opponent. This was followed by an "open" discussion. Those who replied or refuted the speaker in the "open" forum were generally skilled speakers well prepared to refute an opponent. Thus, members in the audience were reassured by hearing their beliefs publicly defended and well defended. This method possibly has the additional advantage of

TABLE 11

MEASURES OF BELIEF IN GROUPS EXPOSED OR NOT TO IMMUNIZING PROCEDURES

| Condition of exposure | First session | Second session |
|---|---|---|
| 1. Subject exposed to counter-arguments only—no prior immunization | — | 5.73 (N = 36) |
| 2. Subjects given immunizing pre-exposure to counter-arguments, followed by exposure to counter-arguments | | |
| a. Pre-exposed to the same counter-arguments | — | 9.25 (N = 20) |
| b. Pre-exposed to alternative counter-arguments | — | 8.70 (N = 27) |
| 3. Subjects given pre-exposure immunization only | 14.34 (N = 73) | 14.15 (N = 26) |
| 4. Control group of subjects—given no immunization and no exposure to counter-arguments | 13.29 (N = 73) | 13.23 (N = 47) |

Note: Numbers represent mean belief strength on a 15 point scale, the higher the number the stronger the adherence to the belief. Numbers in ( ) indicate the number of subjects under each condition.

generating a "fair play" feeling among the audience; it enables members of the organization to claim they hear both sides of an issue.

## unsought continuance

Often we seek, through persuasion or other means, to bring about a discontinuance of behavior. Receivers of our efforts already engage in behavior we wish to bring to an end. This is the dominant goal of all clinical persuasion. It is the present behavior of the alcoholic, the heavy smoker, the over-eater, the stutterer, the thief, and the school failure we wish to reduce or bring to an end. Though persuasion is often combined with other means, such as drugs, to accomplish this goal, it is itself an important means of achieving discontinuance. Another area, in which discontinuance is a prominent goal, is in those instances in which one seeks to alter the *status quo*. Revolutions, for example, begin by seeking the discontinuance of beliefs and actions which favor things as they are.

The lack of conflict favors the continuance of behavior. Without conflict, no counter forces exist which tend to nullify action. For this reason, practices in developing discontinuance in non-clinical situations have emphasized, in the initial phases of a campaign, the discrediting of existing beliefs. The objective is conflict, doubt, uncertainty. Discreditation is looked upon as a prior condition for the discontinuance of behavior. The conflict thus aroused prepares the ground for the reduction of undesired behavior.

## distortion of feedback

The persuader needs information on the success or failure of his efforts. This provides a basis for further activity on his part. This feedback must be in the form of observable and interpretable behavior. For this reason, he seeks to elicit interpretable feedback. Secondly, one would suppose that receiver reaction is at the persuader's disposal to be interpreted, particularly in face-to-face situations. In other media of communication, such as television, it presumably can be obtained through audience research procedures. The notion that feedback is readily available, however, ignores the evidence of experience in trying to obtain and interpret feedback. As receivers, we frequently mask or distort our reactions to messages.

This fact is confirmed in many ways. We recognize it in common remarks: "I didn't want to tell him to his face how I felt," and "I played it close to my chest." Masked and distorted feedback is confirmed by the history and development of attitude and personality testing. Early tests in these fields reflected the naive assumption that if people were asked about themselves, their reactions and beliefs, they would reply unambiguously. Since that time, tests have become more and more indirect or "projective" in character. Some, such as the *Minnesota Multiphasic Personality Inventory,* have built-in lie detectors. Other tests and techniques—the Rorschach Test, the Incomplete Sentences Test, the Thematic Apperception Test and the techniques of forced choice and error choice—attest to our tendency to mask and distort our responses to others. Tests like the Marlow-Crowne measure of our need for social approval were built on the recognition that people frequently respond in a socially approved, and not necessarily a truthful, manner. Furthermore, each society develops a set of conventional reactions for audiences. In some situations, we applaud the speaker, we sit quietly and look interested, or we say "Amen!" These are expected receiver responses which have become conventionalized.

The persuader, then, will experience effects he did not intend, effects which are not particularly helpful as feedback. His observation of receivers involves a problem quite different from observation of other kinds of objects. In observing the physical world, the objects studied do not purposely seek to influence the inferences drawn from observation. In the world of social interaction, and of course persuasion, people do try to affect the inferential process. They do seek to influence the persuader's judgment of their responses. Though it is sometimes asserted that the persuader needs to sharpen his observation of feedback, the masking tendencies of receivers limit the value of direct observation in dealing with feedback. A more productive approach lies in designing messages that elicit more meaningful and interpretable feedback. This means that the persuader must do more than observe any overt responses that occur, must be insightful enough to see what messages or contextual stimuli are useful in provoking responses in which he can have confidence.

## summary

In essence, the goals of persuasion are adoption, deterrence, continuance, and discontinuance. Often, the kind of action or inaction generated by a message can nullify the persuader's goal. He may want receivers to adopt a behavior which for them is new; he may get rejection, resistance, or even excessive adoption. Such responses represent failures of persuasion as a form of influence. Many of these have been identified through research and observation, and methods of circumventing them discussed. Included in this group of unsought actions are: adoption delay, non-adoption, over-adoption, action substitutes, non-deferrence, unsought discontinuance, unsought continuance, and feedback distortion.

# PART THREE

# FUNCTIONAL ANALYSIS IN PERSUASION

# Chapter 12

# Functional Emphasis in the Study of Persuasion

John Lewis, at the age of a college senior, could well be excited by his opportunity. Along with other leaders, he was to speak face-to-face to a tremendous audience—over 200,000 people as it turned out, plus a worldwide television and newspaper audience. As chairman of the Student Nonviolent Coordinating Committee he was accorded a place on the program. The occasion was the Civil Rights March on Washington. He would stand on the steps of the Lincoln Memorial, his audience filling the great mall between it and the Washington Monument. The speech-making was planned as a major feature of the entire demonstration. Doubtless, Lewis in preparing his speech considered the persuasive effects to be sought and the messages suitable to that end. But events did not go as expected. Another demonstration leader objected to some remarks Lewis had planned to make. As Lewis told it to a newsman (Associated Press, August 29, 1963), a meeting of civil rights leaders was called and he was required to delete the objectionable messages.

The incident illustrates a multi-organizational persuasive effort. In this coordinated effort, Mr. Lewis found that some of the functions involved in persuasion were not in his hands. Others had a voice in effects to be sought and messages to be included. It is a goal of this chapter to consider organizational and multi-organizational persuasion, its characteristics and problems, the functions of persuasion disclosed by study of these persuasive efforts, the advantages of functional analysis compared with other types of analysis, and the problem of learning associated with those functions, since multi-organizational persuasion is becoming increasingly predominant in such areas as national development, mass advertising, and social and political campaigns.

## organizational and multi-organizational persuasion

Wires, poles, switchboards and telephones may constitute a communication system, but not an organization engaged in persuasion. A communication system, in itself, does not seek effects, persuasive or otherwise. It may be used by an individual or group for either persuasive or non-persuasive goals. It is the more inclusive man-machine system that is required for an organization. A political organization, for example, may use equipment and machines, but it is these in combination with people that creates an organization. Ackoff (1960) outlined what he considered the essential characteristics of an organization; these are useful in understanding the organizations involved in persuasion. An organization requires that (1) some of its components be human beings; (2) responsibility for choices in achieving a goal be divided among two or more individuals or groups; (3) the functionally distinct subgroups be aware of each other's behavior either through communication or observation; and (4) the organization have some freedom of choice of both means and ends. In a given case, the means chosen to achieve a selected goal may be persuasive.

Frequently the mounting of a persuasive effort requires the talents and products of several organizations. The use of broadcasting as a channel of persuasion, for instance, may involve ad agencies, sponsors, music licensers, transcription and record services, research consultants, unions, station representatives, a broadcasting network, telephone companies, and the F.C.C. One organization may hire the services of several others; for example, in selling its product a corporation may hire the services of an advertising agency, a television network, and a public relations firm. Or several organizations may combine, without one's employing the others, to promote common goals. The civil rights demonstration in Washington, for instance, involved the NAACP, CORE, The Southern Christian Leadership Conference, The National Urban League, and the Student Nonviolent Coordinating Committee in a common effort. In many political campaigns a coalition of organizations—party organization, citizen groups, and financial interests—is formed to achieve goals by various means including persuasion. It is axiomatic in politics that an effective candidacy is more than the expression of individual ambition; it is the focal point of the interests of many men and organizations. In either case, the persuasion is a multi-organizational event, one that involves independent units coordinated to promote the same goals.

### PROMINENCE OF ORGANIZATIONAL PERSUASION

The bulk of effective persuasion is carried on by organizations. Organizations vary, of course, in the degree to which they use messages to produce persuasive effects. Intra-organization messages are often orders from a superior to a subordinate, with authority or power the chief means of influence. The message conveys the desires of the superior; choice of response is frequently limited or non-existent. Also, inter-organizational messages are frequently strategies between competitors and are designed, not to win acceptance but to defeat an opponent (see Chapter 5). Despite these other uses of communication, organizations are a major source of persuasive messages and the foremost source of mass persuasion.

Any index of prominence—money spent, number of messages presented, size of audiences reached—indicates the dominant position of organizational persuasion. Though big numbers tend to lose meaningfulness, a few will reflect the role of organizations in persuasion. The organizational efforts of U.S. advertisers in 1960 involved $11,582,000,000 in newspaper, magazine, television, radio, outdoor and other advertising (*Printers' Ink,* February 17, 1961). Today there are over 11,000 newspapers in America carrying advertisers' messages and presenting messages of their own (*N. W. Ayer and Son's Directory: Newspapers and Periodicals* 1961). In the 1950's about 7,000 magazines were published. At the beginning of the 1960's more than 4,000 radio stations presented millions of persuasive messages to listeners. More than 650 television stations with full schedules provide an awesome number of messages. The number of homes with TV sets exceeds 46 million and those with radios almost exceeds 50 million. It has been estimated that the average American is exposed to as many as 1500 messages daily and that most of them are produced by organizations. In fact, the mass media, which accounts for a very high percentage of the persuasive messages directed at receivers, are used preponderantly by organizations.

This does not mean that the age of the individual persuader is over and that his efforts have little significance. It is a cliché that organizations don't have ideas, only individuals. And it is quite possible that the influence of individuals is superior to that of the mass media and necessary to their success. But these figures do provide evidence that the bulk of persuasive effort is carried on by organizations. Furthermore, though individuals have ideas, it is generally an organization that does the effective promoting of them.

Individual persuaders such as the private citizen speaking publicly, or the minister conducting a revival, have given way to organizations as the instruments through which individuals express themselves effectively, find leadership and guidance, and affect and control their environment. The typical public speaker, as persuader, today represents an organization probably more than himself. Announcements of his speech and a chairman's introduction of him indicate his organizational affiliation. Before the public he cannot easily ignore his organizational role. Mr. Ferris Owen, an Ohio Farm Bureau Federation director, attempted as a private citizen to persuade the public to oppose the right-to-work issue of 1958. He was removed from his directorship (later returned), presumably on the grounds that the public perceived him as a spokesman for the Federation. Regarding the revivalist preacher, Lang and Lang (1960) note his change into an "organization man."

> The modern "revival" is a massive performance. It is carefully organized. . . . The advance preparation, the use of various media of communication, the employment of skilled promoters not only require coordination, but they must be paid for. Jonathan Edwards was able to spark the Great Awakening from his own little acre in Northampton, where he won souls for his own church. The mass evangelist, on the other hand, must be assured of financial and organizational support before he ventures into a strange city.

During the Cuban crisis of 1962, both Adlai Stevenson and USSR delegate Valerian Zorin, in their speeches, were organization men. Decisions regarding effects to be sought, messages to be transmitted, audiences to be reached were not made by these men alone. Attention to the role of organizations in persuasion and in our lives was most extensively brought about by Whyte's *The Organization Man* (1957). This well written best-seller popularized the evidence of our growing dependence upon and involvement in organizational life. Mr. Whyte, of course, deplored this and proposed secret resistance to organizational demands while outwardly approving (and incidentally accepting) the advantages of such a life over self-exile. But, approve or disapprove, he concluded with others that this great change had occurred. Other writers, March and Simon (1958) for example, noted that for most people organizations represent a major part of their lives, and, it might be added, a major means by which they are persuaded and can effectively persuade.

> . . . organizations are important because people spend so much of their time in them. The working force . . . spends more than a third of its waking hours in the organizations by which it is employed. The life of the child [and student] takes place to an almost equal extent in the environment of the school organization; and an uncountable host of other organizations, mostly voluntary, account for a large chunk of the leisure time of child and adult alike. In our society, preschool children and nonworking housewives are the only groups of persons whose behavior is not substantially organizational.

Meerloo (1960) claimed that the many organizations today exist because man needs them.

> In our actual world, with its increasing social and technical complications, it is impossible to have a universal insight and view on everything happening around us. Modern man needs several institutions [newspapers, magazines, television, radio, clinics, planning commissions, bureaus, etc.] as mediators between him and his environment. Therefore, man has created an overwhelming number of organizations to lead and influence him. It starts with the home and ends with the funeral parlor.

## CHARACTERISTICS OF ORGANIZATIONAL PERSUASION

Organizational behavior, including persuasive efforts, is sharply different from that in less structured groups or between individuals. Compare the movement of a worker's grievance in a large manufacturing corporation with the transmission of gossip in a neighborhood. Seldom is gossip transmitted along a single route; its diffusion is not orderly or predictable. Individual neighbors do not have specific communication tasks to carry out. The grievance report, in contrast, is transmitted along definite channels by designated people to specific destinations. Along the route each individual involved has particular responsibilities and functions he is expected to execute. The differences in characteristics warrant study not only in order to understand organizational persuasion, but because they disclose the basic functions involved in the persuasion process. The particular features to be considered are (1) specialization by individuals in the persuasive functions they perform, (2) role-taking—the fulfillment of expected behavior, and (3) the interdependence and coordination of persuasive functions.

SPECIALIZATION OF FUNCTION. The use of and attention to organizations for persuasion as well as other means of influence was exemplified in the Kennedy-for-President campaign. Large numbers of observers were impressed with the size of the organization and the specialization of functions within it. White (1961) reported sufficiently on its make-up to make it evident that each member had particular functions to perform.

The Kennedy campaign organization attracted attention because of its effectiveness, not its novelty. All aspirants for a major party nomination who campaign for public support develop a staff with specialized functions, many of which are basic to persuasion. And, of course, candidates of the major parties and significant splinter groups do the same. Richard Nixon, Republican nominee, developed a counterpart to the Kennedy organization. Even before an aspirant for office tosses his hat in the ring, an organization may be formed to improve as well as investigate his chances for success. This was the case with Nelson Rockefeller in 1960 (White, 1961). His organization was specialized so that a division did reconnaissance work among Republican party and financial leaders; a speech-writing unit gathered information, generated ideas and prepared speeches on national and world issues; an "image" staff of Madison Avenue talents was assigned the problem of personal public relations; a scheduling unit did the "advance" work and arranged Rockefeller's trips and appearances; press relations were entrusted to the Governor's press secretary in Albany; and a citizens' division carried on the function of dealing with potential public supporters.

Specialization of function is by no means unique to political candidates and elected officials. It can be confirmed by examination of the organizational charts and division of work in many group enterprises engaged in persuasion. The U.S. Information Agency, dominantly an organization for persuasion, involves similar specialization. Its former director, Edward R. Murrow (1961), pointed out that

> We embrace a multitude of disciplines and professions. For a quarter of a century I devoted my career to expression in a single medium of communication. USIA employs not one but seven: radio, television, movies, press, book publishing, exhibits, and the arts. We are involved in an entire range of problems: from a press run in Beirut, an exhibition in Turin, a stage performance in Munich and radio relays in Colombo. From a news telecast in Bogota to a sound tracked filmstrip in Paris to a book typeset in Manila. . . .

ROLE-TAKING. Organizational persuasion can be viewed usefully in terms of role theory and some of its major concepts. The perspective they provide contributes to an understanding of the diversification and coordination of tasks in a persuasive effort.

Very probably the increased involvement of people in organizations stimulated the development of role theory. Sociologists, social psychologists, and anthropologists needed the notion of *role* to indicate the relation of the individual to the larger organization. The use of the term in studying organizations led to a coupling of it with institutional terms such as status, office, and position.

The term *role* is not new. It is borrowed from the theatre in the thought that a large segment of behavior, particularly in organizations, could be conceived and described in terms of actors playing parts, of scenes wherein a social situation was acted out, and of a script by which the actors discovered what was expected of them. Since World War II, publications using this theatrical model of behavior have appeared at an increasing rate. In those twenty years it has become highly influential, and its important concepts have been developed and refined. Among those that are most pertinent to organizational persuasion are role, status (position), role-taking, and role expectations.

ROLE: Various meanings for this term are in common use. It is well to note the particular meaning of role in regard to role theory. The theory rejects the notion of role as a series of artificial, insincere acts. When we say of someone, "Oh, he's playing the big shot role," we imply that this person's activities are contrived, deliberately selected in an effort to create a false impression. The actions are inconsistent with our expectations of how the person should act.

Role theory rejects also the concept of role in the theatrical sense. Here the actor's behavior is for the purpose of portraying another person, not himself. Audience expectations regarding the self of the actor are not aroused. The behavior of the actor expected by the audience is oriented around the character portrayed. McGaw (1955), in outlining to the actor the means of discovering what his behavior should be, suggests sources of information all of which are character oriented. The actor studies (1) what the *character* does, (2) what the *character* says, (3) what other characters in the play say about *him,* (4) what actions are suggested in the *character's* lines, and (5) what comments the playwright offers in the stage directions about the *character's* behavior.

Role, as commonly used by those who find role theory useful, is regarded as those actions an individual is expected to provide as a result of occupying a particular status (position) in an organization. It is what he has to do to have his occupation of that status accepted. Note that the behavior of the individual is organized around the position he holds in the organization. Role and position constitute a dyad—like husband and wife, one term cannot be understood or even exist without the other. Sarbin (1954) brings out this union of the two terms in noting that "Roles are defined in terms of the actions performed by the person to validate his occupancy of the position. . . ." *Role-taking,* then, is only a segment of one's behavior, that which is expected and relevant to a position he occupies in an organization.

Each man in his time, of course, plays many roles, many of which are played concurrently. He may in a single day take the role of husband, father, professor, friend, citizen and work associate. Some of these roles are associated with his positions in societal groups such as the family or nation. Others are linked with positions in more formal and task-oriented organizations. It is this latter type of organization that engages in persuasion as an organization. Moreover, role in the task-oriented organization is more precisely spelled out. On this point, March and Simon (1958) write that

> Roles in [task-oriented] organizations, as contrasted with many other roles that individuals fill, tend to be highly elaborated, relatively stable, and defined to a considerable extent in explicit and even written terms. [The formulation of job descriptions provides evidence of this stability and specificity.] Not only is the role defined for the individual who occupies it, but it is known in considerable detail to others in the organization.

Organizational activity, including persuasion, involves a greater number of *must do* and *must not do* behaviors than does the activity of less structured groups. In contrast, there are fewer *may do* behaviors. Young and Lambert (1963) describe some of the contents of the rule book gotten together for marchers in The Civil Rights March in Washington. It illustrates organizational dictation of *must not do* behaviors to those accepting membership in that largely persuasive effort. Marchers' rules include: (1) don't shout slogans; (2) don't sing any other song than the approved march song, *We Shall Overcome;* (3) don't bring placards—headquarters will supply approved signs; and (4) there will be no sit-ins, unofficial marches, or other civil disobedience.

And at least in some instances, marchers were required to pledge that they would indulge in no violence, regardless of provocation.

STATUS (POSITION): Role and status are not synonymous, but denote interdependent concepts. Status refers to the position of an individual in any of society's social groupings or systems. In the case at hand, status directs attention to the position held in an organization engaged in persuasion—terms like speech-writer, speech editor, researcher, audience analyst, and speaker imply position in the persuasion-oriented team. In one way the term "status" is undesirable; it has become confounded with the term "prestige," as in Packard's *The Status Seekers*. Generally, prestige has been used to refer to the value—importance or desirability—of a position, while status identifies or describes a position without evaluating it.

Role theory provides a useful way of describing a status (position) in the form of two sets of expectations. One set consists of those actions expected by others of the occupant of a given position in an organization. A speech editor, for example, may be expected to act as a gatekeeper of messages to be transmitted. The other set of expectations consists of those anticipated by an individual from others in response to his position. The speech editor expects others to accept his decisions on releasing or withholding messages. Both sets of expectations, for the most part, go with the position rather than the person temporarily occupying it. Together these constitute *role-expectations*.

INTERDEPENDENCE. A persuasive effort, by an organization or group of organizations, involves degrees of interdependence not found or required in persuasion by individuals. Within an organization, the greater the specialization of function the greater the interdependence among organizational subunits. Interdependence is reflected in the creation and use of procedures to coordinate the activities of specialists. Generally, these are in abundance in the highly specialized groups.

Similarly, among cooperating organizations, the greater the specialization of function the greater the interdependence. The fifty state political organizations of the same party, though cooperative, do not tend to be specialized. Each has its area of influence and carries on the same persuasive functions as any other. Within a state, however, the financial interests, the party organization and citizen groups are more specialized and more interdependent. The organizations involved in the civil rights movement have, to date, tended toward specialized tasks and means. The NAACP has sought to use the courts to create change; the National Urban League has stressed negotiation and unpublicized pressure to influence; CORE, the Student Non-violent Coordinating Committee and the Southern Christian Leadership Conference have specialized in civil disobedience and other means. It is quite probable that the interdependence thus created has not been matched with the coordination it requires. The March on Washington seemed to be only a beginning in coordination.

## PROBLEMS OF ORGANIZATIONAL PERSUASION

It is not hard to get help in pointing out problems and so-called problems of organizations. The growth of organizational life, as one would expect, has been a determinant of increased interest in the problems it creates. They have become the themes of movies, novels, television plays, and scholarly articles and books. Whyte (1957), March and Simon (1958), Bensman and Rosenberg (1960), and Etzioni (1961) furnish a useful introduction to these problems. It is not the point here, however, that organizations and individuals in them have problems, but that some of these problems bear on the effectiveness of an organization when it engages in persuasion. Furthermore, the selection of problems is governed by the contribution a study of them can make to a study of persuasion. It is with these interests in mind that particular problems are described.

THE MYOPIA OF SPECIALIZATION. Among Nazi documents that fell into allied hands after World War II, some provided a dramatic illustration of the specialist's limited view and his failure to see the relation of his special function to a total effort. On the day Hitler committed suicide and Russian troops were marching through Berlin, officials and clerks in the Reichchancellory were too busy to look out of their windows. Some were engaged in estimating and ordering paper clips for the next fiscal year! (Bensman and Rosenberg, 1960)

When an organizational effort is divided and subdivided into specialized tasks, the individuals engaged in those tasks often fail to comprehend the total program. We say they do not grasp the "big picture." In their nearsightedness they see the smallest details of their own tasks and only fuzzily sense any total program. To them, activities seem chaotic rather than interrelated; the big picture remains with those who oversee the program—the manager and coordinators. Organizations for persuasion, like other structured groups, face this same difficulty. A major determinant of this nearsightedness is the restrictive channeling of information. Individuals are informed about other organizational activities on a need-to-know basis, which often means only what is necessary to carry on their particular functions. Consequently, the more varied will be the perceptions of the total effort among the specialists. Like the blind men in their fabled examination of the elephant, each perceives a different organization.

The wisdom and necessity of diffusing the "big picture" throughout an organization, of course, can be challenged in particular instances. The Manhattan Project at Los Alamos, which produced the first atomic bomb, was an organizational effort in which most workers had no knowledge of its real pupose or of how their work interlocked with that of others. Security was the justification. In another type of situation, it could be argued that the volunteer licking stamps and filling envelopes with campaign literature hardly needs the big picture. These tasks are routine. Probably little inefficiency occurs through not knowing the relation of these tasks to others. Such justifications notwithstanding, there are a large number of situations and tasks in persuasion that would benefit if the individuals involved comprehended more of the total process. Thus, it is desirable that persuasion be studied in a way to promote such comprehension.

LACK OF RESPONSIBILITY. An organization engaged in persuasion, like others pursuing goals by non-persuasive means, develops in members a lack of responsibility for the effects produced. Rank-and-file members in particular feel themselves not responsible for more than obeying orders. The extensive use of authority within the organization promotes the response, "I don't do the thinking around here; I just do my job." As a result, when a situation develops which requires a change from customary procedure, the bureaucratically-oriented individual retreats into "following procedure." Such rigidity, except with tasks that can be completely programmed, reduces the effectiveness of the persuasive effort. In a sales situation, for example, lack of responsibility for adapting to individual customers affects sales.

CONFLICT. Those organizations engaged in persuasion are apt to be hampered by intra-organizational conflicts. In the first place, the persuasive effort requires professionals at tasks such as speech-writing, polling audiences, doing "advance" work, and speaking. We tend to be more ego-involved in these roles than in many less relevant roles. A professional man, for example, may accept without resentment a very modest role as he pushes a food-cart for his wife at a supermarket. Or, he may perform under his wife's supervision numerous household tasks—setting a dining room table, washing dishes, or cleaning up a basement or garage. But in a situation which involves his professional role, he is much more sensitive to the interaction of his role with that of others. White (1961), for instance, concluded that the talented, trained members of Nixon's presidential campaign staff (1960) became disaffected with the candidate and the program because their role expectations were far from fulfilled. Many of these individuals were absentees on leave from professional jobs in American enterprise, yet they found themselves able to contribute little to the functions for which they had been engaged.

The conflict this instance suggests is that which arises between administrative and professional principles of organization. Such a conflict has considerable probability in an organization of persuasive specialists. It grows out of the distinction between employee and professional orientations to work. The employee is hired to do what he is told. Within the limitations of union contracts, the boss has the final word over task assignment; he gets his authority from the position he holds. The employee's orientation is to view his superior as having the legitimate right to decide what is to be done. In contrast, the professional's orientation is that he already knows or will find out what is to be done, and that he does not need to be told how to do it. Authority is not the deciding factor about what is to be done; the decision, in the professional's thinking, goes to the individual with the greater knowledge or with the most convincing argument for his view. When the administrative principle is applied in an organization of professional persuaders, conflict is the likely result.

Furthermore, organizations frequently develop cliques, a source of conflict within the group and a detriment to the official effort. The clique in an organization engaged in persuasion is perhaps most harmful when it is informally responsible for promoting goals which are inconsistent with the official program. The clique has little regard for established procedures, its members communicating with each other and the public without clearance. As a result, future plans are revealed, secrets are no longer secrets, information is leaked to competitors, timing is destroyed, and the structure and effect of a persuasive campaign is damaged. The exposure of secrets, of course, is done by individuals as well as cliques. Those who become disaffected sometimes re-identify with competing organizations or with the audiences the organization seeks to persuade.

## advantages of function analyses

Job analyses, like definitions, vary. It is not a question of which is "right," but which most aids understanding and learning. One approach is to isolate the skills and techniques involved in persuasive efforts. Such an analysis directs attention to skills such as voice control, gesture and body control, outlining techniques, language facility, and memorization. Search for the skills involved and emphasis on their study is generated by this analysis. Another approach is through an analysis which emphasizes functions (activities, behaviors, tasks) as units of a persuasive effort. Search and study is oriented toward identifying those interdependent functions required of an individual or organization that engages in persuasion. The latter is the more rewarding approach. Skills serve functions, not the reverse. Skills and techniques, moreover, have the further disadvantage of being necessary to some persuasive efforts but not to others. Microphone techniques, for example, may be unnecessary in the law court or around the conference table. The analysis of skills, therefore, does not facilitate an understanding of the essential tasks in persuasion.

Persuasion is characterized by interdependence. This is particularly true in persuasion by organizations which, as was earlier remarked, develop considerable specialization of function. But even in persuasion by individuals, functions are still interrelated; one function depends on others. The goals one selects affect the messages selected to accomplish those goals. The point to be stressed, however, is that a functional emphasis provides a continual awareness of interdependence. Functional thinking leads one to consider what other activities are dependent on and depended upon by a particular effort. In contrast, elements like skills can be studied more independently of one another.

Another advantage of investigating persuasion as a set of functions is that it reveals the basic similarity of all persuasive efforts. Miller (1951) held that there is a basic group of functions that must be carried out if a communication, and thus a persuasive process, is to operate. This, he believed, was true even though the components (men or machines) involved might be quite different from case to case. This implies that persuasion by television, the newspaper, or by a public speaker in an auditorium are not basically different. Furthermore, if those functions necessary to every persuasive event were identified, a generalized persuasive process could be described.

Persuasion by television and the face-to-face persuasion of one individual by another may differ in the degree that functions are specialized, in the extent to which they are assigned to machines, in cost, in the extent and types of effects, and in size of audiences. The study of such differences is essential to an understanding and effective use of persuasion. At the same time, the identification of a basic set of functions provides a framework in which comparisons between persuasive efforts can be made. Moreover, this kind of investigation stimulates the use of information gained from the study of one kind of persuasive event in the examination of other kinds.

## basic functions

No "right" set of functions is claimed. Aristotle and later classical writers, who were concerned primarily with the use of speech in persuasion, analyzed the persuasive effort around five canons or basic functions. The basic functions they specified were: (1) invention, finding and selecting the content for a speech; (2) disposition, the arrangement of materials used; (3) style, the linguistic stimuli used in the messages; (4) memory, the retention and recall of materials to be used; and (5) delivery, the auditory and visual attributes of speaking. It seems to me that these canons, identified for speech, are less applicable to other forms of persuasion. They were, moreover, developed as a result of viewing the persuader as an individual and not as an organization with members highly specialized in persuasive tasks. Basic functions with broader applicability are warranted. Hence useful criteria have been established and functions formulated with respect to them. These criteria are: (1) the function is primarily carried on by a source of persuasion; (2) the function should be involved very frequently and even necessarily in all kinds of effective persuasive efforts; (3) the function should be composed of a group of related tasks yet still retain a specialized character; (4) the number of functions in the set should be small enough to promote understanding of the total process; and (5) the set of functions should maximally aid in the analysis and execution of persuasive programs.

### FUNCTIONS COMMON TO VARIOUS PERSUASIVE EFFORTS

The system of interdependent efforts used in a particular situation may acquire functions not generally required. For example, out of the necessity for coordination among specialists in organizations, in contrast with persuasion by individuals, a managerial function develops. This is not a fundamental persuasive function, but one that is necessary to the operation of any organization. It is thus not included in a basic list. Similarly, the Civil Rights March on Washington (August 28, 1963) furnished examples of tasks not required for a persuasive effort though necessary on that particular occasion. Individuals were assigned tasks of crowd control, prevention of medical and sanitation hazards, tasks of feeding, housing and watering large numbers of people, providing security against attacks by antagonists, sealing off infiltrators from the demonstration march, and tasks of mass transport. Such tasks, of course, are not common to most persuasive efforts. For this reason, these and similar activities are excluded from the set of functions considered basic.

### TASK RELATEDNESS

The term "function," as used, typically implies more than a single, highly specific task. The process of persuasion incorporates a great many particular tasks capable of assignment to separate individuals. A listing of these as distinct functions would be more overwhelming than useful. In practice, a group of tasks that go well together often become the role of an individual or unit. The work expected of that role tends to become a professional specialty—reporter, editor, rewrite man, advance man, pollster, announcer. Sometimes, several closely related specialties are combined to accomplish an essential operation in the process of persuasion. For instance, all the tasks and specialties involved in selecting, securing and analyzing audiences may be combined. The audience and the problems it creates is the integrating factor. With this in mind, then, a function is considered that group of tasks selected to promote the best compromise between the advantages of specialization and integration.

### LIST OF BASIC FUNCTIONS

From a consideration of the criteria set up, a functional division of the persuasive effort was made. The order of functions in the list is not meant to suggest a fixed order of tasks.

ENERGIZING AND INITIATING THE PERSUASIVE PROCESS. Though an instance of persuasion may be talked about as an historical event, persuasion is an active, on-going process. As a process, it must be energized and often reenergized. Energy, the product of motivation, tends to be provided primarily by those who bring together an organization for persuasion. These same persons also make the decision to influence through persuasion rather than some other means. When that decision is made, persuasion can be said to be initiated.

SELECTING GOALS. This involves making decisions regarding the specific actions to be sought from receivers. In general, these actions can be categorized into adoption, deterrence, continuance, or discontinuance.

DECIDING WHAT INSTRUMENTAL EFFECTS TO SEEK IN ACHIEVING GOALS. This task involves the determination of what message effects are generative of desired action. Knowledge of relationships between message effects and subsequent actions is required for effectiveness in this function.

SELECTING, SECURING, AND ANALYZING AUDIENCES. This involves decisions as to what receivers are to be persuaded, or who is to receive the bulk of message presentation. Specifying the audience, of course, does not assure access to it; means must be selected to secure the audience. In addition, the selected audience must be analyzed to provide bases for designing a persuasive effort. Audience analysis frequently is carried on before, during, and after message presentation.

ACQUIRING AND ORIGINATING MESSAGE CONTENT. This specialized function is exemplified in the large law firm; research personnel specialize in locating and selecting relevant court cases and other information useful to a prospective persuasive effort. The same specialty is involved in the work of research and survey teams which produce information useful to persuasion.

SELECTING MESSAGES. This task has sometimes been called the "gatekeeper" function. From a pool of available messages, a selection is made of those of greatest potential value to the persuasive effort.

SELECTING AND CREATING CONDITIONS TO FACILITATE MESSAGE EFFECT. Those responsible for this function concern themselves with providing a message-context most likely to enhance message effect. It involves the selection of the speaker, occasion, timing, and other surrounding conditions.

STRUCTURING MESSAGE ELEMENTS IN A SINGLE EFFORT OR CAMPAIGN. In addition to the arrangement of message elements in a single speech or article, this task includes the design of an entire persuasive campaign.

SELECTING MEDIA AND FORMS OF PERSUASION. The term "media" typically refers to radio, telephone, television, newspapers, films, the stage, the public platform. Media selection frequently dictates to some extent the message form. Typical message forms are letters, telegrams, telephone calls, speeches, books, leaflets, plays, and cartoons. In large organizations, this task is apt to become a specialty.

ENCODING MESSAGES. This involves the selection and arrangement of signs (usually words) which constitute the message. Speech writers, commonly used in major persuasive efforts, illustrate this function.

TRANSMITTING MESSAGES. Regardless of message form, it must be transmitted to receivers. Ofttimes this function is provided by agencies not an integral part of a persuasive organization. TV stations, the postal service, telephone and telegraph companies sell transmission service to others. When the message involves speech, however, the speaker is apt to be part of the persuasion team.

SECURING AND INTERPRETING FEEDBACK. Common to all forms of persuasion, a need exists to obtain feedback in order to judge the success of the effort. When feedback is not immediately available, as in radio, television, newspapers, and books, specialists are employed to acquire it from receivers through audience surveys, interviews, and testing.

MAKING ETHICAL DECISIONS. Persuasion, like all other forms of influence, involves ethical decisions regarding ends and means. The function is implicit in all types of persuasion. In organizations, the responsibility is largely with those directing the effort.

## learning of functions

Learning is widely conceived as change of behavior. In persuasion the tasks to be learned include licking and securing postage to envelopes of campaign literature, reading commercials on television, typing a letter, memorizing a speech, analyzing an audience, understanding what effects will be instrumental in promoting a goal, selecting messages to generate those effects, deciding how to handle competing messages, and interpreting the applause, apathy, or silence of an audience. Perhaps by calling all of these "learning," we deceive ourselves. We look for a single explanation, a common set of principles to explain processes with little in common. Hilgard (1956) reviews this possible misunderstanding, noting that some learning theorists recognize the possibility of *several* kinds of learning. This raises the question of what kinds of learning are involved in the execution of persuasion's functions. Is one kind of learning more important than another? The answer to that question determines the way persuasive functions are to be studied and learned.

### LEARNING PROCESSES: SEARCH AND FIXING BEHAVIORS

Learning is a process. It is energized when some obstacle—internal or external—stands between the individual and his goal. One way of distinguishing between learning tasks is to ask what process was emphasized in achieving the goal. In changing his behavior, the individual can focus his efforts on *searching and discovering* a way to attain a goal, or he can concentrate on *fixing or habitualizing* his response to a stimulus situation. In persuasion, examples of the former would include investigating why a campaign is not working, or pre-testing several commercials for the same product to discover which sells best. Examples of the latter are activities such as memorizing the manuscript of a speech, using a typewriter, or learning to spell or pronounce words properly. In these the emphasis is on fixing the correct response.

Some goals require a greater emphasis on one process than on the other. Wickens and Meyer (1955), for example, include both in their view of learning. They note that, "The total process of altering behavior involves three conditions: motivation, variability leading to discovery, and fixation." Coinciding with their discussion of factors involved in fixing a response or path to a goal, learning is viewed as "the more or less permanent modification of the response or responses to a stimulus or to a pattern of stimuli." Here, the emphasis is on fixing or habitualizing response. When we say we finally have learned to pronounce the name "Khrushchev" correctly, we imply effort to fix a response. Elsewhere in their text, these authors shift their focus, pointing out that, "In cases of problem-solving behavior the emphasis is not upon the *fixation* of goal-attaining responses but rather upon their *discovery*."

## PRODUCTS OF LEARNING: HABITS AND KNOWLEDGES

Another way of distinguishing between learning tasks is to ask what is learned, what is the product of the learning process? To this question learning theorists have different answers, possibly because the products of learning, like processes, are quite different and should not be subsumed under a single label. Learning theories largely group themselves into two major families: stimulus-response theories and cognitive theories (Hilgard, 1956). The answer of the former to what is learned is "habit," that of the latter, knowledge, meanings, or in the psychologist's terms "cognitive structures." Both answers are supported by everyday experience. We have observed that we develop useful habits (skills) by practicing them. We become proficient in hitting a golf ball or in looking into the camera when we talk on television. *Responses* are what we learn, practiced until fixation occurs and they become habits. Yet, the answer of cognitive theorists also is verified by experience. If we drive from home to a new supermarket and thus locate it, we can find it as we leave from work, a different starting point, because we *know* where it is. *Facts* are what we learn. Practice and fixation are not needed; the knowledge acquired enables us to develop alternative solutions for reaching a goal. Skills are examples of learned habits; knowledge which generates a knowing of other solutions illustrates the learning product called "cognitive structure."

Furthermore, when either of these processes is used, a greater facility in the use of that process tends to result. By practicing to fix response, we tend to learn something about ways of practicing. Facility in this process, clearly, can be improved by studying what is known about it. Knowing, for example, the techniques of massed versus spaced practice and whole versus part learning help us to improve practice. Similarly, in the search and discovery of solutions to problems, we tend to acquire more useful ways of handling them. This, too, can be supplemented by studying procedures for processing problems. Perhaps the most widely known and influential writer on the problem-solving process has been Dewey (1933). His analysis of the steps in reflective thinking furnishes a procedure for this type of learning. The principal point, however, is that what is learned about process is quite different in these two kinds of learning.

### LEARNING PROCESSES AND PRODUCTS IN PERSUASION

The number and variety of tasks involved in persuasion require different learning processes and products—some call for the process of search, with knowledge and solution the products, and others the process of fixation, with habit and skill the products.

Tasks commonly arise in persuasion in which it is an individual's function to respond to relatively homogeneous situations with a program of activity involving little search, problem-solving, or choice. In a department store, for example, when a person's bill has not been paid on time, a form letter is sent. The form-letter response is routinized; the employee who sends the letter does not need to search for a response to the customer's failure to pay his bill. Similarly, the television announcer responds routinely to the occurrence of transmission difficulties. He need not search for a solution to this problem; a standard response is provided. The viewing audience is told, "Ladies and gentlemen. We have temporarily lost the video portion of the current program. The trouble is not in your set, but at the point of origin. We hope to have the difficulty corrected shortly." This routine message may be read, or transmitted by tape or film by means of a machine in the hands of a technician.

Such programmed responses make up a large part of the behavior of persons engaged in persuasion, and almost all of the behavior of persons in relatively routine positions. The individual's persuasive tasks tend to be governed by response programs. What happens is that situations which face the organization become categorized on the basis of their homogeneity or capacity for being responded to similarly. Programmed responses are prepared and the employee is trained to recognize which situations call for a particular response. The term "programmed response," as used here, is not meant to imply complete rigidity. The television organization will occasionally change the wording of its announcement of transmission difficulties. Or the announcer might add, "We'll be back to the ball game as soon as possible." But the emphasis is on fixed, habitual, routinized behavior. A set of tasks can be viewed as programmed, then, to the extent that search and choice have been reduced in favor of fixed responses. Programmed responses increase economy, and from the viewpoint of an organization, provide control over what is done. The price paid for these advantages is response quality. Being programmed, the response is less adapted to situational differences. This, of course, is less of a problem when the situations assigned a standard response are highly homogeneous.

Fixing responses is facilitated by training and coaching more than by understanding. The coach supplies the correct response; it requires little search and discovery by the learner. In cases where an individual is coached in how to make a particular speech or how to handle himself in a forthcoming television debate, the learning process emphasized is fixation, and the product is behavior which, like habit, has a high probability of occurring. Rehearsals in which individuals are coached similarly seek through repetition a highly predictable response. The response is programmed to produce desired behavior for the forthcoming "real" presentation. Even in the general case of coaching individuals in speech making, speech writing, rebutting arguments, editorial writing, and similar tasks, much of the search task is eliminated by suggestions of the instructor. Such coaching reduces learning time and leads generally to more satisfactory responses. Its value, of course, rests on the coach "knowing," through prior search and discovery, the correct response, and the learner facing little need for further problem-solving. For such situations it is well suited.

On the other hand, many tasks in persuasion call for search and discovery, the product of which is knowledge about and solution of a problem. Many situations are too different to provide economy through programmed responses without sacrificing suitability. The salesman finds the needs of customers too varied for a programmed or memorized sales talk. The trial lawyer becomes associated with court cases so different from each other that each case requires its own persuasive effort. Securing different audiences, selecting messages for particular audiences, creating conditions to facilitate message effects, structuring a persuasive campaign, encoding messages for different receivers, and interpreting feedback require problem-solving more than fixation of procedures. For such tasks, programmed behavior is harmful rather than helpful. The commonplace examples of the habitual back-seat driver and the constantly nagging parent generally illustrate ineffective persuasion because of the misapplication of fixed responses.

Search and discovery—problem solving—is facilitated by information, past experience and concepts relevant and useful to the problem. There is more need for these than training or coaching. They more effectively reduce the difficulties in finding satisfactory solutions. This can be seen in noting the types of difficulties which arise. Among these are: vagueness in defining a problem, erroneous perception of the problem, insufficient information for solution, and the restrictive influence of set in attacking the problem. Concerning problem-solving, Thayer (1961) writes, "Learning can be thought of as an internalization of any information, concept, or new ordering of knowledge that alters one's characteristic way of perceiving the world. . . . Learning literally *changes* the individual from inside out."

Problem-solving as a process is further divided into two types by March and Simon (1958). Both occur commonly in persuasive tasks. One type is labeled "reproductive" and the second "productive." In the first type, the individual faced with a problem searches his memory systematically for solutions that are present there in fairly complete form. He leans heavily on past experience, and little on the generation of new solutions. He seeks an analogous problem in the past for which a solution was developed. In the second type of problem-solving, more novel solutions are constructed from knowledge of the present problem, the ability to perceive the uniqueness of the problem, and the capacity to develop original solutions. This latter type might well be called "creative" problem-solving. It involves the behaviors characterizing creativity. A careful discussion of these may be found in Guilford (1962). In essence, the factors which characterize creative people seem to be: fluency of ideas, flexibility and originality.

## LEARNING FUNCTIONS: ROLE OF INFORMATION AND UNDERSTANDING

While it is true that persuasion involves skills and programmed responses as well as solutions to problems, the nature of those functions basic to persuasive efforts calls for an emphasis on the latter. This puts a premium on information, understanding, and creativity for their role in generating solutions. These functions emphasize such behaviors as selecting, deciding, originating and analyzing. These stress choice rather than habit, solution rather than skill, understanding rather than practice. Thus the student of the persuasive process, in contrast with the skilled performer of selected tasks, achieves his learning objectives from a starting point of more information. For this reason, information about these functions and their interdependence has been stressed in this book.

## summary

Organizations and groups of organizations engage in persuasion as well as communication involving other goals and other means of influence. In modern societies the bulk of significant persuasive efforts is carried on by organizations. For the individual, organizations increasingly have become the instruments through which he seeks to persuade others.

Persuasion by organizations is characterized by specialization: individuals acquire and carry on different tasks in a coordinated enterprise. One or several related tasks become combined into an individual's role (function) in the persuasive effort. The fact that many roles need to be coordinated brings about, in an organization, a condition of interdependence among individuals and a need to understand the total process of persuasion.

Both training in skills and understanding the interrelated tasks of a total process are useful approaches to the question of what needs to be learned. But considering the prominence of organizational persuasion and the complexity of the process, individually or organizationally, one can increase his effectiveness more through understanding than practice. The problem of learning to be more effective is best viewed as a problem-solving activity.

# Glossary

The "definitions" contained in this glossary represent the author's efforts to elicit in readers the meaning he had in mind when using each term. These definitions, thus, are specific to this text, although most of the terms have wide usage in the sense herein used. The glossary contains messages designed to arouse meanings for technical terms used as well as some everyday words that have special meaning to a study of persuasion. For additional terms relevant to persuasion as well as more complete definitions, the reader should examine J. Gould and W. L. Kolb, ed. *A dictionary of the social sciences*. Free Press, 1964.

ACTION SUBSTITUTE. In persuasion, an action-response by a receiver substituted, consciously or not, for the action sought by the persuader.

ADOPTION DELAY. A longer-than-required delay between exposure to a persuasive message and adoption of the proposed action.

ADOPTION GOAL. A goal of a process of influence in which behavior, untried by those to be influenced, is sought.

AFFECTIVE RESPONSE. A response characterized by feeling or mood, whether pleasant or unpleasant to oneself, favorable or unfavorable toward some object, person, or condition.

ALTERNATIVE. An available, possible response to stimulation whether an individual perceives it so or not.

AGITATION. Activities designed, not to develop specific action from others, but to arouse feeling, heighten motivation, and to unstructure the environment of those for whom it is planned.

ASSOCIATION. A connection or functional relation between phenomena such that the occurrence of one tends to evoke the other—e.g. stimulus-response, or sign-referent.

ATTITUDE. An enduring organization of responses—motivational, perceptual, emotional, and cognitive—to some aspect of the individual's world.

AUTHORITY. A form of influence characterized by voluntary obedience to the directives of another perceived to have the legitimate right to direct one's behavior.

BEHAVIORISM. The view that psychologists, as scientists, should study only observable, measurable behavior. Early behaviorists stressed specific, largely reflexive, stimulus-response relationships in which responses were highly predictable.

BOTH-SIDES STRUCTURE. A structure or organization of messages in which unfavorable material to a proposal is included along with favorable material.

CAPTIVE AUDIENCE. An audience highly motivated, by whatever means, to expose itself to messages, and thus characterized by consistent availability.

CHOICE. A capacity providing the individual with more than one possible response, whether he perceives these possibilities or not.

COGNITIVE DISSONANCE. Disharmony or perceived inconsistency among an individual's cognitions—beliefs, assumptions, expectancies, opinions, or items of knowledge.

COGNITIVE RESPONSES. Awareness, beliefs, assumptions, expectancies, opinions, or knowledge about an aspect of one's world.

COGNITIVE RESTRUCTURING. The revision or restructuring of prior meaning as a result of perceiving an altered relation between an object and its context.

COMMITMENT (PUBLIC). A decision to behave in a certain way that is known or can be known by others.

COMMUNICATION. A process involving the selection, production, and transmission of signs in such a way as to help a receiver perceive a meaning similar to that in the mind of the communicator.

CONCEPT. A general idea or a perceived property that characterizes, in common, two or more cases, and permits them to be put into a single class or category. An internal representation of a class of experiences.

CONDITIONED STIMULUS. A stimulus previously incapable of producing a particular response that, during the process of conditioning, comes to be an effective stimulus for that response.

CONDITIONING (CLASSICAL). A learning process in which two specific, external stimuli, occurring closely in time, produce a response to one (conditioned stimulus) that previously could be elicited only by the other (unconditioned stimulus).

CONDITIONING (INSTRUMENTAL). A learning process in which behavior is conditioned by reinforcing it through rewards or removing punishments.

CONFLICT. A condition in which antagonistic rewards, punishments, habits, or feelings have been aroused.

CONGRUITY EFFECT. An effect ascribed to the interaction of differing attitudes toward source and idea from which both will change in such a way that greater harmony between them is brought about.

CONNOTATIVE MEANING. A highly personalized meaning involving the association of attributes with a word or term not critical in determining *genus et differentia.* The use of a word (sign) as a symbol to represent one's conception of an object.

CONSUMMATORY EFFECT. In persuasion, a receiver response to a message which is valued by the persuader as an end in itself and not for its capacity to generate further behavior.

CONTEXT. The circumstances that surround a message that contribute to its meaning, and serve to facilitate or interfere with desired effects.

CONTINUANCE GOAL. A goal of a process of influence in which the repetition or continuation of behavior is sought in those to be influenced.

CORRELATION. A relationship between two phenomena or variables such that a change in one is accompanied by a more or less predictable change in the other. A correlation coefficient is a measure of the extent of this covariation.

COSMOPOLITE. A person who extends his exposure to message sources beyond his locality or his personal contacts.

CREATIVE PROBLEM SOLVING. An ability to construct more novel solutions to a problem and/or to perceive any uniqueness in a problem.

DEMOGRAPHIC. Pertaining to the vital statistics—age, geographic distribution, etc.—of human populations; in research, such statistics with respect to those samples or groups studied.

DENOTATIVE MEANING. Meaning in which a person uses a word (sign) as a signal, i.e. considers those attributes of an object necessary in determining its *genus et differentia.*

DEPENDENT VARIABLE. In experimentation, a variable whose changes are considered the consequence of change in one or more other manipulated variables called independent variables. It is the dependent variable which is observed and whose changes are measured. In persuasion research, the dependent or measured variable is typically the persuasive effect.

DERIVED MOTIVE (SECONDARY MOTIVE). A learned motive that does not directly function in the generation and control of behavior toward the satisfaction of a primary need.

DETERRENCE GOAL. A goal of a process of influence in which a source seeks to prevent the onset of a particular behavior among intended receivers.

DIFFUSION. A process by which a message spreads from a source to receivers not directly exposed to the message-source.

DISASSOCIATION. Specifically, an effect in which source and message, though communicated together, become unconnected for the receiver after a lapse of time.

DISCONTINUANCE GOAL. A goal of a process of influence in which a source seeks to halt the repetition or continuation of a particular behavior among intended receivers.

DISTORTION. Lack of correspondence between the way a message is typically interpreted and the way a given receiver interprets it.

ENCODING. The process of the selection and arrangement of signs undertaken with the intent of directing the meaning aroused by those signs in self or in others.

EXPRESSION. An intra-individual use of signs in the processing of experience involving overt sign usage.

EVENT-MESSAGE. A contrived event intended by the source to function as a message to receivers; a tacit message.

EXTINCTION. Specifically, the progressive reduction of the degree of association between sign and referent.

FEEDBACK. In persuasion, receiver responses to source messages that are perceived by the source. In this sense, feedback serves to provide information on effects sought and contributes inputs which affect future source outputs.

FIXING BEHAVIOR. A learning process in which the products are habits or skills.

FORCE. A form of influence arising in a social relationship such that an individual (or group) can achieve desired behavior in others despite resistance.

FORGETTING. The loss, either temporarily or permanently, of something previously learned.

FREQUENCY DISTRIBUTION. A tabulation of how many events or values occurred in each of several different classes or intervals.

FUNCTION. The activities proper or special to a role.

FUNCTIONAL ANALYSIS. For the persuasive process, an analytical approach emphasizing activities, behaviors, tasks as units.

GALVANIC SKIN RESPONSE. A measure of change in electrical resistance of the skin; a measure of emotional arousal.

GAME BEHAVIOR. Those rational acts in executing a strategy in conflict situations; the rational non-use of force.

GOAL. A state of affairs, existing or anticipated, which satisfies or reduces motivation, or is expected to.

HABIT. Learned behavior which is automatic, consistent, and enduring in character.

HYPODERMIC NEEDLE MODEL. A view which limits the process of message effect to those directly exposed.

ILLUSION. A perception invalidated by the laws of physics or the common experience of others.

ILLUSION OF CHOICE. The notion that the subjective experience of freedom to select responses is a mistaken perception.

INTENDED RECEIVERS. Those in whom a persuader seeks to develop effects instrumental to his goals.

INTERESTED THIRD PARTIES. In persuasion, receivers chiefly interested in source messages in order to produce messages for their own audiences.

INTERMEDIARY SOURCE. A person or group acting as a message source for a persuader in order to get greater message exposure to certain audiences.

INTERNALIZATION. A process by which the norms, ideas, or behavior of another or of society are adopted and accepted as one's own.

INSTRUMENTAL EFFECT. An effect in a receiver generative of that further behavior sought by a persuader.

LANGUAGE. A system of signs underlying a set of responses of which humans are capable.

LATENT NEED. A need commonly satisfied by other responses than action.

LEARNING. A general term for the more or less permanent change in behavior acquired from past experiences.

LOCALITE. A person who limits his exposure to local and personally known message sources.

MANIFEST NEED. A need that typically leads to and is satisfied by action.

MEDIA. Those agencies—radio, television, telephone, telegraph, publishers of newspapers, magazines, and books—which take on the special task of bringing messages to receivers not directly in the presence of sources.

MEANING. In persuasion, a central process in which responses to impinging stimuli occur such that these stimuli are used as signs.

MEDIATION. An intervening, central process between stimuli and responses such that stimuli are used as signs and this use becomes a determinant of response.

MESSAGE. A sign or group of signs—signals and/or symbols—intentionally used by a source to generate signification or symbolization in receivers.

MODEL. A presentation—mathematical, mechanical, diagrammatic, or verbal—which abstracts from the reality it represents certain features for emphasis.

MONITORING FUNCTION. That body of tasks and obligations on behalf of receivers and society designed to control the messages and context used by persuaders.

MOTIVATION (MOTIVES). The nonstimulus variables which generate and control behavior.

MOTIVATION RESEARCH. Research designed to learn what subconscious factors determine the choices people make, and in so doing, produce techniques to use these profitably.

NON-ADOPTION. For the persuader, an unsought effect in which receivers fail to adopt the desired behavior.

OPINION. A cognitive response, a belief expressed in words for oneself and/or others.

OPINION LEADER (INFLUENTIAL). A person, within a group, whose opinions are sought out and valued by others in the group.

ORGANIZATION. A system involving more than one person, and characterized by task specialization, interaction, and some choice of both ends and means for the system.

OVER-ADOPTION. For the persuader, an unsought effect in which receivers are excessive in their adoption of the desired action.

OVERT BEHAVIOR. Activity that can be observed by others in a position to make the observation.

PASSIVE RECEIVERS. The notion that receivers do not energize or reenergize the persuasive process.

PERCEPTION. A process of interpreting stimuli which produces meaning; more than merely sensing a stimulus.

PERCEPTION OF CHOICE. The subjective interpretation of a stimulus situation that several responses are available and that the individual is the principal agent in determining which response is made.

PERSUASION. That body of effects in receivers, relevant and instrumental to source-desired goals and brought about by a process in which messages have been a major determinant of those effects.

PERSUASIVE CAMPAIGN. A structured sequence of persuasive efforts in which message effects in an earlier phase are instrumental to the development of subsequent effects and ultimately to bringing about desired actions in receivers.

PRIVATIZATION. Generalized avoidance of exposure to messages.

PROCESS. The occurrence of changes, consistent in function or direction, in an object or organism.

PROGRAMMED MESSAGE. A pre-worded message designed for use in situations considered similar enough that the same, routine message is acceptable in all.

PROPAGANDA. Effects in receivers, relevant and instrumental to source-desired goals and brought about through the use of any psychological technique based on sign usage.

PSEUDO-RECEIVER. A person masquerading as a legitimate, intended receiver.

PSYCHOTHERAPY. The use of psychological means in the treatment of personality and behavioral problems.

READABILITY. A measure of printed communication setting forth the age or grade level able to understand it.

REASONING. A process of formulating steps in an inferential process in terms of language.

RECALL. A measure of retention. Those measured are instructed to reproduce words or similar material to which they previously have been exposed.

RECOGNITION. A measure of retention. Such a test instructs individuals to choose correctly from two or more answers that item to which they previously have been exposed in some program of learning.

REINFORCEMENT. Any rewarding condition that increases the probability of a response occurring in a given situation as well as occurring later in similar situations.

REJECTION. A tensionless lack of response, or lack of any change in response; an indifferent response.

REPRODUCTIVE PROBLEM-SOLVING. An ability to search one's memory systematically for solutions already present there in fairly complete form.

RESISTANCE (CONTRAST EFFECT). A response, accompanied by tension, in which a receiver maintains his pre-message position or changes in opposition to that desired by a persuader.

REVOLUTION. Rapid, substantial change in thought, behavior, politics, social theory, etc.

ROLE. The behavioral aspect of a status–i.e. what an individual does in putting the rights and duties of his status into effect.

SEARCH BEHAVIOR. A descriptive term for the kind of behavior which characterizes the learning process in solving problems.

SELECTIVE EXPOSURE. A defensive act, by means of avoidance, against messages opposing one's view or otherwise disturbing.

SELECTIVE RECALL. A process in which certain materials, of all those learned or received, are forgotten while others are retained.

SELF-INFLUENCE. Those effects of message production in which the source, intentionally or not, affects himself.

SEMANTIC DIFFERENTIAL. A rating device for measuring the connotative meaning of words or terms in selected groups.

SET. A selective orientation and responsiveness, temporary yet often recurring, toward only some environmental stimuli of all available.

SHILL. A person whose role is to artificially furnish, in the presence of intended receivers, those responses desired by the source.

SIGN. A stimulus used by an individual to indicate or represent something beside itself.

SIGNAL. A stimulus used to indicate the past or present existence or announce the future presence of something beside itself.

SIGNAL RESPONSE. A response to a well conditioned stimulus such that meaning arousal and the perceived exercise of choice do not occur.

SKILL. An habitualized sequence of motor acts that, judged by end results, is considered proficient.

SOCIAL CONTROL. The varying pressures which a group exerts to regulate the behavior of individuals on behalf of the group's goals.

SOCIAL NORMS. Standards of behavior laid down in a group's mores or laws.

SOFT NEWS. Those messages in news media designed largely to obtain and hold an audience for other concurrent messages.

SOURCE. In persuasion, that individual or organization whose motivation and goals primarily are to be satisfied by message effects in receivers.

SPECIALIZATION CHARACTERISTIC OF LANGUAGE. That characteristic of a stimulus which limits the way it achieves effect to the arousal of meaning.

STATISTICAL SIGNIFICANCE. A mathematical statement of the probability that an obtained value could have occurred by chance alone.

STATUS. A culturally determined position in a group.

STIMULUS (EXTERNAL). A change in physical energy impinging on the individual which leads to sensation.

STIMULUS GENERALIZATION. A process in which a learned response to a given stimulus comes to be given to other more or less related stimuli.

SUBLIMINAL STIMULATION. The presentation of stimuli at a level too weak to result in detection or discrimination.

SUGGESTION. (1) The process of arousing uncritical change of attitude toward an idea by means of association with another idea already in the mind. (2) The process by which an idea is aroused in others without direct statement.

SYMBOL. A stimulus used in such a way that a conception of the thing it represents is aroused.

SYSTEM. A combination of identifiable functions, involving more than one person or machine, which are interrelated, interdependent, and have a common direction in the sense of promoting a specific objective.

TENSION-REDUCTION THEORY. The notion that organisms seek to reduce tension which favors the learning and use of tension-reducing behavior.

THERMOSTATIC MODEL. A view of a process which emphasizes the feedback and interaction between parts.

THINKING. The conscious or unconscious processing of stimuli, ideas, and experiences for oneself, usually directed toward practical ends such as the solution of a problem.

UNCONDITIONED STIMULUS. A stimulus capable, without prior learning, of eliciting a specific response.

UNINTENDED EFFECT. In persuasion, an effect dominantly aroused by messages which is undesired by the message source.

UNINTENDED RECEIVERS. Those for whom a persuasive message was not intended, yet in whom unfavorable effects of significance to the persuader may be developed.

VOLUNTARY AUDIENCE. An audience whose availability is uncertain and inconsistent.

# References

Abelson, H. I. *Persuasion*. Springer, 1959.

Abernathy, E. *The advocate: a manual of persuasion*. D. McKay, 1964.

Ackoff, R. L. Systems, organizations, and interdisciplinary research. In D. P. Eckman (Ed.), *Systems: research and design*. Wiley, 1961. Pp. 26–42.

Allport, F. H. *Social psychology*. Houghton Mifflin, 1924.

Asch, S. E. The doctrine of suggestion, prestige, and imitation in social psychology. *Psychol. Rev.*, 1948, **55**, 250–278.

Baldwin, H. W. Managed news: our peacetime censorship. *Atlantic Monthly*, April, 1963, 53–59.

Bauer, R. A. N + 1 ways not to run a railroad. *Amer. Psychologist*, 1960, **15**, 650–655.

Bauer, R. A. The obstinate audience: the influence process from the point of view of social communication. *Amer. Psychologist*, 1964, **19**, 319–328.

Bensman, J., & Rosenberg, B. The meaning of work in bureaucratic society. In Stein, M. and others, *Identity and anxiety*. Free Press, 1960. Pp. 181–197.

Berger, P. L. *Invitation to sociology*. Doubleday-Anchor, 1963.

Berlo, D. K. *The process of communication*. Holt, Rinehart and Winston, 1960.

Berlo, D. K. & Gulley, H. E. Some determinants of the effect of oral communication in producing attitude change and learning. *Speech Monographs*, 1957, **24**, 10–20.

Bettelheim, B. Individual and mass behavior in extreme situations. *J. abnorm. soc. Psychol.*, 1943, **38**, 417–452.

Bettinghaus, E. P. The operation of congruity in an oral communication situation. *Speech Monographs*, 1961, **28**, 131–142.

Bierens de Haan, J. A. Animal language in relation to that of man. *Biol. Rev.*, 1929, **4**, 249–268.

Blackwell, H. R. Comments on "Subliminal projection." *J. Communication*, 1958, **8**, 68–76.

Blau, P. M., & Scott, W. R. *Formal organizations*. Chandler, 1962.

Boorstin, D. J. *The image*. Atheneum, 1962.

Brean, H. Hidden sell techniques are almost here. *Life,* 1958, **44,** 102–104+.

Brembeck, W. L., & Howell, W. S. *Persuasion*. Prentice-Hall, 1952.

Brodbeck, M. The role of small groups in mediating the effects of propaganda, *J. abnorm. soc. Psychol.,* 1956, **52,** 166–170.

Brown, J. A. C. *Techniques of persuasion*. Penguin, 1963.

Bryant, D. C. Rhetoric: its functions and its scope, *Quart. J. Speech,* 1953, **39,** 401–424.

Burke, K. *A rhetoric of motives*. G. Braziller, 1955.

Burton, P. W. *Making media work*. Printers' Ink Books, 1959.

Butler, J. H. Russian rhetoric: a discipline manipulated by Communism. *Quart. J. Speech,* 1964, **50,** 229–239.

Byrne, D. Interpersonal attraction and attitude similarity. *J. abnorm. soc. Psychol.,* 1961, **62,** 713–715.

Campbell, J. H., & Hepler, H. W., *Dimensions in communication*. Wadsworth, 1965.

Carroll, J. B. *Language and thought*. Prentice-Hall, 1964.

Carter, John F. *Power and persuasion*. Duell, Sloan and Pearce, 1960.

Cartwright, D. Some principles of mass persuasion, *Human Relations,* 1949, **2,** 253–267.

Coffin, T. E. Some conditions of suggestion and suggestibility; a study of certain attitudinal and situational factors influencing the process of suggestion, *Psychol. Monogr.,* 1941, **53,** No. 4 (whole No. 241).

Cohen, A. R., Brehm, J., & Latané, B. Choice of strategy and voluntary exposure to information under public and private conditions. *J. Pers.,* 1959, **27,** 63–73.

Condon, R., *Manchurian candidate*. Mentor, 1962.

Coutu, W. An operational definition of meaning. *Quart. J. Speech,* 1962, **48,** 59–64.

Crowne, D. P., & Marlowe, O. A new scale of social desirability independent of psychopathology, *J. consult Psychol.,* 1960, **24,** 349–354.

Cutlip, S. M., & Center, A. H. *Effective public relations*. Prentice-Hall, 3rd ed., 1964.

Deese, J. *Principles of psychology*. Allyn and Bacon, 1964.

Dember, W. N. *The psychology of perception*. Holt, Rinehart, and Winston, 1961.

Dewey, J. *How we think*. D. C. Heath, 1933.

Dollard, J., & Miller, N. *Personality and psychotherapy*. McGraw-Hill, 1950.

Dulles, A. W. The Craft of Intelligence. *Britannica Book of the Year: 1963,* Encyclo. Brit., 1963.

Eastman, M. *Enjoyment of poetry*. Scribners, 1913.

Edwards, A. L. Political frames of reference as a factor influencing recognition. *J. abnorm. soc. Psychol.*, 1941, **36,** 34–61.

Ehrlich, D., Guttman, I., Schonbach, P., & Mills, J. Postdecision exposure to relevant information. *J. abnorm. soc. Psychol.*, 1957, **54,** 98–102.

Eisenson, J., Auer, J., & Irwin, J. *The psychology of communication*. Appleton-Century-Crofts, 1963.

Ellis, W. D. & Seidel, F. *How to win the conference*. Prentice-Hall, 1955.

Emery, H. E., & Katz, F. M. Social theory and minority group behavior. *Austral. J. Psychol.*, 1951, **3,** 22–35.

Etzioni, A. (Ed.) *Complex organizations*. Holt, Rinehart, and Winston, 1961.

Ewing, T. A. Study of certain factors involved in changes of opinion. *J. Soc. Psychol.* 1942, **16,** 63–88.

Fearing, F. Toward a psychological theory of human communications. *J. Pers.*, 1953, **22,** 71–88.

Festinger, L. Informal social communication. *Psychol. Rev.*, 1950, **57,** 271–292.

Festinger, L. *A theory of cognitive dissonance*. Row, Peterson and Co., 1957.

Fotheringham, W. C. Theatre as persuasive communication. *Dramatics*, 1963, **34,** 13–29.

Fine, B. Conclusion-drawing, communicator credibility, and anxiety as factors in opinion change. *J. abnorm. soc. Psychol.*, 1957, **54,** 369–374.

Finestone, H. Cats, kicks, and color. In Stein, M., & others, *Identity and anxiety*. Free Press, 1960. Pp. 435–448.

French, J. R. P., Jr. A formal theory of social power. *Psychol. Rev.*, 1956, **63,** 181–194.

Fromm, E. *The sane society*. Rinehart, 1955.

Gibson, J. W. Direct and indirect attitude scale measurements of positive and negative argumentative communications. Unpublished doctoral dissertation, Ohio State University, 1962.

Gibson, J. J. The useful dimensions of sensitivity. *Amer. Psychologist,* 1963, **18,** 1–15.

Gilbreth, F. B. *Primer of scientific management*. New York, 1912.

Goffman, E. *The presentation of self in everyday life*. Doubleday, 1959.

Goffman, E. Characteristics of total institutions. In Stein, M., & others, *Identity and anxiety*. Free Press, 1960. Pp. 449–479.

Guilford, J. P. *Creativity—its measurement and development, a source book for creative thinking*. Scribner, 1962.

Hall, E. T. *The silent language*. Fawcett Publications, 1959.

Harvey, O. J., & Beverly, G. D. Some personality correlates of concept change through role playing. *J. abnorm. soc. Psychol.*, 1961, **63,** 125–130.

Hastorf, A. H., & Cantril, H. They saw a game: a case study. *J. abnorm. soc. Psychol.*, 1954, **49,** 129–134.

Hebb, D. O., & Thompson, W. R. The social significance of animal studies. In Lindzey, G. (Ed.), *Handbook of social psychology,* vol. 1. Addison-Wesley, 1954. Pp. 532–561.

Heider, F. Attitudes and cognitive organization. *J. Psychol.,* 1946, **21,** 107–112.

Hilgard, E. R. *Theories of learning.* Appleton-Century-Crofts, 2nd ed., 1956.

Hockett, C. F. Animal "language" and human language. In Spuhler, J. N. *The evolution of man's capacity for culture.* Wayne State University Press, 1959.

Hockett, C. F. Logical considerations in the study of animal communication. In Lanyon, W. E., & Tavolga, W. N. *Animal sounds and communication.* Pub. No. 7, The American Institute of Biological Sciences, Washington, D.C., 1960.

Hoffer, E. *The true believer.* New American Library, 1951.

Hoffer, E. *The ordeal of change.* Harper and Row, 1964.

Hovland, C. I. Reconciling conflicting results derived from experimental and survey studies of attitude change. *Amer. Psychologist,* 1959, **14,** 8–17.

Hovland, C. I., Harvey, O. J., & Sherif, M. Assimilation and contrast effects in reactions to communication and attitude change. *J. abnorm. soc. Psychol.,* 1957, **55,** 242–252.

Hovland, C. I., Janis I., & Kelley, H. H. *Communication and persuasion.* Yale Univ. Press, 1953.

Hovland, C. I., Lumsdaine, A. A., & Sheffield, R. D. *Experiments on mass communication.* Princeton Univ. Press, 1949.

Hovland, C. I., & Weiss, W. The influence of source credibility on communication effectiveness. *Publ. Opin. Quart.* 1951, **15,** 635–650.

Immergluck, L. Determinism-Freedom in contemporary psychology. *Amer. Psychologist,* 1964, **19,** 270–281.

Information and Education Division, U.S. War Dept. The effects of presenting "one side" versus "both sides" in changing opinions on a controversial subject. In Newcomb, T. M., Hartley, E. L., & others, *Readings in social psychology.* Holt, 1947, Pp. 566–579.

Insko, C. A. One-sided versus two-sided communications and counter-communications. *J. abnorm. soc. Psychol.,* 1962, **65,** 203–206.

Institute of Practitioners in Advertising, *Subliminal communication.* London, 1958.

Janis, I. and Feshbach, S. The effects of fear-arousing communications. *J. abnorm. soc. Psychol.,* 1953, **48,** 78–92.

Johnson, W. *Your most enchanted listener.* Harper, 1956.

Katz, E., & Feldman, J. J. The debates in the light of research: a survey of surveys. In Kraus, S. (Ed.), *The great debates*. Indiana University Press, 1962. Pp. 173–223.

Katz, E., & Lazarsfeld, P. F. *Personal influence*. Free Press, 1955.

Kelman, H. C. & Hovland, C. I. Reinstatement of the communicator in delayed measurement of opinion change. *J. abnorm. soc. Psychol.*, 1953, **48**, 327–335.

Knower, F. H. Experimental studies of changes in attitude: I. a study of the effect of oral argument on changes of attitude. *J. soc. Psychol.*, 1935, **6**, 315–347.

Knower, F. H. Experimental studies of changes in attitude: III. some incidence of attitude changes. *J. appl. Psychol.*, 1936, **20**, 114–127.

Knower, F. H., Phillips, D., & Koeppel, F. Studies in listening to informative speaking. *J. abnorm. soc. Psychol.*, 1945, **40**, 82–88.

Lang, K., & Lang, G. E. Decisions for Christ: Billy Graham in New York City. In Stein, M., & others, *Identity and anxiety*. Free Press, 1960. Pp. 415–427.

Langer, Susanne K. *Philosophy in a new key*. Mentor, 1951.

Larsen, O., & Hill, R. Mass media and interpersonal communication in the diffusion of a new event. *Amer. Sociol. Rev.*, 1954, **19**, 426–443.

Lasswell, H. D. The structure and function of communications in society. In L. Bryson (Ed), *The communication of ideas*. Harper, 1948. Pp. 37–51.

Lazarsfeld, P., Berelson, B., & Gaudet, H. *The people's choice*. Duell, Sloan and Pearce, 1944.

Le Fleur, M. L., & Larsen, O. N. *The flow of information*. Harper, 1958.

Levine, J. M., & Murphy, G. The learning and forgetting of controversial material. In Newcomb, T. M., Hartley, E. L., & others, *Readings in social psychology*. Holt, 1947. Pp. 108–115.

Lewin, K. Group decision and social change. In Newcomb, T. M., Hartley, E. L., & others, *Readings in social psychology*. Holt, 1947. Pp. 330–344.

Lewis, Helen B. An experiment on the operation of prestige suggestion. In Newcomb, T. M., Hartley, E. L., & others, *Readings in social psychology*. Holt, 1947. Pp. 232–243.

Lifton, R. J. Methods of forceful indoctrination: psychiatric aspects of Chinese Communist thought reform. In Stein, M., & others, *Identity and anxiety*. Free Press, 1960. Pp. 480–492.

Lindeman, B., & Patureau, A. Television ratings on trial. *Saturday Evening Post*, February, 1964. Pp. 13–17.

Lomax, L. E. *The negro revolt*. New American Library, 1963.

Lowenthal, L. Biographies in popular magazines. In Lazarsfeld and Stanton, *Radio research, 1942–43*. Duell, Sloan and Pearce, 1943. Pp. 507–548.

Ludlum, T. S. A Study of Techniques for influencing the credibility of communication. Doctoral dissertation, Ohio State University, 1956.

Luh, C. W. The conditions of retention. In Hovland, C. I., Janis, I. L., & Kelley, H. H. *Communication and persuasion*. Yale University Press, 1953.

Lumsdaine, A. A., & Janis, I. L. Resistance to counterpropaganda produced by a one-sided versus a two-sided propaganda presentation. *Publ. Opin. Quart.*, 1953, **17**, 311–318.

Maier, N. R. F., & Schneirla, T. C. *Principles of animal psychology*. McGraw-Hill, 1935.

Maccoby, N., & Maccoby, E. E. Homeostatic theory in attitude change. *Publ. Opin. Quart.*, 1961, **25**, 535–545.

Manis, M. The interpretation of opinion statements as a function of recipient attitude. *J. abnorm. soc. Psychol.*, 1960, **60**, 340–344.

March, J. G., & Simon, H. A. *Organizations*. Wiley, 1958.

McConnell, J. V., Cutler R. L., & McNeil, E. B. Subliminal stimulation: an overview. *Amer. Psychologist*, 1958, **13**, 229–242.

McGaw, C. *Acting is believing*. Rinehart, 1955.

McGuire, W. J. Resistance to persuasion conferred by active and passive prior refutation of the same and alternate counterarguments. *J. abnorm. soc. Psychol.*, 1961, **63**, 326–332.

McGuire, W. J., & Papageorgis, D. The relative efficacy of various types of prior belief-defense in producing immunity against persuasion. *J. abnorm. soc. Psychol.*, 1961, **62**, 327–337.

McKelvey, J. J. *Handbook of the law of evidence*. (5th ed.) St. Paul: West, 1944.

Meerloo, J. A. M. Brainwashing and menticide: some implications of conscious and unconscious thought control. In Stein, M., & others, *Identity and anxiety*. Free Press, 1960. Pp. 506–520.

Merton, R. K. *Mass persuasion*. Harper, 1946.

Miller, C. R. *The process of persuasion*. Crown, 1946.

Miller, G. A. *Language and communication*. McGraw-Hill, 1951.

Mills, C. W. *White collar*. Oxford University Press, 1956.

Mills, J., Aronson, E., & Robinson, H. Selectivity in exposure to information. *J. abnorm. soc. Psychol.*, 1959, **58**, 250–253.

Minick, W. C. *The art of persuasion*. Houghton-Mifflin, 1957.

Monroe, A. H. *Principles and types of speech*. Scott, Foresman, 1939.

Morris, C. W. *Signs, language, and behavior*. Prentice-Hall, 1946.

Murray, H. A. *Explorations in personality*. Oxford University Press, 1938.

Murrow, E. R. Improved communications for better understanding. Address to the Poor Richard Club, Philadephia, September 14, 1961.

National Association of Broadcasters. *The television code*, 10th ed., 1965.

Neustadt, R. E. *Presidential power*. Signet, 1964.

Newcomb, T. M. An approach to the study of communicative arts. *Psychol. Rev.*, 1953, **60**, 393–404.

Nomad, M. *Aspects of revolt.* Noonday Press, 1959.

Osgood, C. E., & Tannenbaum, P. H. The principle of congruity in the prediction of attitude change. *Psychol. Rev.,* 1955, **62,** 42–55.

Osgood, C. E., Suci, G. J., & Tannenbaum, P. H. *The measurement of meaning.* University of Illinois Press, 1957.

Packard, V. *The hidden persuaders.* Pocket Books, 1957.

Papageorgis, D., & McGuire, W. J. The generality of immunity to persuasion produced by pre-exposure to weakened counterarguments. *J. abnorm. soc. Psychol.,* 1961, **62,** 475–481.

Pillsbury, W. B. *Attention.* Macmillan, 1908.

Potter, S. *One-Upmanship.* Holt, Rinehart, and Winston, 1952.

Rapoport, A. *Fights, games, and debates.* University of Michigan Press, 1960.

Robinson, D. The far right's fight against mental health. *Look,* 1965, **29,** 30–32.

Rogers, E. M. *Diffusion of innovations.* Free Press, 1962.

Rosen, S. Postdecision affinity for incompatible information. *J. abnorm. soc. Psychol.,* 1961, **63,** 188–190.

Rosenberg, H. The orgamerican phantasy. In Stein, M., & others, *Identity and anxiety.* Free Press, 1960. Pp. 319–328.

Rosenberg, M., *et al.* Attitude organization and change. Yale University Press, 1960.

Ross, R. *Speech communication: fundamentals and practice.* Prentice-Hall, 1965.

Rovere, R. H. *Senator Joe McCarthy.* Meridian, 1959.

Sarbin, T. R. Role theory. In Lindzey, G. (Ed.), *Handbook of Social Psychology.* Addison-Wesley, I, 1954. Pp. 223–258.

Schein, E. H. The Chinese indoctrination program for prisoners of war. *Psychiatry,* 1956, **19,** 149–172.

Schein, E. H., Schneier, I., & Barker, C. H. *Coercive persuasion.* W. W. Norton, 1961.

Schelling, T. C. *The strategy of conflict.* Harvard University Press, 1960.

Schramm, W. Why adults read. In Henry, N. B. (Ed.), *Adult reading.* University of Chicago Press, 1956. Pp. 57–88.

Schramm, W. *Responsibility in mass communications.* Harper, 1957.

Sherif, M., & Sherif, C. W. *An outline of social psychology.* Harper, rev. ed., 1956.

Simon, C. W., & Emmons, W. H. Learning during sleep? *Psychol. Bull.* 1955, **52,** 328–342.

Smith, D. H. The perception of mass media attempts to influence behavior and belief. Unpublished paper, 1965.

Smith, H. K. *News and comment.* ABC television, November 11, 1962.

Stagner, R., & Karwoski, T. F. *Psychology.* McGraw-Hill, 1952.

Star, S., & Hughes, H. Report on an educational campaign: the Cincinnati Plan for the United Nations. *Amer. J. Sociol.*, 1950, **55**, 389–400.

Tannenbaum, E. B. *The Action Française*. Wiley, 1962.

Taylor, F. W. *The principles of scientific management*. Harper, 1911.

Thayer, L. O. *Administrative communication*. R. D. Irwin, 1961.

Thistlewaite, D., & Kamenetsky, J. Attitude changes through refutation and elaboration of audience counter-arguments. *J. abnorm. soc. Psychol.*, 1955, **51**, 3–12.

Thistlewaite, D., Kamenetsky, J., & Schmidt, H. Factors influencing attitude change through refutative communications. *Speech Monographs*, 1956, **23**, 14–25.

Turner, R. H., & Killian, L. M. *Collective behavior*. Prentice-Hall, 1957.

Vonier, S. Television—the urban outlook. *Television Quarterly*, 1964, **3**, 24–30.

Wallen, R. Ego-involvement as a determinant of selective forgetting. *J. abnorm. soc. Psychol.*, 1942, **37**, 20–39.

Walster, E., & Festinger, L. The effectiveness of "overheard" persuasive communications. *J. abnorm. soc. Psychol.*, 1962, **65**, 395–402.

Walter, E. V. The politics of decivilization. In Stein, M., & others, *Identity and anxiety*. Free Press, 1960. Pp. 291–308.

Watson, W. S., & Hartman, G. W. The rigidity of a basic attitudinal frame. *J. abnorm. soc. Psychol.*, 1939, **34**, 314–335.

Weaver, C., & Strausbaugh, W. *Fundamentals of speech communication*. American Book, 1964.

White, T. H. *The making of the president 1960*. Pocket Books, 1961.

Whorf, B. L. *Language, thought and reality*. M.I.T.—Wiley, 1956.

Whyte, W. H., Jr. *The organization man*. Doubleday, 1957.

Wickens, D. D. & Meyer, D. R. *Psychology*. Dryden Press, 1955.

Wigmore, J. H. *Wigmore's code of the rules of evidence in trials at law*. Little, Brown, 3rd ed., 1942.

Wilson, J. E., & Arnold, C. C. *Public speaking as a liberal art*. Allyn and Bacon, 1964.

Wolfe, H. D., Brown, J. K., & Thompson, G. C. *Measuring advertising results*. New York: National Industrial Conference Board, 1962.

Wright, C. R. *Mass communication: a sociological perspective*. Random House, 1959.

Wright, J. S., & Warner, D. S. *Advertising*. McGraw-Hill, 1962.

Young, K. *Social psychology*. Appleton-Century-Crofts, 3rd ed., 1956.

Young, W. R., & Lambert, W. Marcher's master plan. *Life*, 1963, **55**, 63–64 +.

# Index